Railways Act 1993

CHAPTER 43

ARRANGEMENT OF SECTIONS

Part I
The Provision of Railway Services

Introductory

Section
1. The Rail Regulator and the Director of Passenger Rail Franchising.
2. Rail users' consultative committees.
3. The Central Rail Users' Consultative Committee.
4. General duties of the Secretary of State and the Regulator.
5. General duties of the Franchising Director.

Licensing of operators of railway assets

6. Prohibition on unauthorised operators of railway assets.
7. Exemptions from section 6.
8. Licences.
9. Conditions of licences: general.
10. Conditions of licences: activities carried on by virtue of a licence exemption.
11. Assignment of licences.

Modification of licences

12. Modification by agreement.
13. Modification references to the Monopolies Commission.
14. Reports on modification references.
15. Modification following report.
16. Modification by order under other enactments.

Access agreements

17. Access agreements: directions requiring facility owners to enter into contracts for the use of their railway facilities.
18. Access agreements: contracts requiring the approval of the Regulator.
19. Access agreements: contracts for the use, on behalf of the Franchising Director, of installations comprised in a network.
20. Exemption of railway facilities from sections 17 and 18.

Section
21. Model clauses for access contracts.
22. Amendment of access agreements.

Franchising of passenger services

23. Passenger services to be subject to franchise agreements.
24. Exemption of passenger services from section 23(1).
25. Public sector operators not to be franchisees.
26. Invitations to tender for franchises.
27. Transfer of franchise assets and shares.
28. Fares and approved discount fare schemes.
29. Other terms and conditions of franchise agreements.
30. Failure to secure subsequent franchise agreement.
31. Leases granted in pursuance of franchise agreements: no security of tenure.

Passenger Transport Authorities and Executives

32. Power of Passenger Transport Executives to enter into agreements with wholly owned subsidiaries of the Board.
33. Re-negotiation of section 20(2) agreements as a result of this Act.
34. Passenger Transport Authorities and Executives: franchising.
35. Termination and variation of section 20(2) agreements by the Franchising Director.
36. Miscellaneous amendments of the Transport Act 1968.

Closures

37. Proposals to discontinue non-franchised etc. passenger services.
38. Proposals to discontinue franchised etc. passenger services.
39. Notification of proposals to close operational passenger networks.
40. Proposals to close passenger networks operated on behalf of the Franchising Director.
41. Notification of proposals to close railway facilities used in connection with passenger services.
42. Proposals to close passenger railway facilities operated on behalf of the Franchising Director.
43. Notification to, and functions of, the Regulator and the relevant consultative committees.
44. Reference to the Secretary of State of decisions of the Regulator concerning proposed closures.
45. Closure conditions: general.
46. Variation of closure conditions.
47. Bus substitution services etc.
48. Experimental railway passenger services.
49. Abolition of former closure procedures, exemptions from new procedures and imposition of alternative procedure.
50. Exclusion of liability for breach of statutory duty.

Supplementary powers of the Franchising Director etc.

51. Performance of the Franchising Director's duties to secure the provision of services etc.
52. Contracts between the Franchising Director and the Board etc. for the provision of non-franchised railway passenger services.

Section
53. Powers of the Franchising Director to form and finance companies and to acquire and dispose of assets.
54. Exercise of functions for purpose of encouraging investment in the railways.

Enforcement by the Regulator and the Franchising Director

55. Orders for securing compliance.
56. Procedural requirements.
57. Validity and effect of orders.
58. Power to require information etc.

Railway administration orders, winding up and insolvency

59. Meaning and effect of railway administration order.
60. Railway administration orders made on special petitions.
61. Restriction on making winding-up order in respect of protected railway company.
62. Restrictions on voluntary winding up and insolvency proceedings in the case of protected railway companies.
63. Government financial assistance where railway administration orders made.
64. Guarantees under section 63.
65. Meaning of "company" and application of provisions to unregistered, foreign and other companies.

Consumer protection

66. Amendments of the Fair Trading Act 1973.
67. Respective functions of the Regulator and the Director General of Fair Trading, and functions of the Monopolies Commission.

Other functions of the Regulator

68. Investigatory functions.
69. General functions.
70. Code of practice for protection of interests of rail users who are disabled.
71. Publication of information and advice.

Registers and reports of the Regulator and the Franchising Director

72. Keeping of register by the Regulator.
73. Keeping of register by the Franchising Director.
74. Annual and other reports of the Regulator.
75. Annual reports of the Franchising Director.

The Central Committee and the consultative committees

76. General duties of the Central Committee.
77. General duties of consultative committees.
78. Functions under section 56 of the Transport Act 1962.
79. Annual reports by the Central Committee and the consultative committees.

Information

Section
80. Duty of certain persons to furnish information to the Franchising Director on request.

Interpretation

81. Meaning of "railway".
82. Meaning of "railway services" etc.
83. Interpretation of Part I.

PART II

RE-ORGANISATION OF THE RAILWAYS

New companies, transfer schemes and disposals

84. Powers of the Board to form companies.
85. Powers of the Board to make transfer schemes.
86. Powers of the Franchising Director to make transfer schemes.
87. Transfer to the Secretary of State or the Franchising Director of the Board's function of making transfer schemes.
88. Transfers of interests in certain companies: provisions supplemental to sections 84 to 87.
89. Disposals by the Board and its subsidiaries.
90. Directions to the Board about the exercise of rights conferred by holdings in companies.

Transfer schemes: supplemental provision

91. Transfer schemes: general.
92. Functions under local or private legislation etc.
93. Assignment of employees to particular parts of undertakings.
94. Accounting provisions.
95. Power of the Secretary of State or the Franchising Director to require provision of information in connection with transfer schemes.
96. Functions of the Secretary of State in relation to transfer schemes.
97. Supplementary provisions as to transfers by transfer scheme.

Ownership of successor companies

98. Initial share holding in successor companies.
99. Government investment in securities of successor companies.
100. Exercise of functions through nominees.
101. Target investment limit for Government shareholding in certain successor companies.

Finances of successor companies

102. Temporary restrictions on borrowings etc.
103. Government lending to certain successor companies.
104. Treasury guarantees for loans made to certain successor companies.
105. Grants to certain successor companies.
106. Extinguishment of certain liabilities of successor companies.

Provisions with respect to flotation

Section
107. Responsibility for composite listing particulars of certain licensed successor companies.
108. Application of Trustee Investments Act 1961 in relation to investment in certain licensed successor companies.

Other financial provisions

109. Grants to the Board.
110. Application of sections 19 to 21A of the Transport Act 1962 to wholly owned subsidiaries of the Board.
111. Financial limits on loans.

Stamp duty and stamp duty reserve tax

112. Stamp duty and stamp duty reserve tax.

Supplemental

113. Objectives of the Secretary of State and corresponding duties of the Board.
114. The Secretary of State, the Franchising Director and the Board not to be regarded as shadow directors of certain railway companies etc.
115. Parliamentary disqualification.
116. Interpretation of Part II.

Part III

Miscellaneous, General and Supplemental Provisions

Safety, emergencies, security etc.

117. Safety of railways and other guided transport systems.
118. Control of railways in time of hostilities, severe international tension or great national emergency.
119. Security: power of Secretary of State to give instructions.
120. Security: enforcement notices.
121. Security: inspections.

Statutory authority

122. Statutory authority as a defence to actions in nuisance etc.

Miscellaneous and general

123. No person to be common carrier by railway.
124. Carriage of mail by railway.
125. Railway heritage.
126. General duties and powers of the Board.
127. Power of the Board to provide business support services for other operators.
128. Amendment of section 13 of the Transport Act 1962.
129. Bye-laws.
130. Penalty fares.
131. Modification of Restrictive Trade Practices Act 1976.

Transport police

Section
132. Schemes for the organisation etc. of transport police.
133. Terms and conditions of employment of transport police.

Pensions and other benefits

134. Pensions.
135. Concessionary travel for railway staff etc.

Financial provisions

136. Grants and subsidies.
137. Payments by the Secretary of State in respect of track access charges in connection with railway goods services.
138. Grants and other payments towards facilities for public passenger transport to and from airports, harbours etc.
139. Grants to assist the provision of facilities for freight haulage by railway.
140. Grants to assist the provision of facilities for freight haulage by inland waterway.
141. Financial assistance for employees seeking to acquire franchises or parts of the Board's undertaking etc.
142. General financial provisions.

Supplemental

143. Regulations and orders.
144. Directions.
145. General restrictions on disclosure of information.
146. Making of false statements etc.
147. Offences by bodies corporate or Scottish partnerships.
148. Proceedings in Scotland.
149. Service of documents.
150. Crown application.
151. General interpretation.
152. Minor and consequential amendments, transitional provisions and repeals.
153. Power to make consequential modifications in other Acts etc.
154. Short title, commencement and extent.

SCHEDULES:

Schedule 1—The Regulator and the Franchising Director.
Schedule 2—Rail users' consultative committees.
Schedule 3—The Central Rail Users' Consultative Committee.
Schedule 4—Access agreements: applications for access contracts.
Schedule 5—Alternative closure procedure.
Schedule 6—Railway administration orders.
   Part I—Modifications of the 1986 Act.
   Part II—Further modifications of the 1986 Act: application in relation to foreign companies.
   Part III—Supplemental.
Schedule 7—Transfer of relevant activities in connection with railway administration orders.
Schedule 8—Transfers by transfer scheme.
Schedule 9—Stamp duty and stamp duty reserve tax.

Schedule 10—Transport police: consequential provisions.
Schedule 11—Pensions.
Schedule 12—Minor and consequential amendments.
Schedule 13—Transitional provisions and savings.
Schedule 14—Repeals.

ELIZABETH II   c. 43

Railways Act 1993

1993 CHAPTER 43

An Act to provide for the appointment and functions of a Rail Regulator and a Director of Passenger Rail Franchising and of users' consultative committees for the railway industry and for certain ferry services; to make new provision with respect to the provision of railway services and the persons by whom they are to be provided or who are to secure their provision; to make provision for and in connection with the grant and acquisition of rights over, and the disposal or other transfer and vesting of, any property, rights or liabilities by means of which railway services are, or are to be, provided; to amend the functions of the British Railways Board; to make provision with respect to the safety of railways and the protection of railway employees and members of the public from personal injury and other risks arising from the construction or operation of railways; to make further provision with respect to transport police; to make provision with respect to certain railway pension schemes; to make provision for and in connection with the payment of grants and subsidies in connection with railways and in connection with the provision of facilities for freight haulage by inland waterway; to make provision in relation to tramways and other guided transport systems; and for connected purposes.

[5th November 1993]

BE IT ENACTED by the Queen's most Excellent Majesty, by and with the advice and consent of the Lords Spiritual and Temporal, and Commons, in this present Parliament assembled, and by the authority of the same, as follows:—

Part I

Part I

The Provision of Railway Services

Introductory

The Rail Regulator and the Director of Passenger Rail Franchising.

1.—(1) The Secretary of State shall appoint—

(a) an officer to be known as "the Rail Regulator" (in this Act referred to as "the Regulator"), and

(b) an officer to be known as "the Director of Passenger Rail Franchising" (in this Act referred to as "the Franchising Director"),

for the purpose of carrying out the functions assigned or transferred to the Regulator, or (as the case may be) the Franchising Director, by or under this Act.

(2) An appointment of a person to hold office as the Regulator or the Franchising Director shall be for a term not exceeding five years; but previous appointment to either of those offices shall not affect eligibility for re-appointment (or for appointment to the other of them).

(3) The Secretary of State may remove any person from office as the Regulator or the Franchising Director on the ground of incapacity or misbehaviour.

(4) Subject to subsections (2) and (3) above, a person appointed as the Regulator or the Franchising Director shall hold and vacate office as such in accordance with the terms of his appointment.

(5) The Franchising Director shall be a corporation sole by the name of "The Director of Passenger Rail Franchising".

(6) The provisions of Schedule 1 to this Act shall have effect with respect to the Regulator and the Franchising Director.

Rail users' consultative committees.
1962 c. 46.
1984 c. 32.

2.—(1) The Area Transport Users Consultative Committees established under section 56 of the Transport Act 1962 are hereby abolished and the London Regional Passengers' Committee established under section 40 of the London Regional Transport Act 1984 (which is treated by virtue of section 41 of that Act as such a committee for certain purposes) shall accordingly cease to be treated as one of those committees for any purpose.

(2) The Regulator shall establish a number of committees, not exceeding nine at any one time, to be known as Rail Users' Consultative Committees (in this Part referred to as "consultative committees").

(3) There shall be one consultative committee for Scotland, and one for Wales.

(4) In addition to the consultative committees established under subsection (2) above, the London Regional Passengers' Committee shall be treated as the consultative committee for the Greater London area for all purposes of this Part other than—

(a) subsections (2) and (3) above and subsections (6) to (8) below;

(b) section 79 below; and

(c) Schedule 2 to this Act;

and references in this Part to a consultative committee shall be construed accordingly.

(5) Subject to subsections (3) and (4) above—

(a) each consultative committee shall be appointed for such area as the Regulator may from time to time assign to it; and

(b) the Regulator shall so assign areas to consultative committees as to secure that every place in Great Britain forms part of the area of a consultative committee, and that no place forms part of the area of two or more consultative committees.

(6) Each consultative committee established under subsection (2) above shall consist of—

(a) a chairman appointed by the Secretary of State after consultation with the Regulator; and

(b) such other members, being not less than ten nor more than twenty in number, as the Regulator may from time to time appoint, after consultation with the Secretary of State and the chairman.

(7) The chairman and other members of a consultative committee established under subsection (2) above shall hold and vacate office in accordance with the terms of the instruments appointing them and shall, on ceasing to hold office, be eligible for re-appointment.

(8) The provisions of Schedule 2 to this Act shall have effect with respect to each of the consultative committees established under subsection (2) above.

(9) Unless the Secretary of State, after consultation with the Regulator, otherwise directs, "the Greater London area" means, for the purposes of this section, the area for which, immediately before the coming into force of this section, the London Regional Passengers' Committee was treated, by virtue of section 41(1) of the London Regional Transport Act 1984, as the Area Transport Users Consultative Committee for the purposes there mentioned.

1984 c. 32.

3.—(1) The Central Transport Consultative Committee for Great Britain, established under section 56 of the Transport Act 1962, is hereby abolished.

The Central Rail Users' Consultative Committee.

(2) There shall be a committee, to be known as the Central Rail Users' Consultative Committee (in this Part referred to as "the Central Committee").

(3) The Central Committee shall consist of—

(a) a chairman, appointed by the Secretary of State after consultation with the Regulator;

(b) every person who for the time being holds office as chairman of a consultative committee established under section 2(2) above or as chairman of the London Regional Passengers' Committee; and

(c) not more than six other members, appointed by the Regulator after consultation with the Secretary of State and the chairman.

(4) The chairman of the Central Committee and any members appointed under subsection (3)(c) above shall hold and vacate office in accordance with the terms of the instruments appointing them and shall, on ceasing to hold office, be eligible for re-appointment.

PART I

(5) The provisions of Schedule 3 to this Act shall have effect with respect to the Central Committee.

General duties of the Secretary of State and the Regulator.

4.—(1) The Secretary of State and the Regulator shall each have a duty to exercise the functions assigned or transferred to him under or by virtue of this Part in the manner which he considers best calculated—

(a) to protect the interests of users of railway services;

(b) to promote the use of the railway network in Great Britain for the carriage of passengers and goods, and the development of that railway network, to the greatest extent that he considers economically practicable;

(c) to promote efficiency and economy on the part of persons providing railway services;

(d) to promote competition in the provision of railway services;

(e) to promote measures designed to facilitate the making by passengers of journeys which involve use of the services of more than one passenger service operator;

(f) to impose on the operators of railway services the minimum restrictions which are consistent with the performance of his functions under this Part;

(g) to enable persons providing railway services to plan the future of their businesses with a reasonable degree of assurance.

(2) Without prejudice to the generality of subsection (1)(a) above, the Secretary of State and the Regulator shall each have a duty, in particular, to exercise the functions assigned or transferred to him under or by virtue of this Part in the manner which he considers is best calculated to protect—

(a) the interests of users and potential users of services for the carriage of passengers by railway provided by a private sector operator otherwise than under a franchise agreement, in respect of—

(i) the prices charged for travel by means of those services, and

(ii) the quality of the service provided,

in cases where the circumstances appear to the Secretary of State or, as the case may be, the Regulator to be such as to give rise, or be likely to give rise, to a monopoly situation in the passenger transport market; and

(b) the interests of persons providing services for the carriage of passengers or goods by railway in their use of any railway facilities which are for the time being vested in a private sector operator, in respect of—

(i) the prices charged for such use; and

(ii) the quality of the service provided.

(3) The Secretary of State and the Regulator shall each be under a duty in exercising the functions assigned or transferred to him under or by virtue of this Part—

(a) to take into account the need to protect all persons from dangers arising from the operation of railways, taking into account, in particular, any advice given to him in that behalf by the Health and Safety Executive; and

(b) to have regard to the effect on the environment of activities connected with the provision of railway services.

(4) The Secretary of State shall also be under a duty, in exercising the functions assigned or transferred to him under or by virtue of this Part, to promote the award of franchise agreements to companies in which qualifying railway employees have a substantial interest, "qualifying railway employees" meaning for this purpose persons who are or have been employed in an undertaking which provides or provided the services to which the franchise agreement in question relates at a time before those services begin to be provided under that franchise agreement.

(5) The Regulator shall also be under a duty in exercising the functions assigned or transferred to him under this Part—

(a) until 31st December 1996, to take into account any guidance given to him from time to time by the Secretary of State;

(b) to act in a manner which he considers will not render it unduly difficult for persons who are holders of network licences to finance any activities or proposed activities of theirs in relation to which the Regulator has functions under or by virtue of this Part (whether or not the activities in question are, or are to be, carried on by those persons in their capacity as holders of such licences); and

(c) to have regard to the financial position of the Franchising Director in discharging his functions under this Part.

(6) In performing his duty under subsection (1)(a) above so far as relating to services for the carriage of passengers by railway or to station services, the Regulator shall have regard, in particular, to the interests of persons who are disabled.

(7) Without prejudice to the generality of paragraph (e) of subsection (1) above, any arrangements for the issue and use of through tickets shall be regarded as a measure falling within that paragraph.

(8) For the purposes of this section, "monopoly situation" has the same meaning as it has in the Fair Trading Act 1973 (in this Part referred to as "the 1973 Act"), except that in relation to the passenger transport market—

(a) the expression includes a monopoly situation which is limited to the passenger transport market in some part of the United Kingdom; and

(b) in the application of section 7 of the 1973 Act (monopoly situation in relation to the supply of services) for the purposes of paragraph (a) above, references in that section to the United Kingdom shall accordingly be taken to include references to a part of the United Kingdom.

(9) In this section—

"environment" has the meaning given by section 1(2) of the Environmental Protection Act 1990;

PART I

"the passenger transport market" means the market for the supply of services for the carriage of passengers, whether by railway or any other means of transport;

"through ticket" means—

(a) a ticket which is valid for a journey which involves use of the services of more than one passenger service operator; or

(b) a combination of two or more tickets issued at the same time which are between them valid for such a journey.

General duties of the Franchising Director.

5.—(1) It shall be the duty of the Franchising Director to exercise any functions assigned or transferred to him under or by virtue of this Act in the manner which he considers best calculated—

(a) to fulfil, in accordance with such instructions and guidance as may be given to him from time to time by the Secretary of State, any objectives given to him from time to time by the Secretary of State with respect to—

(i) the provision of services for the carriage of passengers by railway in Great Britain; or

(ii) the operation of additional railway assets under or by virtue of any franchise agreement or any provision of sections 30 and 37 to 49 below;

(b) to ensure that any payments to which this paragraph applies are such as he reasonably considers will achieve economically and efficiently any objectives given to him by the Secretary of State under paragraph (a) above.

(2) The payments to which paragraph (b) of subsection (1) above applies are—

(a) any payments which the Franchising Director may be required to make pursuant to a franchise agreement;

(b) any payments which the Franchising Director may make with a view to securing—

(i) the provision of any services, or

(ii) the operation of any network, station or light maintenance depot, or any part of a network, station or light maintenance depot,

in pursuance of any provision of sections 30, 37 to 42 and 52 below; and

(c) any payments which it falls to the Franchising Director to make to passenger service operators as mentioned in section 136(7) below.

(3) Where the Secretary of State gives the Franchising Director any objectives under subsection (1)(a) above, the Secretary of State shall—

(a) lay a copy of a statement of those objectives before each House of Parliament; and

(b) arrange for copies of that statement to be published in such manner as he may consider appropriate.

Licensing of operators of railway assets

Prohibition on unauthorised operators of railway assets.

6.—(1) Any person who acts as the operator of a railway asset is guilty of an offence unless—

(a) he is authorised to be the operator of that railway asset by a licence; or

(b) he is exempt, by virtue of section 7 below, from the requirement to be so authorised.

(2) In this Part—

"operator", in relation to any railway asset, means the person having the management of that railway asset for the time being;

"railway asset" means—

(a) any train being used on a network, whether for the purpose of carrying passengers or goods by railway or for any other purpose whatsoever;

(b) any network;

(c) any station; or

(d) any light maintenance depot.

(3) Any person who is guilty of an offence under this section shall be liable—

(a) on summary conviction, to a fine not exceeding the statutory maximum;

(b) on conviction on indictment, to a fine.

(4) No proceedings shall be instituted in England and Wales in respect of an offence under this section except by or on behalf of the Secretary of State or the Regulator.

Exemptions from section 6.

7.—(1) The Secretary of State may, after consultation with the Regulator, by order grant exemption from the requirement to be authorised by licence to be the operator of such railway assets, or of railway assets of such a class or description, as may be specified in the order, but subject to compliance with such conditions (if any) as may be so specified.

(2) A licence exemption under subsection (1) above may be granted either—

(a) to persons of a particular class or description; or

(b) to a particular person;

and a licence exemption granted to persons of a particular class or description shall be published in such manner as the Secretary of State considers appropriate for bringing it to the attention of persons of that class or description.

(3) If any person makes an application under this subsection to the Regulator for the grant of an exemption from the requirement to be authorised by licence to be the operator of such railway assets, or of railway assets of such a class or description, as he may specify in the application, the Regulator, after consultation with the Secretary of State—

(a) may either grant or refuse the exemption, whether wholly or to such extent as he may specify in the exemption; and

PART I

(b) if and to the extent that he grants it, may do so subject to compliance with such conditions (if any) as he may so specify.

(4) Before granting a licence exemption under subsection (3) above, the Regulator shall give notice—

(a) stating that he proposes to grant the licence exemption,

(b) stating the reasons why he proposes to grant the licence exemption; and

(c) specifying the time (not being less than 28 days from the date of publication of the notice) within which representations or objections with respect to the proposed licence exemption may be made,

and shall consider any representations or objections which are duly made and not withdrawn.

(5) A notice under subsection (4) above shall be given by publishing the notice in such manner as the Regulator considers appropriate for bringing it to the attention of persons likely to be affected by the grant of the licence exemption.

(6) If any condition (the "broken condition") of a licence exemption is not complied with—

(a) the Secretary of State, in the case of a licence exemption under subsection (1) above, or

(b) the Regulator, in the case of a licence exemption under subsection (3) above,

may give to any relevant person a direction declaring that the licence exemption is revoked, so far as relating to that person, to such extent and as from such date as may be specified in the direction.

(7) For the purposes of subsection (6) above—

"condition", in relation to a licence exemption, means any condition subject to compliance with which the licence exemption was granted;

"relevant person", in the case of any licence exemption, means a person who has the benefit of the licence exemption and who—

(a) is a person who failed to comply with the broken condition or with respect to whom the broken condition is not complied with; or

(b) is the operator of any of the railway assets in relation to which the broken condition is not complied with.

(8) Where the Secretary of State or the Regulator gives a direction under subsection (6) above to any person, he may also direct that person to refrain from being the operator of any railway assets or of such railway assets, or railway assets of such a class or description, as may be specified in the direction by virtue of this subsection.

(9) Subject to subsection (6) above, a licence exemption, unless previously revoked in accordance with any term contained in the licence exemption, shall continue in force for such period as may be specified in, or determined by or under, the licence exemption.

(10) A licence exemption may be granted under subsection (1) above only if—

(a) the licence exemption is to come into force on the day on which section 6(1) above comes into force; or

(b) the licence exemption is to be granted on or before that day but is not to come into force until after that day;

and a licence exemption may be granted under subsection (3) above only if the licence exemption is not to come into force until after that day.

(11) Any application for a licence exemption under subsection (3) above must be made in writing; and where any such application is made, the Regulator may require the applicant to furnish him with such information as the Regulator may consider necessary to enable him to decide whether to grant or refuse the licence exemption.

(12) Licence exemptions may make different provision, or be granted subject to compliance with different conditions, for different cases.

(13) In this Part "licence exemption" means an exemption, granted under any provision of this section in respect of a railway asset or in respect of railway assets of any class or description, from the requirement to be authorised by licence to be the operator of that railway asset or, as the case may be, railway assets of that class or description.

8.—(1) Subject to the following provisions of this section— Licences.

(a) the Secretary of State after consultation with the Regulator, or

(b) the Regulator with the consent of, or in accordance with a general authority given by, the Secretary of State,

may grant to any person a licence authorising the person to be the operator of such railway assets, or of railway assets of such a class or description, as may be specified in the licence.

(2) Any general authority given to the Regulator under subsection (1)(b) above may include a requirement for the Regulator to consult with, or obtain the approval of, the Secretary of State before granting a licence.

(3) Any application for a licence—

(a) shall be made in the prescribed manner;

(b) shall be accompanied by such fee (if any) as may be prescribed in the case of a licence of the description in question; and

(c) shall, if the Secretary of State so requires, be published by the applicant in the prescribed manner and within such period as may be notified to the applicant by the Secretary of State;

and, on any such application, the Secretary of State or, as the case may be, the Regulator may either grant or refuse the licence.

(4) Before granting a licence, the Secretary of State or the Regulator shall give notice—

(a) stating that he proposes to grant the licence,

(b) stating the reasons why he proposes to grant the licence, and

PART I

(c) specifying the time (not being less than 28 days from the date of publication of the notice) within which representations or objections with respect to the proposed licence may be made,

and shall consider any representations or objections which are duly made and not withdrawn.

(5) A notice under subsection (4) above shall be given by publishing the notice in such manner as the Secretary of State or the Regulator considers appropriate for bringing it to the attention of persons likely to be affected by the grant of the licence.

(6) A licence shall be in writing and, unless previously revoked or surrendered in accordance with any terms contained in the licence, shall continue in force for such period as may be specified in or determined by or under the licence; and a licence shall not be capable of being surrendered without the consent of the Regulator if it is—

(a) a passenger licence;

(b) a network licence;

(c) a station licence; or

(d) a light maintenance depot licence.

(7) As soon as practicable after the granting of a licence, the grantor shall send a copy—

(a) in the case of a licence granted by the Secretary of State, to the Regulator and to the Health and Safety Executive; or

(b) in the case of a licence granted by the Regulator, to the Health and Safety Executive.

(8) Any power to make regulations by virtue of subsection (3) above shall only be exercisable by the Secretary of State after consultation with the Regulator and the Franchising Director.

(9) Different fees may be prescribed under subsection (3) above in respect of licences authorising a person to be the operator of railway assets of different classes or descriptions.

(10) None of the following, that is to say—

(a) the requirement to consult imposed by subsection (1) above,

(b) the requirements of paragraphs (a) to (c) of subsection (3) above, and

(c) subsections (4) and (5) above,

shall apply to applications for, or the grant of, any licences which, having regard to the provisions of section 6 above, need to be granted before the coming into force of that section.

(11) Any sums received by the Secretary of State or the Regulator under this section shall be paid into the Consolidated Fund.

Conditions of licences: general.

9.—(1) A licence may include—

(a) such conditions (whether or not relating to the licence holder's being the operator of railway assets under the authorisation of the licence) as appear to the grantor to be requisite or expedient having regard to the duties imposed by section 4 above; and

(b) conditions requiring the rendering to—

(i) the Secretary of State,

(ii) the Regulator, or

(iii) any other person, or any other person of a class or description, specified in the licence, except a Minister of the Crown or Government department,

of a payment on the grant of the licence, or payments during the currency of the licence, or both, of such amount or amounts as may be determined by or under the licence.

(2) Conditions included in a licence by virtue of subsection (1)(a) above—

(a) may require the licence holder to enter into any agreement with any person for such purposes as may be specified in the conditions; and

(b) may include provision for determining the terms on which such agreements are to be entered into.

(3) Conditions included in a licence by virtue of subsection (1)(a) above may require the licence holder—

(a) to comply with any requirements from time to time imposed by a qualified person with respect to such matters as are specified in the licence or are of a description so specified;

(b) except in so far as a qualified person consents to his doing or not doing them, not to do or to do such things as are specified in the licence or are of a description so specified;

(c) to refer for determination by a qualified person such questions arising under the licence as are specified in the licence or are of a description so specified;

(d) to refer for approval by a qualified person such things falling to be done under the licence as are specified in the licence or are of a description so specified;

(e) to furnish to a qualified person such documents or other information as he may require for the purpose of exercising any functions conferred or imposed on him under or by virtue of the licence;

(f) to furnish to the Secretary of State or the Regulator such documents or other information as he may require for the purpose of exercising the functions assigned or transferred to him under or by virtue of this Part.

(4) Conditions included in a licence may contain provision for the conditions to cease to have effect or be modified at such times, in such manner and in such circumstances as may be specified in or determined by or under the conditions; and any provision included by virtue of this subsection in a licence shall have effect in addition to the provision made by this Part with respect to the modification of the conditions of a licence.

(5) Subsections (2) to (4) above are without prejudice to the generality of subsection (1)(a) above.

(6) Any reference in subsection (3) above to a "qualified person" is a reference to—

(a) a person specified in the licence in question for the purpose in question, or

PART I

(b) a person of a description so specified,

and includes a reference to a person nominated for that purpose by such a person pursuant to the licence.

(7) Any sums received by the Secretary of State or the Regulator in consequence of the provisions of any condition of a licence shall be paid into the Consolidated Fund.

Conditions of licences: activities carried on by virtue of a licence exemption.

10.—(1) If and so long as a person is a licence exempt operator—

(a) there shall not be included in any licence granted to him any condition which relates to his licence exempt activities, except to the extent permitted by virtue of subsection (2) below; and

(b) any such condition which is included in a licence which has been granted to him shall, except to that extent, be of no effect so far as so relating.

(2) A condition which relates to both—

(a) a licensed activity carried on by a person ("the licensee"), and

(b) a licence exempt activity carried on by him,

may be included in a licence, but only if and to the extent that, in the opinion of the person granting the licence, the condition must, in consequence of the licensee's carrying on of a mixed activity, necessarily have effect in relation to the whole, or some part, of so much of the mixed activity as consists of the licence exempt activity if the condition is to have full effect in relation to so much of the mixed activity as consists of the licensed activity.

(3) There shall not be included in a licence any condition relating to the fares that may be charged in respect of train journeys involving licence exempt travel, other than train journeys which also involve—

(a) licensed travel; and

(b) at least two consecutive scheduled calls at stations during any one continuous spell of licensed operation.

(4) For the purposes of subsection (3) above and this subsection—

"call" means any stop at a station for the purpose of allowing passengers to board or leave the train (including the stops at the stations at the beginning and end of the train journey in question);

"licence exempt travel" means travel by means of a train whose operator is, by virtue of a licence exemption, exempt from the requirement to be authorised by licence to be the operator of that train for the whole, or for some part, of the train journey in question;

"licensed travel" means travel by means of a train whose operator is authorised by licence to be the operator of that train for some part of the train journey in question;

"spell of licensed operation", in the case of any train journey, means any part of the journey throughout which the operator of the train in question lawfully acts as such by virtue only of holding one or more licences;

"train journey" means a journey between any two stations which is scheduled to be made by means of one train (irrespective of where the train in question begins or ends its journey).

(5) Subsection (3) above has effect notwithstanding anything in subsection (1) or (2) above; and section 9 above is subject to the provisions of this section.

(6) In this section—

"licence exempt activity" means any activity which a person carries on in his capacity as a licence exempt operator;

"licence exempt operator" means an operator of railway assets, or railway assets of a class or description, who is, by virtue of a licence exemption, exempt from the requirement to be authorised by licence to be the operator of those railway assets or of railway assets of that class or description;

"licensed activity" means any activity which a person carries on in his capacity as a licence holder;

"mixed activity" means any activity which is carried on by a person who is both a licence holder and a licence exempt operator and which is carried on by him in part as a licensed activity and in part as a licence exempt activity.

11.—(1) A licence shall be capable of being assigned, but only if it includes a condition authorising assignment.

Assignment of licences.

(2) A licence shall not be capable of being assigned except with the consent of that one of the relevant authorities who is specified for the purpose in the licence.

(3) The "relevant authorities" for the purposes of this section are—

(a) the Secretary of State; and

(b) the Regulator.

(4) Any consent under subsection (2) above may be given subject to compliance with such conditions as the person giving the consent thinks fit to impose, which may include conditions modifying, or requiring or otherwise providing for the making of modifications to, the conditions of the licence.

(5) A licence may include conditions which must be complied with before the licence can be assigned.

(6) An assignment, or purported assignment, of a licence shall be void—

(a) if the licence is not capable of assignment;

(b) if the assignment, or purported assignment, is in breach of a condition of the licence; or

(c) if there has, before the assignment or purported assignment, been a contravention of a condition subject to compliance with which the consent required by subsection (2) above is given.

(7) A licence shall not be capable of being assigned under or by virtue of any other provision of this Act, other than paragraph 4 of Schedule 7 to this Act.

PART I

(8) In this section "assignment" includes any form of transfer and cognate expressions shall be construed accordingly.

(9) Any reference in this section to "assignment" shall be construed in Scotland as a reference to assignation.

Modification of licences

Modification by agreement.

12.—(1) Subject to the following provisions of this section, the Regulator may modify the conditions of a licence if the holder of the licence consents to the modifications.

(2) Before making modifications under this section, the Regulator shall give notice—

(a) stating that he proposes to make the modifications and setting out their effect,

(b) stating the reasons why he proposes to make the modifications, and

(c) specifying the period (not being less than 28 days from the date of publication of the notice) within which representations or objections with respect to the proposed modifications may be made,

and shall consider any representations or objections which are duly made and not withdrawn.

(3) A notice under subsection (2) above shall be given—

(a) by publishing the notice in such manner as the Regulator considers appropriate for the purpose of bringing the notice to the attention of persons likely to be affected by the making of the modifications; and

(b) by serving a copy of the notice on the holder of the licence.

(4) As soon as practicable after making any modifications under this section, the Regulator shall send a copy of those modifications to the Health and Safety Executive.

Modification references to the Monopolies Commission.

13.—(1) The Regulator may make to the Monopolies and Mergers Commission (in this Act referred to as the "Monopolies Commission") a reference which is so framed as to require the Commission to investigate and report on the questions—

(a) whether any matters which—

(i) relate to the provision of any railway services by means of a railway asset, or railway assets of a class or description, whose operator acts as such by virtue of a licence, and

(ii) are specified in the reference,

operate, or may be expected to operate, against the public interest; and

(b) if so, whether the effects adverse to the public interest which those matters have or may be expected to have could be remedied or prevented by modifications of the conditions of the licence.

(2) The Regulator may, at any time, by notice given to the Monopolies Commission vary a reference under this section by adding to the matters specified in the reference or by excluding from the reference some or all of the matters so specified; and on receipt of any such notice the Commission shall give effect to the variation.

(3) The Regulator may specify in a reference under this section, or a variation of such a reference, for the purpose of assisting the Monopolies Commission in carrying out the investigation on the reference—

(a) any effects adverse to the public interest which, in his opinion, the matters specified in the reference or variation have or may be expected to have; and

(b) any modifications of the conditions of the licence by which, in his opinion, those effects could be remedied or prevented.

(4) As soon as practicable after making a reference under this section or a variation of such a reference, the Regulator—

(a) shall serve a copy of the reference or variation on the holder of the licence; and

(b) shall publish particulars of the reference or variation in such manner as he considers appropriate for the purpose of bringing the reference or variation to the attention of persons likely to be affected by it.

(5) The Regulator shall also send a copy of a reference under this section, or a variation of such a reference, to the Secretary of State; and if, before the end of the period of 28 days beginning with the day on which the Secretary of State receives the copy of the reference or variation, the Secretary of State directs the Monopolies Commission not to proceed with the reference or, as the case may require, not to give effect to the variation, the Commission shall comply with the direction.

(6) It shall be the duty of the Regulator, for the purpose of assisting the Monopolies Commission in carrying out an investigation on a reference under this section, to give to the Commission—

(a) any information in his possession which relates to matters falling within the scope of the investigation and—

(i) is requested by the Commission for that purpose; or

(ii) is information which, in his opinion, it would be appropriate for that purpose to give to the Commission without any such request; and

(b) any other assistance which the Commission may require, and which it is within his power to give, in relation to any such matters;

and the Commission, for the purpose of carrying out any such investigation, shall take account of any information given to them for that purpose under this subsection.

(7) In determining for the purposes of this section whether any particular matter operates, or may be expected to operate, against the public interest, the Monopolies Commission shall have regard to the matters as respects which duties are imposed on the Secretary of State and the Regulator by section 4 above.

(8) Sections 70 (time limit for report on merger reference), 81 (procedure in carrying out investigations) and 85 (attendance of witnesses and production of documents) of the 1973 Act, Part II of Schedule 3 to that Act (performance of functions of the Monopolies Commission) and section 24 (modifications of provisions about performance of such functions) of the Competition Act 1980 (in this Part referred to as "the 1980 Act") shall apply in relation to references under this section as if—

(a) the functions of the Commission in relation to those references were functions under the 1973 Act;

(b) the expression "merger reference" included a reference under this section;

(c) in the said section 70, references to the Secretary of State were references to the Regulator and the reference to three months were a reference to six months;

(d) in paragraph 11 of the said Schedule 3, the reference to section 71 of the 1973 Act were a reference to subsection (2) above; and

(e) paragraph 16(2) of that Schedule were omitted.

(9) Nothing in this section applies in relation to any term of a licence to the extent that it makes provision for the revocation or surrender of the licence.

Reports on modification references.

14.—(1) In making a report on a reference under section 13 above, the Monopolies Commission—

(a) shall include in the report definite conclusions on the questions comprised in the reference together with such an account of their reasons for those conclusions as in their opinion is expedient for facilitating a proper understanding of those questions and of their conclusions;

(b) where they conclude that any of the matters specified in the reference operate, or may be expected to operate, against the public interest, shall specify in the report the effects adverse to the public interest which those matters have or may be expected to have; and

(c) where they conclude that any adverse effects so specified could be remedied or prevented by modifications of the conditions of the licence, shall specify in the report modifications by which those effects could be remedied or prevented.

(2) Where, on a reference under section 13 above, the Monopolies Commission conclude that the holder of the licence is a party to an agreement to which the Restrictive Trade Practices Act 1976 applies, the Commission, in making their report on that reference, shall exclude from their consideration the question whether the provisions of that agreement, in so far as they are provisions by virtue of which it is an agreement to which that Act applies, operate, or may be expected to operate, against the public interest; and paragraph (b) of subsection (1) above shall have effect subject to the provisions of this subsection.

(3) Section 82 of the 1973 Act (general provisions as to reports) shall apply in relation to reports of the Monopolies Commission on references under section 13 above as it applies to reports of the Commission under that Act.

(4) A report of the Monopolies Commission on a reference under section 13 above shall be made to the Regulator.

(5) Subject to subsection (6) below, the Regulator—

(a) shall, on receiving such a report, send a copy of it to the holder of the licence to which the report relates and to the Secretary of State; and

(b) shall, not less than 14 days after that copy is received by the Secretary of State, publish the report in such manner as he considers appropriate for bringing the report to the attention of persons likely to be affected by it.

(6) If it appears to the Secretary of State that the publication of any matter in such a report would be against the public interest or the commercial interests of any person, he may, before the end of the period of 14 days mentioned in paragraph (b) of subsection (5) above, direct the Regulator to exclude that matter from every copy of the report to be published by virtue of that paragraph.

(7) Nothing in this section applies in relation to any term of a licence to the extent that it makes provision for the revocation or surrender of the licence.

15.—(1) Where a report of the Monopolies Commission on a reference under section 13 above—

(a) includes conclusions to the effect that any of the matters specified in the reference operate, or may be expected to operate, against the public interest,

(b) specifies effects adverse to the public interest which those matters have or may be expected to have,

(c) includes conclusions to the effect that those effects could be remedied or prevented by modifications of the conditions of the licence, and

(d) specifies modifications by which those effects could be remedied or prevented,

the Regulator shall, subject to the following provisions of this section, make such modifications of the conditions of that licence as appear to him requisite for the purpose of remedying or preventing the adverse effects specified in the report.

Modification following report.

(2) Before making modifications under this section, the Regulator shall have regard to the modifications specified in the report.

(3) Before making modifications under this section, the Regulator shall give notice—

(a) stating that he proposes to make the modifications and setting out their effect,

(b) stating the reasons why he proposes to make the modifications, and

(c) specifying the period (not being less than 28 days from the date of publication of the notice) within which representations or objections with respect to the proposed modifications may be made,

and shall consider any representations or objections which are duly made and not withdrawn.

(4) A notice under subsection (3) above shall be given—

(a) by publishing the notice in such manner as the Regulator considers appropriate for the purpose of bringing the matters to which the notice relates to the attention of persons likely to be affected by the making of the modifications; and

(b) by serving a copy of the notice on the holder of the licence.

(5) As soon as practicable after making any modifications under this section, the Regulator shall send a copy of those modifications to the Health and Safety Executive.

(6) Nothing in this section applies in relation to any term of a licence to the extent that it makes provision for the revocation or surrender of the licence.

Modification by order under other enactments.

16.—(1) Where, in the circumstances mentioned in subsection (2) below, the Secretary of State by order exercises any of the powers specified in—

(a) Parts I and II of Schedule 8 to the 1973 Act, or

(b) section 10(2)(a) of the 1980 Act,

the order may also provide for the modification of the conditions of a licence to such extent as may appear to him to be requisite or expedient for the purpose of giving effect to or of taking account of any provision made by the order.

(2) Subsection (1) above shall have effect where—

(a) the circumstances are as mentioned in section 56(1) of the 1973 Act (order on report on monopoly reference) and either—

(i) the monopoly situation exists in relation to the supply of any railway service; or

(ii) the monopoly situation exists in relation to the supply of transport services and at least one of the persons in whose favour the monopoly situation exists has been engaged in the supply of railway services;

(b) the circumstances are as mentioned in section 73(1) of that Act (order on report on merger reference) and at least one of the two or more enterprises which ceased, or (in the application of that provision as it has effect by virtue of section 75(4)(e) of that Act) which would cease, to be distinct enterprises was or, as the case may be, is engaged in the supply of railway services; or

(c) the circumstances are as mentioned in section 10(1) of the 1980 Act (order on report on competition reference) and the anti-competitive practice relates to the supply of any railway service.

(3) As soon as practicable after making any modifications under this section, the Secretary of State shall send a copy of those modifications to the Regulator and to the Health and Safety Executive.

(4) Nothing in this section applies in relation to any term of a licence to the extent that it makes provision for the revocation or surrender of the licence.

(5) In this section expressions which are also used in the 1973 Act or the 1980 Act have the same meaning as in that Act.

Access agreements

17.—(1) The Regulator may, on the application of any person, give directions to a facility owner requiring him to enter into an access contract with the applicant for the purpose specified in subsection (2) below; but no such directions shall be given if and to the extent that—

> Access agreements: directions requiring facility owners to enter into contracts for the use of their railway facilities.

(a) the facility owner's railway facility is, by virtue of section 20 below, an exempt facility;

(b) performance of the access contract, if entered into, would necessarily involve the facility owner in being in breach of an access agreement or an international railway access contract; or

(c) as a result of an obligation or duty owed by the facility owner which arose before the coming into force of this section, the consent of some other person is required by the facility owner before he may enter into the access contract.

(2) The purpose for which directions may be given is that of enabling the beneficiary to obtain (whether for himself alone or for himself and, so far as may be applicable, associates of his)—

(a) from a facility owner whose railway facility is track, permission to use that track for the purpose of the operation of trains on that track by the beneficiary;

(b) from a facility owner whose railway facility is a station, permission to use that station for or in connection with the operation of trains by the beneficiary;

(c) from a facility owner whose railway facility is a light maintenance depot, permission to use that light maintenance depot for the purpose of obtaining light maintenance services for or in connection with the operation of trains by the beneficiary, whether the facility owner is to provide those services himself or to secure their provision by another;

(d) from any facility owner, permission to use the facility owner's railway facility for the purpose of stabling, or otherwise temporarily holding, rolling stock in connection with the operation of trains on any track by the beneficiary; or

(e) from any facility owner, permission to use the facility owner's railway facility for or in connection with the operation of a network, station or light maintenance depot by the beneficiary;

but this subsection is subject to the limitations imposed by subsection (3) below.

(3) In subsection (2) above—

(a) paragraph (a) does not extend to obtaining permission to use track for the purpose of providing network services on that track;

(b) paragraph (b) does not extend to obtaining permission to use a station for the purpose of operating that station;

(c) paragraph (c) does not extend to obtaining permission to use a light maintenance depot for the purpose of enabling the beneficiary to carry out light maintenance;

(d) if and to the extent that the railway facility mentioned in paragraph (e) is track, that paragraph does not extend to obtaining permission to use that track for the purpose—

(i) of providing network services on that track, or

(ii) of operating any network in which that track is comprised,

except where the purpose for which directions are sought is to enable the beneficiary to operate on behalf of the Franchising Director a network in which the track in question is comprised;

(e) if and to the extent that the railway facility mentioned in that paragraph is a station, that paragraph does not extend to obtaining permission to use that station for the purpose—

(i) of providing station services at that station, or

(ii) of operating that station,

except where the purpose for which directions are sought is to enable the beneficiary to operate the station on behalf of the Franchising Director;

(f) if and to the extent that the railway facility mentioned in that paragraph is a light maintenance depot, that paragraph does not extend to obtaining permission to use that light maintenance depot for the purpose—

(i) of carrying out light maintenance at that light maintenance depot, or

(ii) of operating that light maintenance depot,

except where the purpose for which directions are sought is to enable the beneficiary to operate the light maintenance depot on behalf of the Franchising Director.

(4) Any reference in this section to a person operating a network, station or light maintenance depot "on behalf of the Franchising Director" is a reference to his operating the network, station or light maintenance depot in pursuance of any agreement or other arrangements made by the Franchising Director for the purpose of performing a duty imposed upon him, or exercising a power conferred upon him, under or by virtue of this Part to secure the operation of that network, station or light maintenance depot.

(5) Nothing in this section authorises the Regulator to give directions to any person requiring him to grant a lease of the whole or any part of a railway facility.

(6) In this Part—

"access contract" means—

(a) a contract under which—

(i) a person (whether or not the applicant), and

(ii) so far as may be appropriate, any associate of that person,

obtains permission from a facility owner to use the facility owner's railway facility; or

(b) a contract conferring an option, whether exercisable by the applicant or some other person, to require a facility owner to secure that—

(i) a person (whether or not the applicant or that other), and

(ii) so far as may be appropriate, any associate of that person,

obtains permission from the facility owner to use his railway facility;

and any reference to an "access option" is a reference to an option falling within paragraph (b) above;

"facility owner" means any person—

(a) who has an estate or interest in, or right over, a railway facility; and

(b) whose permission to use that railway facility is needed by another before that other may use it;

and any reference to a facility owner's railway facility is a reference to the railway facility by reference to which he is a facility owner.

(7) In this section—

"the applicant" means the person making the application for directions;

"associate", in relation to any person, includes—

(a) any servant, agent or independent contractor of his;

(b) any passenger of his;

(c) any person engaged in the provision of goods or services to or for him; and

(d) any other person who deals or has business with him;

"the beneficiary" means the person mentioned in paragraph (a)(i) or, as the case may be, paragraph (b)(i) of the definition of "access contract" in subsection (6) above, according to the description of access contract in question;

"directions" means directions under this section;

"the Directive" means the Directive of the Council of the European Communities dated 29th July 1991 on the development of the Community's railways;

91/440/EEC.

"implementing regulation" means a provision contained in subordinate legislation made for the purpose of implementing the Directive;

"international railway access contract" means an access contract entered into as a result of—

(a) an application made under an implementing regulation by an international grouping to an infrastructure manager for access and transit rights, or for transit rights, for the provision of international services between the member States where the undertakings constituting the international grouping are established; or

(b) an application made under an implementing regulation by a railway undertaking established, or to be established, in a member State other than the United

Kingdom to an infrastructure manager for the grant of access for the purpose of the operation of international combined transport goods services;

and expressions used in paragraph (a) or (b) above and in the Directive have the same meaning in that paragraph as they have in the Directive;

"lease" includes an underlease or sublease and an agreement for a lease, underlease or sublease.

(8) Any reference in this section to obtaining permission to use a railway facility includes—

(a) a reference to obtaining, in connection with any such permission, power to obtain the provision of ancillary services relating to that railway facility, whether the facility owner in question is to provide those services himself or to secure their provision by another; and

(b) a reference to obtaining permission—

(i) to enter upon the facility land, with or without vehicles,

(ii) to bring things on to that land and keep them there,

(iii) to carry out works on that land, and

(iv) to use and maintain any things kept, or buildings or other works constructed, on that land (whether by the beneficiary or another) or any amenities situated on that land,

"facility land" meaning in this paragraph the land which constitutes the railway facility in question;

and, in subsection (2)(c) above, the reference to obtaining permission to use a light maintenance depot includes a reference to obtaining power to obtain light maintenance services at that light maintenance depot, whether the facility owner is to provide those services himself or to secure their provision by another.

(9) Any reference in this section to a railway facility includes a reference to a part of a railway facility.

(10) Schedule 4 to this Act shall have effect with respect to applications for directions.

(11) Any sums required for the making by the Franchising Director of payments in respect of an access contract entered into pursuant to directions under this section shall, if the access contract is one—

(a) in relation to which the Franchising Director is the person who made the application under this section, or

(b) under which an access option is exercisable by the Franchising Director,

be paid by the Secretary of State out of money provided by Parliament.

Access agreements: contracts requiring the approval of the Regulator.

18.—(1) A facility owner shall not enter into an access contract to which this section applies unless—

(a) he does so pursuant to directions under section 17 above; or

(b) the Regulator has approved the terms of the access contract and the facility owner enters into the contract pursuant to directions under this section;

and any access contract to which this section applies which is entered into otherwise than in compliance with paragraph (a) or (b) above shall be void.

(2) The access contracts to which this section applies are those under which the beneficiary obtains, or, in the case of an access contract conferring an access option, may obtain, (whether for himself alone or for himself and associates of his)—

- (a) from a facility owner whose railway facility is track, permission to use that track for the purpose of the operation of trains on that track by the beneficiary;
- (b) from a facility owner whose railway facility is a station, permission to use that station, for or in connection with the operation of trains by the beneficiary;
- (c) from a facility owner whose railway facility is a light maintenance depot, permission to use that light maintenance depot for the purpose of obtaining light maintenance services for or in connection with the operation of trains by the beneficiary, whether the facility owner is to provide those services himself or to secure their provision by another;
- (d) from any facility owner, permission to use the facility owner's railway facility for the purpose of stabling, or otherwise temporarily holding, rolling stock in connection with the operation of trains on any track by the beneficiary; or
- (e) from any facility owner, permission to use the facility owner's railway facility for or in connection with the operation of a network, station or light maintenance depot by the beneficiary;

but this subsection is subject to subsections (3) and (4) below.

(3) This section does not apply to an access contract—

- (a) if and to the extent that the railway facility to which the access contract relates is, by virtue of section 20 below, an exempt facility; or
- (b) if and to the extent that the access contract is an international railway access contract.

(4) In subsection (2) above—

- (a) paragraph (a) does not extend to permission to use track for the purpose of providing network services on that track;
- (b) paragraph (b) does not extend to permission to use a station for the purpose of operating that station;
- (c) paragraph (c) does not extend to permission to use a light maintenance depot for the purpose of enabling the beneficiary to carry out light maintenance;
- (d) if and to the extent that the railway facility mentioned in paragraph (e) is track, that paragraph does not extend to obtaining permission to use that track for the purpose—
    - (i) of providing network services on that track, or

(ii) of operating any network in which that track is comprised,

unless the purpose of entering into the access contract is to enable the beneficiary to operate on behalf of the Franchising Director a network in which the track in question is comprised;

(e) if and to the extent that the railway facility mentioned in that paragraph is a station, that paragraph does not extend to obtaining permission to use that station for the purpose—

(i) of providing station services at that station, or

(ii) of operating that station,

unless the purpose of entering into the access contract is to enable the beneficiary to operate the station on behalf of the Franchising Director;

(f) if and to the extent that the railway facility mentioned in that paragraph is a light maintenance depot, that paragraph does not extend to obtaining permission to use that light maintenance depot for the purpose—

(i) of carrying out light maintenance at that light maintenance depot, or

(ii) of operating that light maintenance depot,

unless the purpose of entering into the access contract is to enable the beneficiary to operate the light maintenance depot on behalf of the Franchising Director.

(5) In any case where—

(a) a facility owner and another person (the "other party") have agreed the terms on which they propose to enter into an access contract to which this section applies, but

(b) the circumstances are such that, by virtue of subsection (1)(b) above, those terms must be approved, and directions must be given, by the Regulator before the facility owner may enter into the proposed access contract,

it shall be for the facility owner to submit the proposed access contract to the Regulator for approval of its terms.

(6) If, on the submission of a proposed access contract pursuant to subsection (5) above, the Regulator approves its terms, he shall issue directions to the facility owner—

(a) requiring him to enter into the proposed access contract within such period as may be specified for the purpose in the directions; but

(b) releasing him from his duty to do so if the other party fails to enter into the proposed access contract within such period as may be specified for the purpose in the directions;

and the Regulator shall send a copy of the directions to the other party.

(7) If, on the submission of a proposed access contract pursuant to subsection (5) above, the Regulator does not consider it appropriate to approve its terms without modification (or to reject it), he may, after consultation with the facility owner and the other party, issue directions to the facility owner—

(a) approving the terms of the proposed access contract, but subject to such modifications as may be specified in the directions; and

(b) requiring the facility owner to enter into the proposed access contract on those terms, as so modified; but

(c) releasing him from his duty to do so if either—

(i) the facility owner gives the Regulator notice of objection before the expiration of the period of fourteen days beginning with the day after that on which the directions are issued; or

(ii) the other party fails to enter into the proposed access contract, on the terms as modified under this subsection, before the date specified for the purpose in the directions;

and the Regulator shall send a copy of the directions to the other party.

(8) In this section, "associate", "the beneficiary", "international railway access contract" and "lease" have the same meaning as they have in section 17 above.

(9) The following provisions of section 17 above, that is to say—

(a) subsection (4),

(b) subsection (8)(a) and (b), and

(c) subsection (9),

apply for the purposes of this section as they apply for the purposes of that section; and the words following paragraph (b) of subsection (8) of that section apply in relation to subsection (2)(c) of this section as they apply in relation to subsection (2)(c) of that section.

(10) This section shall not prevent a facility owner from granting a lease of any land which consists of or includes the whole or any part of his railway facility.

(11) Any sums required for the making by the Franchising Director of payments in respect of an access contract entered into pursuant to directions under this section shall, if the access contract is one—

(a) to which the Franchising Director is a party, but in relation to which he is not the facility owner, or

(b) under which the Franchising Director is the person by whom an access option is exercisable,

be paid by the Secretary of State out of money provided by Parliament.

19.—(1) The Regulator may, on the application of any person, give directions to an installation owner requiring him to enter into an installation access contract with the applicant for the purpose of enabling the beneficiary to obtain (whether for himself alone or for himself and, so far as may be applicable, associates of his) permission to use the installation owner's network installation for the purpose of operating, on behalf of the Franchising Director, the network in which the network installation is comprised.

Access agreements: contracts for the use, on behalf of the Franchising Director, of installations comprised in a network.

(2) Directions shall not be given under subsection (1) above in the case of any network installation if and to the extent that, as a result of an obligation or duty owed by the installation owner which arose before the coming into force of this section, the consent of some other person is required by the installation owner before he may enter into the installation access contract.

PART I

(3) An installation owner shall not enter into an installation access contract to which this subsection applies unless—

(a) he does so pursuant to directions under subsection (1) above; or

(b) the Regulator has approved the terms of the installation access contract and the installation owner enters into the contract pursuant to directions given by virtue of subsection (5) below;

and any installation access contract to which this subsection applies which is entered into otherwise than in compliance with paragraph (a) or (b) above shall be void.

(4) The installation access contracts to which subsection (3) above applies are those under which the beneficiary obtains (whether for himself alone or for himself and associates of his) from an installation owner permission to use the installation owner's network installation for the purpose of operating, on behalf of the Franchising Director, the network in which the network installation is comprised.

(5) Subsections (5) to (7) of section 18 above shall apply in relation to installation access contracts to which subsection (3) of this section applies as they apply in relation to access contracts to which that section applies, but with the following modifications, that is to say—

(a) for any reference to a facility owner there shall be substituted a reference to an installation owner;

(b) for any reference to an access contract to which that section applies there shall be substituted a reference to an installation access contract to which subsection (3) above applies;

(c) for the reference to subsection (1)(b) of that section there shall be substituted a reference to subsection (3)(b) of this section.

(6) Nothing in this section—

(a) authorises the Regulator to give directions to an installation owner requiring him to grant a lease of the whole or any part of his network installation; or

(b) prevents an installation owner from granting a lease of any land which consists of or includes the whole or any part of his network installation.

(7) Any reference in this section to a person operating a network "on behalf of the Franchising Director" is a reference to his operating the network in pursuance of any agreement or other arrangements made by the Franchising Director for the purpose of performing a duty imposed upon him, or exercising a power conferred upon him, under or by virtue of this Part to secure the operation of that network.

(8) Any reference in this section to obtaining permission to use a network installation includes—

(a) a reference to obtaining, in connection with any such permission, power to obtain the provision of ancillary services relating to that network installation, whether the installation owner in question is to provide those services himself or to secure their provision by another; and

(b) a reference to obtaining permission—

(i) to enter upon the installation land, with or without vehicles,

(ii) to bring things on to that land and keep them there,

(iii) to carry out works on that land, and

(iv) to use and maintain any things kept, or buildings or other works constructed, on that land (whether by the beneficiary or another) or any amenities situated on that land;

and in paragraph (b) above "installation land" means the land which constitutes the network installation in question.

(9) In this Part—

"installation access contract" means a contract under which—

(a) a person (whether or not the applicant), and

(b) so far as may be appropriate, any associate of that person,

obtains permission from an installation owner to use the installation owner's network installation;

"installation owner" means any person—

(a) who has an estate or interest in, or right over, a network installation; and

(b) whose permission to use that network installation is needed by another before that other may use it;

and any reference to an installation owner's network installation is a reference to the network installation by reference to which he is an installation owner.

(10) In this section—

"ancillary service" means any service which is necessary or expedient for giving full effect to any permission or right which a person may have to use a network installation;

"the applicant" means the person making the application for directions under subsection (1) above;

"associate" has the meaning given by section 17(7) above;

"the beneficiary" means the person mentioned in paragraph (a) of the definition of "installation access contract" in subsection (9) above;

"lease" includes an underlease or sublease and an agreement for a lease, underlease or sublease;

"network installation" means any installation (other than track) which is comprised in a network.

(11) Any reference in this section to a network installation includes a reference to a part of a network installation.

(12) Schedule 4 to this Act shall have effect with respect to applications for directions under subsection (1) above as it has effect with respect to applications for directions under section 17 above, but with the following modifications, that is to say—

(a) for any reference to an access contract, there shall be substituted a reference to an installation access contract;

(b) any reference to an application for directions under section 17 above shall be taken as a reference to an application for directions under subsection (1) above;

PART I

(c) for any reference to the facility owner, there shall be substituted a reference to the installation owner mentioned in subsection (1) above;

(d) for any reference to section 17 above (but not to any specific provision of that section) there shall be substituted a reference to this section.

(13) There shall be paid by the Secretary of State out of money provided by Parliament any sums required for the making by the Franchising Director of payments in respect of—

(a) an installation access contract—

(i) which is entered into pursuant to directions under subsection (1) above; and

(ii) in relation to which the Franchising Director is the person who made the application under this section; and

(b) an installation access contract—

(i) which is entered into pursuant to directions given by virtue of subsection (5) above; and

(ii) to which the Franchising Director is a party, but in relation to which he is not the installation owner.

Exemption of railway facilities from sections 17 and 18.

20.—(1) The Secretary of State may, after consultation with the Regulator, by order grant exemption from sections 17 and 18 above in respect of such railway facilities as may be specified in the order, but subject to compliance with such conditions (if any) as may be so specified.

(2) A facility exemption under subsection (1) above may be granted—

(a) to persons of a particular class or description or to a particular person; and

(b) in respect of railway facilities of a particular class or description or a particular railway facility, or in respect of part only of any such railway facilities or facility;

and a facility exemption granted to persons of a particular class or description shall be published in such manner as the Secretary of State considers appropriate for bringing it to the attention of persons of that class or description.

(3) If a facility owner makes an application under this subsection to the Regulator for the grant of an exemption from sections 17 and 18 above in respect of the whole or any part of his railway facility, the Regulator, after consultation with the Secretary of State—

(a) may either grant or refuse the exemption, whether wholly or to such extent as he may specify in the exemption; and

(b) if and to the extent that he grants it, may do so subject to compliance with such conditions (if any) as he may so specify.

(4) Before granting a facility exemption under subsection (3) above, the Regulator shall give notice—

(a) stating that he proposes to grant the facility exemption,

(b) stating the reasons why he proposes to grant the facility exemption, and

(c) specifying the time (not being less than 28 days from the date of publication of the notice) within which representations or objections with respect to the proposed facility exemption may be made,

and shall consider any representations or objections which are duly made and not withdrawn.

(5) A notice under subsection (4) above shall be given by publishing the notice in such manner as the Regulator considers appropriate for bringing it to the attention of persons likely to be affected by the grant of the facility exemption.

(6) If any condition (the "broken condition") of a facility exemption is not complied with—

(a) the Secretary of State, in the case of a facility exemption under subsection (1) above, or

(b) the Regulator, in the case of a facility exemption under subsection (3) above,

may give to any relevant person a direction declaring that the facility exemption is revoked, so far as relating to that person, to such extent and as from such date as may be specified in the direction.

(7) For the purposes of subsection (6) above—

"condition", in relation to a facility exemption, means any condition subject to compliance with which the facility exemption was granted;

"relevant person", in the case of any facility exemption, means a person who has the benefit of the facility exemption and who—

(a) is a person who failed to comply with the broken condition or with respect to whom the broken condition is not complied with; or

(b) is the facility owner in the case of the railway facility in relation to which the broken condition is not complied with.

(8) Subject to subsection (6) above, a facility exemption, unless previously revoked in accordance with any term contained in the facility exemption, shall continue in force for such period as may be specified in, or determined by or under, the facility exemption.

(9) Subsection (1) above applies in relation to the grant of any facility exemption which is to become effective on the day on which sections 17 and 18 above come into force; and subsection (3) above applies in relation to the grant of any facility exemption which is not to become effective until after that day.

(10) Any application for a facility exemption under subsection (3) above must be made in writing; and where any such application is made, the Regulator may require the applicant to furnish him with such information as the Regulator may consider necessary to enable him to decide whether to grant or refuse the facility exemption.

(11) Facility exemptions may make different provision, or be granted subject to compliance with different conditions, for different cases.

(12) A facility exemption may be granted in respect of the whole or any part of a railway facility notwithstanding that the railway facility or the part is one which—

(a) is proposed to be constructed; or

(b) is in the course of construction;

and any reference in this section to a railway facility or part of a railway facility shall be construed accordingly.

(13) In this Part "facility exemption" means an exemption from sections 17 and 18 above granted under any provision of this section in respect of the whole or any part of a railway facility; and a railway facility is an "exempt facility" if and to the extent that it is the subject of such an exemption.

Model clauses for access contracts.

21.—(1) The Regulator may prepare and publish model clauses for inclusion in access contracts.

(2) Different model clauses may be prepared and published in relation to different classes or descriptions of railway facility.

(3) The Regulator may from time to time revise any model clauses published under this section and may publish those clauses as so revised.

(4) In preparing or revising any model clauses under this section, the Regulator may consult such persons as he thinks fit.

(5) The Regulator shall encourage, and may require, the use of any model clauses of his in access contracts wherever he considers it appropriate.

Amendment of access agreements.

22.—(1) Any amendment, or purported amendment, of an access agreement shall be void unless the amendment has been approved by the Regulator.

(2) The Regulator may, for the purposes of subsection (1) above, give the parties to any particular access agreement his general approval to the making to that access agreement of amendments of a description specified in the approval; and any approval so given shall not be revoked.

(3) The Regulator may, for the purposes of subsection (1) above, give his general approval to the making to access agreements, or to access agreements of a particular class or description, of amendments of a description specified in the approval.

(4) Where the Regulator gives or revokes a general approval under subsection (3) above, he shall publish the approval or revocation (as the case may be) in such manner as he considers appropriate.

(5) The revocation of a general approval given under subsection (3) above shall not affect the continuing validity of any amendment made in accordance with, and before the revocation of, that approval.

(6) The Regulator shall not have power to direct or otherwise require amendments to be made to an access agreement.

Franchising of passenger services

Passenger services to be subject to franchise agreements.

23.—(1) It shall be the duty of the Franchising Director from time to time to designate as eligible for provision under franchise agreements such services for the carriage of passengers by railway as he may determine (other than services which are, by virtue of section 24 below, exempt from designation under this subsection).

(2) The Franchising Director may perform his duty under subsection (1) above by designating particular services or services of a class or description.

(3) In this Part—

"franchise agreement" means an agreement with the Franchising Director under which another party undertakes either—

(a) to provide, or

(b) to secure that a wholly owned subsidiary of his provides,

throughout the franchise term those services for the carriage of passengers by railway to which the agreement relates;

"franchise operator", in relation to any franchise agreement, means the person (whether the franchisee or, as the case may be, the wholly owned subsidiary of the franchisee) who is to provide the franchised services;

"franchise period", in relation to any franchise agreement, means the franchise term, except where the franchise agreement is terminated before the end of that term, in which case it means so much of that term as ends with that termination;

"franchise term", in relation to any franchise agreement, means the period specified in the franchise agreement as the period throughout which the franchisee is to provide, or secure that a wholly owned subsidiary of his provides, the franchised services, and includes any such extension of that period as is mentioned in section 29(3) below;

"franchised services", in relation to any franchise agreement, means the services for the carriage of passengers by railway which are to be provided under that franchise agreement;

"franchisee" means—

(a) in relation to a franchise agreement under which a party undertakes to secure that a wholly owned subsidiary of his provides the franchised services, the party so undertaking; or

(b) in relation to any other franchise agreement, the person who is to provide the franchised services.

(4) Any reference in this Part to the provision of services under a franchise agreement is a reference to the provision of those services by the franchise operator; and where the franchise operator is, or is to be, a wholly owned subsidiary of the franchisee, any reference to the provision of services by the franchisee under a franchise agreement shall accordingly be construed as a reference to his securing their provision by the franchise operator.

24.—(1) The Secretary of State may by order grant exemption from designation under section 23(1) above in respect of such services for the carriage of passengers by railway as may be specified in the order, but subject to compliance with such conditions (if any) as may be so specified.

Exemption of passenger services from section 23(1).

(2) A franchise exemption under subsection (1) above may be granted—

(a) to persons of a particular class or description or to a particular person; and

(b) in respect of services generally, services of a particular class or description or a particular service, or in respect of part only of any such services or service;

and a franchise exemption granted to persons of a particular class or description shall be published in such manner as the Secretary of State considers appropriate for bringing it to the attention of persons of that class or description.

(3) If a person who provides, or who proposes to introduce, services for the carriage of passengers by railway makes an application to the Secretary of State under this subsection for the grant of an exemption from designation under section 23(1) above in respect of any such service which he provides or proposes to introduce, the Secretary of State, after consultation with the Regulator and the Franchising Director—

(a) may either grant or refuse the exemption, whether wholly or to such extent as he may specify in the exemption; and

(b) if and to the extent that he grants it, may do so subject to compliance with such conditions (if any) as he may so specify.

(4) Before granting a franchise exemption under subsection (3) above, the Secretary of State shall give notice—

(a) stating that he proposes to grant the franchise exemption,

(b) stating the reasons why he proposes to grant the franchise exemption, and

(c) specifying the time (not being less than 28 days from the date of publication of the notice) within which representations or objections with respect to the proposed franchise exemption may be made,

and shall consider any representations or objections which are duly made and not withdrawn.

(5) A notice under subsection (4) above shall be given by publishing the notice in such manner as the Secretary of State considers appropriate for bringing it to the attention of persons likely to be affected by the grant of the franchise exemption.

(6) If any condition (the "broken condition") of a franchise exemption is not complied with, the Secretary of State may give to any relevant person a direction declaring that the franchise exemption is revoked, so far as relating to that person, to such extent and as from such date as may be specified in the direction.

(7) For the purposes of subsection (6) above—

"condition", in relation to a franchise exemption, means any condition subject to compliance with which the franchise exemption was granted;

"relevant person", in the case of any franchise exemption, means a person who has the benefit of the franchise exemption and who—

(a) is a person who failed to comply with the broken condition or with respect to whom the broken condition is not complied with; or

(b) provides any of the services in relation to which the broken condition is not complied with.

(8) Subject to subsection (6) above, a franchise exemption, unless previously revoked in accordance with any term contained in the franchise exemption, shall continue in force for such period as may be specified in, or determined by or under, the franchise exemption.

(9) Any application for a franchise exemption under subsection (3) above must be made in writing; and where any such application is made, the Secretary of State may require the applicant to furnish him with such information as the Secretary of State may consider necessary to enable him to decide whether to grant or refuse the franchise exemption.

(10) Any franchise exemption granted under subsection (3) above shall be in writing.

(11) Subsections (1) and (3) above apply in relation to the grant of a franchise exemption whether it is to become effective on, or after, the day on which section 23(1) above comes into force.

(12) Franchise exemptions may make different provision for different cases.

(13) In this Part, "franchise exemption" means an exemption from designation under section 23(1) above granted under any provision of this section in respect of any service for the carriage of passengers by railway.

25.—(1) The following bodies and persons (in this Part referred to as "public sector operators") shall not be franchisees—

 (a) any Minister of the Crown, Government department or other emanation of the Crown;

 (b) any local authority;

 (c) any metropolitan county passenger transport authority;

 (d) any body corporate whose members are appointed by a Minister of the Crown, a Government department, a local authority or a metropolitan county passenger transport authority or by a body corporate whose members are so appointed;

 (e) a company—

   (i) a majority of whose issued shares are held by or on behalf of any of the bodies or persons falling within paragraphs (a) to (d) above;

   (ii) in which the majority of the voting rights are held by or on behalf of any of those bodies or persons;

   (iii) a majority of whose board of directors can be appointed or removed by any of those bodies or persons; or

   (iv) in which the majority of the voting rights are controlled by any of those bodies or persons, pursuant to an agreement with other persons;

 (f) a subsidiary of a company falling within paragraph (e) above.

Public sector operators not to be franchisees.

(2) Expressions used in sub-paragraphs (i) to (iv) of subsection (1)(e) above and in section 736 of the Companies Act 1985 have the same meaning in those sub-paragraphs as they have in that section.

1985 c. 6.

(3) Subject to the following provisions of this section, subsection (1) above shall not prevent—

 (a) the British Railways Board (in this Act referred to as "the Board"), or

(b) a wholly owned subsidiary of the Board,

from being a franchisee.

(4) Subject to the following provisions of this section, whenever the Franchising Director proposes to issue invitations to tender under section 26 below in respect of any particular services for the carriage of passengers by railway, he may, after consultation with the Board and the Regulator, determine that neither the Board nor any wholly owned subsidiary of the Board shall be eligible for inclusion among the persons to whom the invitations are to be issued or who may be selected as the franchisee.

(5) The Franchising Director shall not make a determination under subsection (4) above unless he considers that it is desirable to do so—

(a) for the purpose of promoting competition for franchises;

(b) for the purpose of promoting the award of franchise agreements to companies in which qualifying railway employees have a substantial interest;

(c) for the purpose of encouraging new entry to the passenger railway industry; or

(d) for the purpose of preventing or reducing the dominance of any person or persons in the market for the provision in Great Britain, or in a part of Great Britain, of services for the carriage of passengers by railway.

(6) The Franchising Director shall—

(a) give notice of any determination under subsection (4) above to the Board; and

(b) publish notice of the determination in such manner as he thinks fit.

(7) Nothing in subsection (5) above shall be taken to affect the matters which the Franchising Director may take into account in determining the other persons whom he invites to tender for franchise agreements or whom he selects as franchisees.

(8) No objectives, instructions or guidance shall be given under section 5 above by the Secretary of State to the Franchising Director with respect to the exercise of his functions under this section.

(9) In this section—

"competition for franchises" means competition to become franchisees under franchise agreements;

"encouraging new entry to the passenger railway industry" means encouraging private sector operators who do not currently provide services for the carriage of passengers by railway to commence doing so;

"qualifying railway employees", in the case of any franchise agreement, means persons who are or have been employed in an undertaking which provides or provided the services to which the franchise agreement relates at a time before those services begin to be provided under that franchise agreement.

PART I
Invitations to tender for franchises.

26.—(1) Unless the Secretary of State otherwise directs, the person who is to be the franchisee under any franchise agreement shall be selected by the Franchising Director from among those who submit tenders in response to an invitation to tender under this section for the right to provide, or to secure that a wholly owned subsidiary provides, services for the carriage of passengers by railway under that franchise agreement.

(2) The Franchising Director shall prepare any such invitation to tender and shall issue that invitation to such persons as he may, after consultation with the Regulator, think fit.

(3) The Franchising Director shall not issue an invitation to tender under this section to (or entertain such a tender from) any person unless he is of the opinion that the person has, or is likely by the commencement of the franchise term to have, an appropriate financial position and managerial competence, and is otherwise a suitable person, to be the franchisee.

Transfer of franchise assets and shares.

27.—(1) It shall be the duty of the Franchising Director before entering into a franchise agreement to satisfy himself that if the franchise agreement is entered into—

(a) the initial franchise assets (if any) for that franchise agreement will be vested in the person who is to be the franchise operator; and

(b) if the franchise agreement is to be one under which the franchisee undertakes to secure that a wholly owned subsidiary of his provides the franchised services, that the franchise operator will be a wholly owned subsidiary of the franchisee.

(2) After a franchise agreement has been entered into, it shall be the duty of the Franchising Director, before any property, rights or liabilities are subsequently designated as franchise assets in accordance with the terms of, or by amendment to, the franchise agreement, to satisfy himself that, if the property, rights or liabilities in question are so designated, they will be vested in the franchise operator.

(3) Without the consent of the Franchising Director, the franchise operator shall not—

(a) if and to the extent that the franchise assets are property or rights—

(i) transfer or agree to transfer, or create or agree to create any security over, any franchise assets or any interest in, or right over, any franchise assets; or

(ii) create or extinguish, or agree to create or extinguish, any interest in, or right over, any franchise assets; and

(b) if and to the extent that the franchise assets are liabilities, shall not enter into any agreement under which any such liability is released or discharged, or transferred to some other person.

(4) Where the franchise agreement is one under which the franchisee undertakes to secure that a wholly owned subsidiary of his provides the franchised services, the franchisee shall not, without the consent of the Franchising Director, take any action which would result in the franchise operator ceasing to be a wholly owned subsidiary of his.

(5) Any transaction which is entered into in contravention of subsection (3) or (4) above shall be void.

Part I

(6) In England and Wales, no execution or other legal process may be commenced or continued, and no distress may be levied, against any property which is, or rights which are, franchise assets in the case of any franchise agreement.

(7) In Scotland, no diligence or other legal process may be carried out or continued against any property which is, or rights which are, franchise assets in the case of any franchise agreement.

(8) In any case where—

(a) there are to be initial franchise assets in relation to a franchise agreement,

(b) a franchise agreement is to be one which provides for subsequent designation of property, rights or liabilities as franchise assets, or

(c) property, rights or liabilities are to be designated as franchise assets by an amendment made to a franchise agreement,

the Franchising Director shall ensure that the franchise agreement includes provision specifying, or providing for the determination of, amounts to be paid in respect of the property, rights and liabilities which, immediately before the end of the franchise period, constitute the franchise assets in relation to that franchise agreement if and to the extent that they are transferred by transfer scheme at or after the end of that period.

(9) Without prejudice to the generality of the provisions that may be included in a franchise agreement with respect to the acquisition, provision, disposal or other transfer of property, rights or liabilities (whether franchise assets or not), the Franchising Director may undertake in a franchise agreement to exercise his powers under Part II below to transfer franchise assets to himself or another in such circumstances as may be specified in the franchise agreement.

(10) The Franchising Director shall ensure that every franchise agreement includes such provision (if any) as he may consider appropriate in the particular case for the purpose of securing—

(a) that the franchise assets are adequately maintained, protected and preserved; and

(b) that, at the end of the franchise period, possession of such of the franchise assets as may be specified for the purpose in the agreement, or by the Franchising Director in accordance with the agreement, is delivered up to the Franchising Director or such other person as may be so specified.

(11) In this Part, "franchise assets", in relation to any franchise agreement, means—

(a) any property, rights or liabilities which are designated as franchise assets in the franchise agreement as originally made (in this section referred to as the "initial franchise assets"), and

(b) any property, rights or liabilities which, after the making of the franchise agreement, are designated as franchise assets in accordance with the terms of, or by an amendment made to, the franchise agreement,

but does not include any property, rights or liabilities which, in accordance with the terms of, or by an amendment made to, the franchise agreement, have for the time being ceased to be designated as franchise assets.

(12) No rights or liabilities under contracts of employment shall be designated as franchise assets.

(13) In this section "security" has the meaning given by section 248(b) of the Insolvency Act 1986.

1986 c. 45.

(14) Any sums required by the Franchising Director for making payments for or in connection with the acquisition, transfer or disposal of property, rights or liabilities in pursuance of provisions contained in a franchise agreement shall be paid by the Secretary of State out of money provided by Parliament.

(15) Any sums received by the Franchising Director for or in connection with the acquisition, transfer or disposal of property, rights or liabilities in pursuance of provisions contained in a franchise agreement shall be paid into the Consolidated Fund.

28.—(1) A franchise agreement may include provision with respect to the fares to be charged for travel by means of the franchised services.

Fares and approved discount fare schemes.

(2) Subject to the other provisions of this Act, if it appears to the Franchising Director that the interests of persons who use, or who are likely to use, franchised services so require, he shall ensure that the franchise agreement in question contains any such provision as he may consider necessary for the purpose of securing that any fares, or any fares of a class or description, which are to be charged are, in his opinion, reasonable in all the circumstances of the case.

(3) Every franchise agreement shall include provision requiring the franchise operator—

(a) to participate in every approved discount fare scheme,

(b) to charge fares, in cases to which such a scheme applies, at rates which are not in excess of the levels or, as the case may be, the maximum levels set by the scheme, and

(c) otherwise to comply with the requirements of every such scheme,

if and to the extent that the franchised services are services, or services of a class or description, in relation to which the approved discount fare scheme in question applies.

(4) The discount fare schemes which are to be regarded for the purposes of this section as "approved" are those which are from time to time approved for the purposes of this section by the Franchising Director.

(5) In this section—

"discount fare scheme" means any scheme for enabling persons who are young, elderly or disabled to travel by railway at discounted fares, subject to compliance with such conditions (if any) as may be imposed by or under the scheme;

Part I

"discounted fare" means a lower fare than the standard fare for the journey in question;

"scheme" includes any agreement or arrangements.

Other terms and conditions of franchise agreements.

29.—(1) The Franchising Director may enter into a franchise agreement on conditions requiring—

(a) the rendering to the Franchising Director by the franchisee or the franchise operator of payments of such amounts and at such intervals as may be specified in, or determined by or under, the franchise agreement; or

(b) the payment to the franchisee or the franchise operator of grants of such amounts and at such intervals as may be specified in, or determined by or under, the franchise agreement.

(2) A franchise agreement may include provision requiring the franchisee—

(a) to operate any additional railway asset; or

(b) to secure the operation of any additional railway asset by the franchise operator or any other wholly owned subsidiary of the franchisee.

(3) A franchise agreement shall include provision specifying the franchise term and may include provision enabling that term to be extended by such further term as may be specified in the franchise agreement.

(4) Without prejudice to the generality of the provisions relating to property, rights and liabilities that may be included in a franchise agreement, a franchise agreement may include provision requiring the franchise operator—

(a) to acquire from such person as may be specified in the franchise agreement, and to use, such property or rights as may be so specified; or

(b) to undertake such liabilities as may be so specified.

(5) Subject to any requirements imposed by or under this Act, a franchise agreement may contain any such provisions as the Franchising Director may think fit.

(6) Any sums received by the Franchising Director in consequence of the conditions of a franchise agreement shall be paid into the Consolidated Fund.

(7) Any sums required by the Franchising Director for the payment of any grant, or for the making of any other payment, in consequence of any condition or other provision of a franchise agreement shall be paid by the Secretary of State out of money provided by Parliament.

(8) In this Part, "additional railway asset" means any network, station or light maintenance depot, and any reference to an additional railway asset includes a reference to any part of an additional railway asset.

Failure to secure subsequent franchise agreement.

30.—(1) In any case where—

(a) a franchise agreement is terminated or otherwise comes to an end, but

Part I

(b) no further franchise agreement has been entered into in respect of services for the carriage of passengers by railway formerly provided under that franchise agreement,

it shall, subject to subsection (3) below, be the duty of the Franchising Director to secure the provision of those services until such time as they again begin to be provided under a franchise agreement.

(2) In any case where a franchise agreement which includes provision in respect of the operation of any additional railway assets is terminated or otherwise comes to an end, but—

(a) no further franchise agreement has been entered into which makes provision in respect of the operation of the additional railway assets formerly operated under or by virtue of that franchise agreement, or

(b) such further franchise agreement as has been entered into in respect of the operation of those additional railway assets makes provision in respect of the operation of some but not all of those additional railway assets,

the Franchising Director shall, subject to subsection (4) below, have the power to secure the operation of any additional railway asset with respect to the operation of which no further franchise agreement has been entered into, until such time as it again begins to be operated under or by virtue of a franchise agreement.

(3) Subsection (1) above does not—

(a) require the Franchising Director to secure the provision of any services, if and to the extent that, in his opinion, adequate alternative railway passenger services are available;

(b) preclude him from giving notice under subsection (5) of section 38 below in relation to any of the services in question, in which case his duty under this section to secure the provision of the services to which the notice relates will (subject to subsections (5) and (6) of that section) terminate on the day specified in the notice in pursuance of paragraph (b) of that subsection; or

(c) preclude him from ceasing to secure the provision of any of the services in question in any case falling within any of paragraphs (a) to (d) of subsection (2) of that section.

(4) The Franchising Director's power under subsection (2) above to secure the operation of any additional railway asset shall come to an end—

(a) where the Franchising Director publishes a notice under subsection (5) of section 40 or subsection (4) of section 42 below in respect of the additional railway asset in question, on the date mentioned in paragraph (b) of the subsection in question;

(b) where the Franchising Director discontinues the operation of the additional railway asset in question in circumstances in which he is entitled to do so without notice under or by virtue of subsection (2) of section 40 or 42 below, on the date on which that discontinuance takes place;

(c) where the operator of the additional railway asset in question gives notice to the Franchising Director in respect of that additional railway asset under section 39 or 41 below, on the

PART I

date specified by the operator pursuant to subsection (4)(b) of section 39 or subsection (3)(b) of section 41 below, as the case may be; or

(d) where the operator of the additional railway asset in question discontinues the operation of that additional railway asset in circumstances in which he is entitled to do so without notice, under or by virtue of subsection (1), (2) or (3) of section 39 or subsection (1) or (2) of section 41 below, on the date on which that discontinuance takes place.

Leases granted in pursuance of franchise agreements: no security of tenure.

31.—(1) In any case where—

(a) a franchise agreement makes provision for the franchisee, the franchise operator or a wholly owned subsidiary of the franchisee to enter into an agreement ("the contemplated agreement") with a person who has an interest in a network or a railway facility,

(b) the network or railway facility is to be used for or in connection with the provision of any of the franchised services, and

(c) the contemplated agreement creates a tenancy of any property which (whether in whole or in part) constitutes, or is comprised in, the network or railway facility,

1954 c. 56.
1949 c. 25.

neither Part II of the Landlord and Tenant Act 1954 (security of tenure of business premises) nor the Tenancy of Shops (Scotland) Act 1949 (security of tenure of shop premises in Scotland) shall apply to that tenancy.

(2) For the purposes of this section, a person shall be regarded as having an interest in a network or railway facility if he has an estate or interest in, or right over, any of the property which constitutes, or is comprised in, the network or railway facility.

(3) Any reference in this section to a network or a railway facility includes a reference to any part of a network or railway facility.

(4) In this section—

"agreement" includes a lease, underlease or sublease (as well as a tenancy agreement or an agreement for a lease, underlease or sublease);

"tenancy" has the same meaning as it has in Part II of the Landlord and Tenant Act 1954 or, in Scotland, as it has in the Tenancy of Shops (Scotland) Act 1949.

Passenger Transport Authorities and Executives

Power of Passenger Transport Executives to enter into agreements with wholly owned subsidiaries of the Board.
1968 c. 73.

32.—(1) The Transport Act 1968 shall have effect with the following amendments, which are made for the purpose of enabling Passenger Transport Executives to enter into agreements under section 20(2)(b) of that Act (securing provision of railway services considered appropriate to meet public transport requirements for the Executive's area) with wholly owned subsidiaries of the Board, as well as with the Board.

(2) In section 10(1)(vi) (power of Executive to make payments to the Board for certain services)—

(a) after the words "Railways Board" there shall be inserted the words ", or any wholly-owned subsidiary of that Board,"; and

(b) after the words "the Board" there shall be inserted the words "or the subsidiary (as the case may be)".

(3) In section 15(1)(d) (Executive to obtain the Authority's approval of any agreement proposed to be entered into otherwise than under section 20(2)(b) with the Board for the provision by the Board of certain services)—

(a) after the words "Railways Board" there shall be inserted the words "or a wholly-owned subsidiary of that Board"; and

(b) after the words "the Board" there shall be inserted the words "or the wholly-owned subsidiary".

(4) In section 20(2)(b)—

(a) after the words "section 10 of this Act" there shall be inserted the words "and subject to sections 33 and 34 of the Railways Act 1993";

(b) after the words "that Board" there shall be inserted the words ", or with any wholly-owned subsidiary of that Board,"; and

(c) for the words "the Board" there shall be substituted the words ", between them, the Board and their wholly-owned subsidiaries".

(5) In section 20(4) (payments to the Board)—

(a) after the words "to the Railways Board" there shall be inserted the words "or a wholly-owned subsidiary of that Board"; and

(b) after the words "provided by the Board" there shall be inserted the words "or the subsidiary".

(6) In section 20(6) (resolution of disputes)—

(a) after the words "Railways Board" there shall be inserted the words "or any wholly-owned subsidiary of that Board"; and

(b) after the words "the Board" there shall be inserted the words "or the subsidiary".

33.—(1) It shall be the duty of the Board and of every Passenger Transport Authority and every Passenger Transport Executive to co-operate with each other with a view to reaching agreement about—

(a) the changes that need to be made to existing section 20(2) agreements as a result of the provisions of this Act or anything done or to be done pursuant to any such provision;

(b) whether those changes can best be made by amending the existing section 20(2) agreements or by terminating those agreements and entering into new section 20(2) agreements in their place; and

(c) the amendments that need to be made to the existing section 20(2) agreements or, as the case may be, the provisions that need to be contained in the new section 20(2) agreements.

(2) The Secretary of State may give notice to the Board, and to the Passenger Transport Authority and the Passenger Transport Executive for any passenger transport area, specifying the date by which they are—

Re-negotiation of section 20(2) agreements as a result of this Act.

(a) to have reached agreement on the matters specified in paragraphs (a) to (c) of subsection (1) above, so far as relating to the existing section 20(2) agreement with which they are concerned; and

(b) to have made to that existing section 20(2) agreement the amendments mentioned in paragraph (c) of that subsection or, as the case may be, to have entered into a new section 20(2) agreement, containing the provisions mentioned in that paragraph, in place of the existing section 20(2) agreement.

(3) If, in a case where the Secretary of State has given notice under subsection (2) above, the requirements of paragraphs (a) and (b) of that subsection have not been complied with by the date specified in that notice, he may issue directions to the Board and to the Passenger Transport Executive in question requiring them—

(a) to make to the existing section 20(2) agreement in question amendments determined by him and specified in the directions, or

(b) to enter into a new section 20(2) agreement, on terms determined by him and specified in the directions, in place of the existing section 20(2) agreement,

by such date as may be specified in the directions.

(4) The Board or any Passenger Transport Executive may refer to the Secretary of State any dispute which arises in the course of negotiations concerning the matters specified in paragraphs (a) to (c) of subsection (1) above; and on any such reference the Secretary of State may give such directions as he thinks fit to the Board and to the Passenger Transport Executive in question.

(5) Without prejudice to the generality of the directions that may be given on a reference under subsection (4) above, the Secretary of State may, on any such reference, give directions to the Board and to the Passenger Transport Executive in question requiring the Board and that Executive—

(a) to make to the existing section 20(2) agreement in question amendments determined by him and specified in the directions; or

(b) to enter into a new section 20(2) agreement, on terms determined by him and specified in the directions, in place of the existing section 20(2) agreement,

by such date as may be specified in the directions.

(6) Where the Secretary of State gives directions under this section with respect to the amendments that are to be made to an existing section 20(2) agreement or the terms on which a new section 20(2) agreement is to be entered into, any requirement for the consent of the Passenger Transport Authority in question to be obtained to the making of those amendments or that agreement shall be dispensed with.

(7) This section shall apply in relation to any section 20(2) agreement which has been amended or entered into pursuant to this section as it applies in relation to an existing section 20(2) agreement, and "existing section 20(2) agreement" shall be construed accordingly.

(8) In this section—

"section 20(2) agreement" means an agreement made between the Board and a Passenger Transport Executive pursuant to section 20(2)(b) of the Transport Act 1968 (whether or not the agreement has been amended or entered into pursuant to this section);

1968 c. 73.

"existing section 20(2) agreement", subject to subsection (7) above, means a section 20(2) agreement entered into before the coming into force of this section;

"new section 20(2) agreement" means a section 20(2) agreement made at or after the coming into force of this section;

and any reference to the Board includes a reference to a wholly owned subsidiary of the Board.

34.—(1) The fact that any services for the carriage of passengers by railway are, or are to be, provided by the Board or a wholly owned subsidiary of the Board under a section 20(2) agreement does not preclude the designation of those services under section 23(1) above as eligible for provision under a franchise agreement.

Passenger Transport Authorities and Executives: franchising.

(2) Subsection (1) above does not affect the continuing validity of any section 20(2) agreement and, accordingly, no services provided, or to be provided, under such an agreement shall begin to be provided under a franchise agreement until such time as the section 20(2) agreement in question has terminated.

(3) Subject to section 35(7) below, a Passenger Transport Executive shall continue to have power to enter into section 20(2) agreements with the Board or any wholly owned subsidiary of the Board for the provision of services for the carriage of passengers by railway until such time as the services in question first begin to be provided under a franchise agreement; and, accordingly, once the services first begin to be so provided, the Executive in question shall cease to have power to enter into a section 20(2) agreement for the provision of those services.

(4) The Franchising Director—

(a) before issuing an invitation to tender under section 26 above in respect of any services for the carriage of passengers by railway within the passenger transport area of a Passenger Transport Executive, or

(b) in a case where the Secretary of State has given a direction under section 26(1) above which has effect in relation to any such services, before entering into a franchise agreement in respect of any of those services,

shall comply with the requirements imposed upon him by subsection (5) below.

(5) The requirements mentioned in subsection (4) above are that the Franchising Director must give notice to the Passenger Transport Executive for the area in question—

(a) of his intentions with respect to the inclusion, in any franchise agreement contemplated by that subsection, of provisions relating to the operation of any additional railway assets wholly or partly within the area in question, and

(b) of his intention—

(i) in a case falling within paragraph (a) of that subsection, to issue the invitation to tender, or

(ii) in a case falling within paragraph (b) of that subsection, to enter into the franchise agreement,

and must, in either of the cases mentioned in paragraph (b) above, consult that Executive, which may, before the expiration of the period of 60 days immediately following the date specified in that notice as its date of issue, submit to him a statement under this subsection.

(6) A statement under subsection (5) above—

(a) shall specify the services for the carriage of passengers by railway which the Passenger Transport Authority for the area in question considers it appropriate to secure to meet any public transport requirements within that area, so far as relating to the provision of services of the same description as those in respect of which the Franchising Director proposes—

(i) to issue the invitation to tender mentioned in paragraph (b)(i) of that subsection, or

(ii) to enter into the franchise agreement mentioned in paragraph (b)(ii) of that subsection,

as the case may be;

(b) may specify the minimum level of quality to which any services so specified are to be provided;

(c) may (subject to section 28(3) above) specify requirements with respect to the fares to be charged to persons using any services so specified; and

(d) may specify the minimum level of quality with respect to the operation of any station (but not any other additional railway asset) which may be required by any such franchise agreement as is mentioned in subsection (5)(a) above.

(7) A Passenger Transport Executive which has submitted a statement under subsection (5) above to the Franchising Director may from time to time amend that statement by giving notice of the amendments to the Franchising Director; and where any such statement is so amended, any reference in this section to the statement submitted under subsection (5) above shall be taken as a reference to that statement as for the time being amended.

(8) Where a Passenger Transport Executive has submitted a statement under subsection (5) above to the Franchising Director, the Franchising Director shall ensure that the services, and any minimum levels of quality or requirements with respect to fares, specified in that statement—

(a) in a case falling within paragraph (a) of subsection (4) above, are included in the specification of the services in respect of which the invitation to tender is issued; or

(b) in a case falling within paragraph (b) of that subsection, are provided for in any franchise agreement into which he may enter in respect of the services mentioned in that paragraph.

(9) A Passenger Transport Executive shall be a party to any franchise agreement which relates, whether in whole or in part, to the provision, within the Executive's passenger transport area, of services specified in a statement under subsection (5) above.

(10) The Franchising Director and any Passenger Transport Executive may enter into agreements with each other as to the terms on which franchise agreements to which the Executive is a party are to be entered into.

(11) Before entering into a franchise agreement, a Passenger Transport Executive for a passenger transport area shall submit to the Passenger Transport Authority for that area, and obtain that Passenger Transport Authority's approval of, the proposed franchise agreement.

(12) It shall be the duty of every Passenger Transport Authority and every Passenger Transport Executive to facilitate the attainment by the Franchising Director of the objective of securing expeditiously that franchise agreements are entered into in respect of any services for the carriage of passengers by railway within their passenger transport area—

(a) which are for the time being the subject of section 20(2) agreements; but

(b) which are designated under section 23(1) above as eligible for provision under franchise agreements.

(13) In any case where —

(a) any services ("the PTA services") are included, in consequence of a statement under subsection (5) above, among those which are to be provided under a franchise agreement or a franchise agreement requires the operation of any additional railway assets as mentioned in paragraph (a) of that subsection,

(b) the franchise agreement does not make provision for the Passenger Transport Executive for the area in question to make payments to the franchisee or the franchise operator in respect of the provision of the PTA services or the operation of the additional railway assets, and

(c) payments by way of grant in respect of the provision of the PTA services or the operation of the additional railway assets fall to be made by the Franchising Director pursuant to conditions contained in the franchise agreement by virtue of section 29(1)(b) above,

the Passenger Transport Executive shall pay to the Franchising Director, at or before the time at which any such payment as is mentioned in paragraph (c) above is made, a sum equal to the amount of that payment.

(14) Where, pursuant to section 30 above, the Franchising Director is under a duty to secure the provision of any services for the carriage of passengers by railway, or is empowered to secure the operation of any additional railway assets, within the passenger transport area of a Passenger Transport Executive, the Executive—

(a) shall have power to enter into agreements with the Franchising Director with respect to the securing by him of—

(i) the provision of any of the services in question, or

(ii) the operation of any of the additional railway assets in question,

until such time as they are again provided under a franchise agreement;

(b) shall make to the Franchising Director in respect of—

(i) the provision of any of the services in question whose provision he secures pursuant to section 30 above, and

(ii) the operation of any of the additional railway assets in question whose operation he secures pursuant to section 30 above,

payments of such amounts, and at such times, as may be agreed between the Executive and the Franchising Director or, in default of agreement, of such amounts and at such times as the Secretary of State may direct; but

(c) shall not have power to enter into agreements with the Board or any wholly owned subsidiary of the Board for—

(i) the provision of any of the services in question, or

(ii) the operation of any of the additional railway assets in question.

(15) Without prejudice to the generality of the provisions which may be included in any agreement made between the Franchising Director and a Passenger Transport Executive under paragraph (a) of subsection (14) above, such an agreement may, in particular, contain provisions concerning—

(a) the services for the carriage of passengers by railway which the Passenger Transport Authority for the passenger transport area in question considers it appropriate to secure to meet any public transport requirements within that area,

(b) the minimum level of quality to which any such services are to be provided,

(c) the fares to be charged to persons using any such services, or

(d) the minimum level of quality to which the operation of any station (but not of any other additional railway asset) is to be secured under sub-paragraph (ii) of that paragraph.

(16) The Secretary of State shall not direct a Passenger Transport Executive to make any payment under subsection (14)(b) above, except in respect of—

(a) any service—

(i) which is provided under an agreement entered into by the Franchising Director pursuant to his duty under section 30 above, and

(ii) which under the terms of that agreement is required to involve calls at more than one station within the passenger transport area of the Executive, or

(b) any additional railway asset which is operated under an agreement entered into by the Franchising Director pursuant to his power under that section,

"call" meaning for this purpose any stop at a station for the purpose of allowing passengers to board or leave the train (including the stops at the stations at the beginning and end of any journey to which the service relates).

(17) If any dispute arises between the Franchising Director and a Passenger Transport Executive in connection with—

(a) a proposal by the Franchising Director to issue an invitation to tender, or to enter into a franchise agreement, in respect of services for the carriage of passengers by railway within the passenger transport area of that Executive, or

(b) any franchise agreement which has been entered into in respect of any such services, or in respect of any such services and any additional railway asset,

either of them may refer the dispute to the Secretary of State for determination and on any such reference the Secretary of State may give to the Franchising Director or the Passenger Transport Executive such directions with respect to the dispute as he may think fit.

(18) Without prejudice to subsection (17) above—

(a) if the Franchising Director considers it desirable to do so for the purpose of securing expeditiously that a franchise agreement is entered into in respect of services for the carriage of passengers by railway within the passenger transport area of a Passenger Transport Executive, he may apply to the Secretary of State for directions under this subsection; or

(b) if a Passenger Transport Executive for any passenger transport area considers it desirable to do so for the purpose of securing expeditiously that a franchise agreement is entered into in respect of services for the carriage of passengers by railway within that passenger transport area, the Executive may apply to the Secretary of State for directions under this subsection;

and on any such application, the Secretary of State may give for that purpose such directions as he may think fit to the Franchising Director or the Executive.

(19) Without prejudice to the generality of the directions that may be given under subsection (17) or (18) above, but subject to subsection (20) below, the Secretary of State may, in particular, give a direction under either of those subsections—

(a) requiring the Franchising Director or the Executive to enter into a franchise agreement on such terms as may be specified in the direction;

(b) providing that any one or more of subsections (4) to (11) and (13) above, or any part of any of those subsections, shall not have effect with respect to a franchise agreement; or

(c) requiring the Executive to make payments in respect of—

(i) the provision under a franchise agreement of services for the carriage of passengers by railway within their passenger transport area, whether or not the inclusion of those services among the services which are to be provided under the franchise agreement is in consequence of a statement submitted under subsection (5) above by the Executive and whether or not the Executive is a party to the franchise agreement; or

(ii) the operation under or by virtue of a franchise agreement of additional railway assets wholly or partly within their passenger transport area, whether or not the Executive is a party to the franchise agreement;

and, without prejudice to any other provision of this Act, any reference in paragraph (b) or (c) above to a franchise agreement includes a reference to a proposed franchise agreement.

(20) The Secretary of State shall not give a direction under subsection (19)(c) above requiring a Passenger Transport Executive to make payments in respect of the provision under a franchise agreement of services for the carriage of passengers by railway, or the operation under or by virtue of a franchise agreement of additional railway assets, except in respect of—

(a) such of those services as are required by the terms of the franchise agreement—

(i) to be provided during the relevant period in the case of that direction, and

(ii) to involve calls at more than one station within the passenger transport area of the Executive, or

(b) such of those additional railway assets as are required by or under the terms of the franchise agreement to be operated during the relevant period in the case of that direction,

"call" having the same meaning in this subsection as it has in subsection (16) above.

(21) For the purposes of subsection (20) above, the "relevant period", in the case of any direction, is the period which is made up of—

(a) the financial year in which the direction is given,

(b) the financial year immediately preceding that in which the direction is given, and

(c) the financial year immediately following that in which the direction is given,

"financial year" meaning for this purpose the period of twelve months ending with 31st March.

(22) In this section—

"public transport requirements" has the same meaning as it has in the Transport Act 1968;

"section 20(2) agreement" has the same meaning as in section 33 above.

(23) Any sums received by the Franchising Director under this section shall be paid into the Consolidated Fund.

Termination and variation of section 20(2) agreements by the Franchising Director.

35.—(1) This section applies in any case where services for the time being provided under a section 20(2) agreement by the Board or a wholly owned subsidiary of the Board have been designated under section 23(1) above as eligible for provision under a franchise agreement.

(2) If, in a case where this section applies, a franchise agreement is entered into in respect of all the services for the time being provided under the section 20(2) agreement, the Franchising Director shall serve a notice on the parties to the section 20(2) agreement terminating that agreement on such date ("the termination date") as may be specified in the notice.

(3) Where notice is served under subsection (2) above, the parties to the section 20(2) agreement—

(a) shall be taken to have agreed to terminate that agreement on the termination date, and

(b) shall accordingly be released from the performance of their obligations under that agreement after that date,

and the section 20(2) agreement shall not have effect after the termination date, except so far as relating to anything done, or required to be done, pursuant to the agreement on or before that date.

(4) If, in a case where this section applies, a franchise agreement is entered into in respect of some, but not all, of the services for the time being provided under the section 20(2) agreement, the Franchising Director may serve a notice on the parties to the section 20(2) agreement varying the terms of that agreement.

(5) Where notice is served under subsection (4) above—

(a) the parties to the section 20(2) agreement shall be taken to have agreed to a variation of the section 20(2) agreement such that the services to be provided under the franchise agreement shall, after such date as may be specified in the notice, no longer be provided under the section 20(2) agreement; and

(b) the section 20(2) agreement shall have effect with such further modifications which are necessary to give effect to, or are consequential on, the variation referred to in paragraph (a) above as the parties may agree or, in default of agreement, as may be determined on a reference to arbitration.

(6) For the purposes of subsection (5)(b) above—

(a) either party to the section 20(2) agreement may refer the matter in dispute to arbitration after giving the other not less than fourteen days' notice of his intention to do so; and

(b) if the parties are unable to agree on the appointment of a person as the arbitrator, either of them, after giving the other not less than fourteen days' notice of his intention to do so, may by notice request the Franchising Director to appoint a person as the arbitrator.

(7) Where a section 20(2) agreement is terminated or varied by virtue of this section, the Passenger Transport Executive in question shall not have power to enter into another such agreement for the provision of the services which are to be provided under the franchise agreement referred to in subsection (2) or (4) above (as the case may be) without the consent of the Franchising Director.

(8) Where a section 20(2) agreement has been entered into, but services have not begun to be provided under it, this section shall have effect in relation to the services which are to be provided as it has effect in relation to services for the time being provided under a section 20(2) agreement.

PART I

(9) Any reference in this section to an arbitrator shall, in Scotland, be taken as a reference to an arbiter.

(10) In this section, "section 20(2) agreement" has the same meaning as it has in section 33 above.

Miscellaneous amendments of the Transport Act 1968.
1968 c. 73.

36.—(1) In section 10 of the Transport Act 1968, in subsection (1) (which specifies the powers of Passenger Transport Executives) after paragraph (vi) there shall be inserted—

> "(via) with the approval of the Authority, to enter into and carry out agreements with any person who is the operator of, or who has an estate or interest in, or right over, a network, station or light maintenance depot or some part of a network, station or light maintenance depot, in connection with the building, replacement, redevelopment, refurbishment, repair, maintenance, operation or staffing of the network, station or light maintenance depot or any part thereof;".

(2) After paragraph (viii) of that subsection there shall be inserted—

> "(viiia) to let locomotives and other rolling stock on hire to any person who is (within the meaning of Part I of the Railways Act 1993) the franchisee or the franchise operator under a franchise agreement to which the Executive is a party;
>
> (viiib) to let locomotives and other rolling stock on hire to a person not falling within paragraph (viiia) above—
>
>> (a) for or in connection with the provision of railway passenger services within that area or within the permitted distance; or
>>
>> (b) with the written consent of the Secretary of State, for or in connection with the provision of railway passenger services outside that area and beyond the permitted distance;
>
> (viiic) with the approval of the Authority, to enter into and carry out agreements with the owner of any locomotive or other rolling stock concerning the persons to whom, or the terms on which, the locomotive or other rolling stock may be let on hire;".

(3) In section 20(2) of that Act, in paragraph (a) (duty of Passenger Transport Executive to keep under review the railway passenger services provided by the Railways Board for meeting the needs of persons travelling between places in the Executive's passenger transport area etc) for the words "by the Railways Board" there shall be substituted the words "by passenger service operators (within the meaning of Part I of the Railways Act 1993)".

(4) After section 23 of that Act there shall be inserted—

"Interpretation of certain provisions of this Part relating to railways.

23A.—(1) For the purposes of sections 10, 15 and 20 of this Act—

(a) "light maintenance depot", "locomotive", "network", "railway passenger services", "rolling stock" and "station" have the meaning given in section 83(1) of the Railways Act 1993; and

(b) "operator" has the meaning given in section 6(2) of that Act.

(2) For the purposes of sections 10(1)(vi), 15(1)(d) and 20(2)(b), (4) and (6) of this Act "wholly-owned subsidiary" has the meaning given by section 736 of the Companies Act 1985.". 1985 c. 6.

(5) In section 159(1) of that Act (general interpretation), in the definition of "subsidiary" and "wholly-owned subsidiary", for the words "subject to section 51(5)" there shall be substituted the words "subject to sections 23A(2) and 51(5)".

Closures

37.—(1) In any case where— Proposals to discontinue non-franchised etc. passenger services.

(a) all the railway passenger services on any line or from any station are provided otherwise than in satisfaction of requirements imposed by a franchise agreement and otherwise than on behalf of the Franchising Director, and

(b) the person providing those services (in this section referred to as "the service operator") proposes to discontinue all such services on that line or from that station (in this section referred to as a closure),

then, unless the closure is certified by the Regulator as being a minor closure, the service operator shall give notice of the proposal to the Franchising Director not less than three months before the date specified pursuant to subsection (3)(b) below as that on which the service operator will cease providing the services (the "service operator's withdrawal date") and shall not discontinue those services before that date.

(2) In determining for the purposes of paragraph (a) of subsection (1) above whether all the railway passenger services on a line or from a station are provided as mentioned in that paragraph, there shall be left out of account any services—

(a) which involve travel through the Channel Tunnel;

(b) which are experimental passenger services, within the meaning of section 48 below, or which are provided on an experimental basis, for the purposes of section 56A of the Transport Act 1962; 1962 c. 46.

(c) which are provided otherwise than as regular scheduled services for that line or for that station, as the case may be; or

(d) which are designated, or which are of a class or description designated, by order under section 49(2) below as services in relation to which this section is not to have effect;

and this section shall not have effect in relation to any services falling within paragraphs (a) to (d) above.

(3) A notice under subsection (1) above shall be accompanied by a statement of—

(a) the service operator's reasons for the proposal;

(b) the date on which he will cease providing the services in question; and

(c) any alternative transport services which appear to the service operator to be available.

(4) Where notice is given to the Franchising Director under subsection (1) above, he must consider, and form an opinion on, the question whether the proposed closure should or should not be permitted to take effect.

(5) If the Franchising Director is of the opinion that the proposed closure should not be permitted to take effect, he shall be under a duty to secure the provision of the services in question after the service operator's withdrawal date.

(6) If the Franchising Director is of the opinion that the proposed closure should be permitted to take effect, he shall publish in two successive weeks in a local newspaper circulating in the area affected and in two national newspapers, and in such other manner as appears to him to be appropriate, a notice containing—

(a) particulars of the proposal to effect the closure,

(b) particulars of the date on which it is proposed that the closure will take effect,

(c) particulars of any alternative transport services which appear to him to be available,

(d) the addresses of the premises at which a statement of the reasons for the proposed closure can be inspected, or from which a copy of that statement can be obtained, and any fees payable for copies of the statement,

(e) a statement that objections to the proposed closure may be lodged with the Regulator within such period as may be specified for the purpose in the notice (being not less than six weeks from the date of the last publication of the notice in a local newspaper),

and shall be under a duty during the interim period to secure the provision of the services to which the proposed closure relates.

(7) The reasons contained in the statement referred to in subsection (6)(d) above may consist of or include the reasons included in the statement under subsection (3) above, with or without other reasons of the Franchising Director's.

(8) Without prejudice to the provisions of section 38 below in relation to the services in question—

(a) if the final decision on the closure question is that the proposed closure will not be allowed to take effect, the Franchising Director shall be under a duty to secure the provision of those services after the interim period; and

(b) if the final decision on the closure question is that the proposed closure will be allowed to take effect subject to compliance with conditions, the Franchising Director shall be under a duty to comply with those conditions or to secure that they are complied with.

(9) In this section—

"the area affected" means the area in which is situated the station or, as the case may be, the line mentioned in subsection (1) above;

"the final decision on the closure question" means—

(a) in a case where the decision of the Regulator under section 43(9) below with respect to the proposed closure is not referred to the Secretary of State under section 44 below, that decision; or

(b) in a case where that decision is referred to the Secretary of State under section 44 below, the disposal of that reference by the Secretary of State;

"the interim period" means the period beginning immediately after the service operator's withdrawal date and ending four weeks after the date of the final decision on the closure question;

"minor closure" means the discontinuance of services on any stretch of line along which there is no station (or no station in use) where the circumstances are, in the opinion of the Regulator, such that—

(a) any trains that would otherwise use that stretch of line in travelling between any two stations will instead pass along an alternative route; and

(b) any passengers travelling on any such trains will not be required to make any additional change of train and will not incur any significant increase in the time which their journey takes.

(10) The railway passenger services which are to be regarded for the purposes of this section as provided on behalf of the Franchising Director are those whose provision he is for the time being under a duty to secure in consequence of—

(a) section 30 above,

(b) subsection (5) or (8)(a) above,

(c) section 38(6)(a) below, or

(d) any closure condition imposed under section 43(9) or 44(2) below.

(11) Any sums received by the Franchising Director under this section shall be paid into the Consolidated Fund.

38.—(1) This section applies in any case where— *Proposals to discontinue franchised etc. passenger services.*

(a) any railway passenger services on any line or from any station are provided on behalf of the Franchising Director and he proposes to discontinue those services, or

(b) any railway passenger services on any line or from any station are provided in satisfaction of requirements imposed by a franchise agreement, but—

(i) the person so providing those services intends not to continue to provide them when the requirement so to provide them comes to an end, and

(ii) the Franchising Director proposes that they should then be discontinued;

and any reference in this section to a closure is a reference to a discontinuance falling within paragraph (a) or (b) above.

(2) If in a case to which this section applies—

(a) the closure is certified by the Regulator as being a minor closure,

(b) the closure in question is one in respect of which, in consequence of the application of section 49(6) below, neither section 37 above nor Schedule 5 to this Act is to apply,

(c) the closure is one in respect of which neither of the conditions in subsection (3) below is satisfied, and any requirement imposed by a franchise agreement to provide the services in question has come to an end, or

(d) the services in question fall within any of paragraphs (a) to (c) of subsection (4) below,

the Franchising Director may discontinue the services in question, notwithstanding any duty imposed on him by or under this Part to secure their provision, and subsections (5) and (6) below shall not apply in relation to the closure.

(3) The conditions mentioned in subsection (2)(c) above are—

(a) that all the railway passenger services on the line or from the station in question are provided on behalf of the Franchising Director and he proposes to discontinue all such services on that line or from that station; or

(b) that all the railway passenger services on the line or from the station in question are provided in satisfaction of requirements imposed by a franchise agreement, and—

(i) the person so providing those services intends not to continue providing them when the requirement so to provide them comes to an end, and

(ii) the Franchising Director proposes that all such services on that line or from that station should then be discontinued.

(4) In determining, for the purposes of paragraph (a) or (b) of subsection (3) above, whether all the railway passenger services on a line or from a station are provided as mentioned in that paragraph there shall be left out of account any services—

(a) which involve travel through the Channel Tunnel;

(b) which are provided otherwise than as regular scheduled services for that line or for that station, as the case may be;

(c) which are designated, or which are of a class or description designated, by order under section 49(2) below as services in relation to which section 37 above is not to have effect; or

(d) which are experimental passenger services, within the meaning of section 48 below, or which are provided on an experimental basis, for the purposes of section 56A of the Transport Act 1962;

and this section shall not have effect in relation to any services falling within paragraph (d) above.

(5) Subject to subsection (2) above, where this section applies, the Franchising Director shall publish in two successive weeks in a local newspaper circulating in the area affected and in two national newspapers, and in such other manner as appears to him to be appropriate, a notice containing—

  (a) particulars of the proposal to effect the closure,

  (b) the date on which it is proposed that the closure will take effect,

  (c) particulars of any alternative transport services which appear to him to be available,

  (d) the addresses of the premises at which a statement of the reasons for the proposed closure can be inspected, or from which a copy of that statement can be obtained, and any fees payable for copies of the statement,

  (e) a statement that objections to the proposed closure may be lodged with the Regulator within such period as may be specified for the purpose in the notice (being not less than six weeks from the date of the last publication of the notice in a local newspaper),

and shall be under a duty during the interim period to secure the provision of the services to which the proposed closure relates.

(6) Without prejudice to any subsequent application of this section in relation to the services in question—

  (a) if the final decision on the closure question is that the proposed closure will not be allowed to take effect, the Franchising Director shall be under a duty to secure the provision of those services after the interim period; and

  (b) if the final decision on the closure question is that the proposed closure will be allowed to take effect subject to compliance with conditions, the Franchising Director shall be under a duty to comply with those conditions or to secure that they are complied with.

(7) In this section—

"the area affected" means the area in which is situated the station or, as the case may be, the line mentioned in subsection (1) above;

"the final decision on the closure question" means—

  (a) in a case where the decision of the Regulator under section 43(9) below with respect to the proposed closure is not referred to the Secretary of State under section 44 below, that decision; or

  (b) in a case where that decision is referred to the Secretary of State under section 44 below, the disposal of that reference by the Secretary of State;

"the interim period" means—

  (a) in a case falling within paragraph (a) of subsection (1) above, the period beginning with the date mentioned in subsection (5)(b) above and ending four weeks after the date of the final decision on the closure question; or

(b) in a case falling within paragraph (b) of that subsection, the period beginning immediately after the requirement mentioned in sub-paragraph (i) of that paragraph comes to an end and ending four weeks after the date of the final decision on the closure question;

"minor closure" has the same meaning as it has in section 37 above.

(8) The services which are to be regarded for the purposes of this section as provided on behalf of the Franchising Director are the same services as are to be so regarded for the purposes of section 37 above.

(9) Any sums received by the Franchising Director under this section shall be paid into the Consolidated Fund.

Notification of proposals to close operational passenger networks.

39.—(1) Subject to subsection (2) below, in any case where—

(a) the operator of a network proposes to discontinue the operation of the network or some part of it (in this section referred to as a "closure"),

(b) the network or, as the case may be, the part of the network in question has, at any time within the preceding five years, been used for or in connection with the provision of any services for the carriage of passengers by railway, and

(c) the network or, as the case may be, the part of the network in question is not one which is operated on behalf of the Franchising Director,

then, unless the closure is certified by the Regulator as being a minor closure, the operator shall give notice of the proposal to the Franchising Director not less than three months before the date specified pursuant to subsection (4)(b) below as the date on which it is proposed that the closure should take effect and shall not discontinue the operation of the network or, as the case may be, the part of the network in question before that date.

(2) This section does not apply if and to the extent that the proposal mentioned in subsection (1) above is a proposal to discontinue the operation of part of a multiple track railway between any two places, where the circumstances are such that the railway line in question will continue to be at least a single track railway between those two places.

(3) In determining for the purposes of subsection (1)(b) above whether the network or, as the case may be, the part of the network in question has at any time within the period there mentioned been used for or in connection with the provision of services for the carriage of passengers by railway, there shall be left out of account any use for or in connection with the provision of services—

(a) which involve travel through the Channel Tunnel;

(b) which are experimental passenger services, within the meaning of section 48 below, or which are provided on an experimental basis, for the purposes of section 56A of the Transport Act 1962; or

1962 c. 46.

(c) which are provided otherwise than as regular scheduled services on that network or, as the case may be, the part of the network in question;

and this section shall not have effect in relation to any networks which are designated, or which are of a class or description designated, by order under section 49(4) below as networks in relation to which this section is not to have effect.

(4) A notice under subsection (1) above shall be accompanied by a statement of—

(a) the operator's reasons for the proposal;

(b) the date on which it is proposed that the closure will take effect; and

(c) any alternative transport services which appear to him to be available.

(5) Where notice is given to the Franchising Director under subsection (1) above, he must consider, and form an opinion on, the question whether the proposed closure should or should not be permitted to take effect.

(6) If the Franchising Director is of the opinion that the proposed closure should not be permitted to take effect, he shall be under a duty to secure the continued operation of the network or, as the case may be, the part of the network in question after the date on which the operator proposes that the closure should take effect.

(7) If the Franchising Director is of the opinion that the proposed closure should be permitted to take effect, he shall publish in two successive weeks in a local newspaper circulating in the area affected and in two national newspapers, and in such other manner as appears to him to be appropriate, a notice containing—

(a) particulars of the proposal to effect the closure,

(b) the date on which it is proposed that the closure will take effect,

(c) particulars of any alternative transport services which appear to him to be available,

(d) the addresses of the premises at which a statement of the reasons for the proposed closure can be inspected, or from which a copy of that statement can be obtained, and any fees payable for copies of the statement,

(e) a statement that objections to the proposed closure may be lodged with the Regulator within such period as may be specified for the purpose in the notice (being not less than six weeks from the date of the last publication of the notice in a local newspaper),

and shall be under a duty during the interim period to secure the operation of the network or, as the case may be, the part of the network to which the proposed closure relates.

(8) The reasons contained in the statement referred to in subsection (7)(d) above may consist of or include the reasons included in the statement under subsection (4) above, with or without other reasons of the Franchising Director's.

(9) Without prejudice to the provisions of section 40 below in relation to the network or the part of the network in question—

(a) if the final decision on the closure question is that the proposed closure will not be allowed to take effect, the Franchising Director shall be under a duty to secure the operation of the network or, as the case may be, the part of the network after the interim period; and

(b) if the final decision on the closure question is that the proposed closure will be allowed to take effect subject to compliance with conditions, the Franchising Director shall be under a duty to comply with those conditions or to secure that they are complied with.

(10) In this section—

"the area affected" means the area in which is situated the network or, as the case may be, the part of the network in question;

"the final decision on the closure question" means—

(a) in a case where the decision of the Regulator under section 43(9) below with respect to the proposed closure is not referred to the Secretary of State under section 44 below, that decision; or

(b) in a case where that decision is referred to the Secretary of State under section 44 below, the disposal of that reference by the Secretary of State;

"the interim period" means the period beginning with the date mentioned in subsection (7)(b) above and ending four weeks after the date of the final decision on the closure question;

"minor closure" means discontinuance of the operation of—

(a) any part of a network which consists of a stretch of track, or installations associated with a stretch of track, along which there is no station (or no station in use) where the circumstances are, in the opinion of the Regulator, such that—

(i) any trains that would otherwise use that part of the network in travelling between any two stations will instead pass along an alternative route; and

(ii) any passengers travelling on any such trains will not be required to make any additional change of train and will not incur any significant increase in the time which their journey takes; or

(b) any part of a network (other than track) which, in the opinion of the Regulator, is not necessary for the use of the network for or in connection with the provision of services for the carriage of passengers by railway;

"multiple track railway" means a railway line between any two places which consists of two or more continuous sets of track taking the same route between those two places;

"single track railway" means a railway line between any two places which consists of one continuous set of track between the two places.

(11) The networks, and the parts of networks, which are to be regarded for the purposes of this section as operated on behalf of the Franchising Director are those whose operation he is for the time being under a duty to secure, in consequence of—

(a) subsection (6) or (9)(a) above,

(b) section 40(6)(a) below, or

(c) any closure condition imposed under section 43(9) or 44(2) below,

and those whose operation he is for the time being securing in pursuance of his power under section 30 above.

(12) Any sums received by the Franchising Director under this section shall be paid into the Consolidated Fund.

40.—(1) This section applies in any case where—

(a) a network or a part of a network is operated on behalf of the Franchising Director; and

(b) the Franchising Director proposes to discontinue the operation of the network or, as the case may be, the part of the network in question (in this section referred to as a "closure").

Proposals to close passenger networks operated on behalf of the Franchising Director.

(2) If in a case where this section applies—

(a) the closure is certified by the Regulator as being a minor closure,

(b) the closure is one to which subsection (3) below applies,

(c) the network or, as the case may be, the part of the network in question has at no time within the preceding five years been used for or in connection with the provision of any services for the carriage of passengers by railway, or

(d) the network in question is one of those which are designated, or which are of a class or description designated, by order under section 49(4) below as networks in relation to which section 39 above is not to have effect,

the Franchising Director may discontinue the operation of the network or, as the case may be, the part of the network in question, notwithstanding any duty imposed upon him by or under this Part to secure its operation, and subsections (5) and (6) below shall not apply in relation to the closure.

(3) This subsection applies to a closure if and to the extent that it is the closure of part of a multiple track railway running between any two places, where the circumstances are such that the railway line in question will continue to be at least a single track railway between those two places.

(4) In determining for the purposes of subsection (2)(c) above whether the network or, as the case may be, the part of the network in question has at any time within the period there mentioned been used for or in connection with the provision of services for the carriage of passengers by railway, there shall be left out of account any use for or in connection with the provision of services—

(a) which involve travel through the Channel Tunnel;

(b) which are experimental passenger services, within the meaning of section 48 below, or which are provided on an experimental basis, for the purposes of section 56A of the Transport Act 1962; or

(c) which are provided otherwise than as regular scheduled services on that network or, as the case may be, the part of the network in question.

(5) Subject to subsection (2) above, where this section applies, the Franchising Director shall publish in two successive weeks in a local newspaper circulating in the area affected and in two national newspapers, and in such other manner as appears to him to be appropriate, a notice containing—

(a) particulars of the proposal to effect the closure,

(b) the date on which it is proposed that the closure will take effect,

(c) particulars of any alternative transport services which appear to him to be available,

(d) the addresses of the premises at which a statement of the reasons for the proposed closure can be inspected, or from which a copy of that statement can be obtained, and any fees payable for copies of the statement,

(e) a statement that objections to the proposed closure may be lodged with the Regulator within such period as may be specified for the purpose in the notice (being not less than six weeks from the date of the last publication of the notice in a local newspaper),

and shall be under a duty during the interim period to secure the operation of the network or, as the case may be, the part of the network to which the proposed closure relates.

(6) Subject to subsection (2) above and without prejudice to any subsequent application of this section in relation to the network or the part of the network in question—

(a) if the final decision on the closure question is that the proposed closure will not be allowed to take effect, the Franchising Director shall be under a duty to secure the operation of the network or, as the case may be, the part of the network after the interim period; and

(b) if the final decision on the closure question is that the proposed closure will be allowed to take effect subject to compliance with conditions, the Franchising Director shall be under a duty to comply with those conditions or to secure that they are complied with.

(7) In this section—

"the area affected" means the area in which is situated the network or, as the case may be, the part of the network in question;

"the final decision on the closure question" means—

(a) in a case where the decision of the Regulator under section 43(9) below with respect to the proposed closure is not referred to the Secretary of State under section 44 below, that decision; or

(b) in a case where that decision is referred to the Secretary of State under section 44 below, the disposal of that reference by the Secretary of State;

"the interim period" means the period beginning with the date mentioned in subsection (5)(b) above and ending four weeks after the date of the final decision on the closure question;

"minor closure", "multiple track railway" and "single track railway" have the same meaning as they have in section 39 above.

(8) The networks and parts of networks that are to be regarded for the purposes of this section as operated on behalf of the Franchising Director are the same networks and parts of networks as are to be so regarded for the purposes of section 39 above.

(9) Any sums received by the Franchising Director under this section shall be paid into the Consolidated Fund.

41.—(1) In any case where—

(a) the operator of a station or light maintenance depot ("the relevant facility") proposes to terminate the use of that station or light maintenance depot, or some part of it, as such (in this section referred to as a "closure"),

(b) the relevant facility or, as the case may be, the part of the relevant facility in question has, at any time within the preceding five years, been used in connection with the provision of any services for the carriage of passengers by railway, and

(c) the relevant facility or, as the case may be, the part of the relevant facility in question is not one which is operated on behalf of the Franchising Director,

then, unless the closure is certified by the Regulator as being a minor closure, the operator shall give notice of the proposal to the Franchising Director not less than three months before the date specified pursuant to subsection (3)(b) below as the date on which it is proposed that the closure should take effect and shall not terminate the use of the relevant facility or, as the case may be, the part of the relevant facility in question before that date.

Notification of proposals to close railway facilities used in connection with passenger services.

(2) In determining for the purposes of subsection (1)(b) above whether the relevant facility or, as the case may be, the part of the relevant facility in question has at any time within the period there mentioned been used in connection with the provision of services for the carriage of passengers by railway, there shall be left out of account any use in connection with the provision of services—

(a) which involve travel through the Channel Tunnel;

(b) which are experimental passenger services, within the meaning of section 48 below, or which are provided on an experimental basis, for the purposes of section 56A of the Transport Act 1962; or

1962 c. 46.

(c) which are provided otherwise than as regular scheduled services;

and this section shall not have effect in relation to any stations or light maintenance depots which are designated, or which are of a class or description designated, by order under section 49(5) below as stations or light maintenance depots in relation to which this section is not to have effect.

(3) A notice under subsection (1) above shall be accompanied by a statement of—

(a) the operator's reasons for the proposal;

(b) the date on which it is proposed that the closure will take effect; and

(c) any alternative facilities which appear to the operator to be available for the provision of services corresponding to those provided by means of the relevant facility or, as the case may be, the part of the relevant facility in question.

(4) Where notice is given to the Franchising Director under subsection (1) above, he must consider, and form an opinion on, the question whether the proposed closure should or should not be permitted to take effect.

(5) If the Franchising Director is of the opinion that the proposed closure should not be permitted to take effect, he shall be under a duty to secure the continued operation of the relevant facility or, as the case may be, the part of the relevant facility in question after the date on which the operator proposes that the closure should take effect.

(6) If the Franchising Director is of the opinion that the proposed closure should be permitted to take effect, he shall publish in two successive weeks in a local newspaper circulating in the area affected and in two national newspapers, and in such other manner as appears to him to be appropriate, a notice containing—

(a) particulars of the proposal to effect the closure,

(b) the date on which it is proposed that the closure will take effect,

(c) particulars of any alternative facilities which appear to him to be available for the provision of services corresponding to those provided by means of the relevant facility or, as the case may be, the part of the relevant facility in question,

(d) the addresses of the premises at which a statement of the reasons for the proposed closure can be inspected, or from which a copy of that statement can be obtained, and any fees payable for copies of the statement,

(e) a statement that objections to the proposed closure may be lodged with the Regulator within such period as may be specified for the purpose in the notice (being not less than six weeks from the date of the last publication of the notice in a local newspaper),

and shall be under a duty during the interim period to secure the operation of the relevant facility or, as the case may be, the part of the relevant facility to which the proposed closure relates.

(7) The reasons contained in the statement referred to in subsection (6)(d) above may consist of or include the reasons included in the statement under subsection (3) above, with or without other reasons of the Franchising Director's.

(8) Without prejudice to the provisions of section 42 below in relation to the relevant facility or the part of the relevant facility in question—

- (a) if the final decision on the closure question is that the proposed closure will not be allowed to take effect, the Franchising Director shall be under a duty to secure the operation of the relevant facility or, as the case may be, the part of the relevant facility after the interim period; and

- (b) if the final decision on the closure question is that the proposed closure will be allowed to take effect subject to compliance with conditions, the Franchising Director shall be under a duty to comply with those conditions or to secure that they are complied with.

(9) In this section—

"the area affected"—

- (a) in a case where the relevant facility is a station, means the area served by the station; and

- (b) in a case where the relevant facility is a light maintenance depot, means the area in which the light maintenance depot is situated;

"the final decision on the closure question" means—

- (a) in a case where the decision of the Regulator under section 43(9) below with respect to the proposed closure is not referred to the Secretary of State under section 44 below, that decision; or

- (b) in a case where that decision is referred to the Secretary of State under section 44 below, the disposal of that reference by the Secretary of State;

"the interim period" means the period beginning with the date mentioned in subsection (6)(b) above and ending four weeks after the date of the final decision on the closure question;

"minor closure"—

- (a) in relation to a station, means discontinuance of the operation of a part of the station which, in the opinion of the Regulator, is not necessary for the use of the station for the purpose of, or in connection with, the provision of services for the carriage of passengers by railway; and

- (b) in relation to a light maintenance depot, means any such discontinuance as would not, in the opinion of the Regulator, jeopardise the provision of any services for the carriage of passengers by railway.

(10) The stations and light maintenance depots, and the parts of stations or light maintenance depots, which are to be regarded for the purposes of this section as operated on behalf of the Franchising Director are those whose operation he is for the time being under a duty to secure, in consequence of—

- (a) subsection (5) or (8)(a) above,

(b) section 42(5)(a) below, or

(c) any closure condition imposed under section 43(9) or 44(2) below,

and those whose operation he is for the time being securing in pursuance of his power under section 30 above.

(11) Any sums received by the Franchising Director under this section shall be paid into the Consolidated Fund.

Proposals to close passenger railway facilities operated on behalf of the Franchising Director.

42.—(1) This section applies in any case where—

(a) the whole or some part of a station or light maintenance depot ("the relevant facility") is operated on behalf of the Franchising Director; and

(b) the Franchising Director proposes to discontinue the operation of the relevant facility or of some part of the relevant facility (in this section referred to as a "closure").

(2) If in a case where this section applies—

(a) the closure is certified by the Regulator as being a minor closure,

(b) the relevant facility or, as the case may be, the part of the relevant facility in question has at no time within the preceding five years been used in connection with the provision of any services for the carriage of passengers by railway, or

(c) the relevant facility is, or is part of, one of those stations or light maintenance depots which are designated, or which are of a class or description designated, by order under section 49(5) below as stations or light maintenance depots in relation to which section 41 above is not to have effect,

the Franchising Director may discontinue the operation of the relevant facility or, as the case may be, the part of the relevant facility in question, notwithstanding any duty imposed upon him by or under this Part to secure its operation, and subsections (4) and (5) below shall not apply in relation to the closure.

(3) In determining for the purposes of subsection (2)(b) above whether the relevant facility or, as the case may be, the part of the relevant facility in question has at any time within the period there mentioned been used in connection with the provision of services for the carriage of passengers by railway, there shall be left out of account any use in connection with the provision of services—

(a) which involve travel through the Channel Tunnel;

(b) which are experimental passenger services, within the meaning of section 48 below, or which are provided on an experimental basis, for the purposes of section 56A of the Transport Act 1962; or

1962 c. 46.

(c) which are provided otherwise than as regular scheduled services.

(4) Subject to subsection (2) above, where this section applies, the Franchising Director shall publish in two successive weeks in a local newspaper circulating in the area affected and in two national newspapers, and in such other manner as appears to him to be appropriate, a notice containing—

(a) particulars of the proposal to effect the closure,

(b) the date on which it is proposed that the closure will take effect,

(c) particulars of any alternative facilities which appear to him to be available for the provision of services corresponding to those provided by means of the relevant facility or, as the case may be, the part of the relevant facility in question,

(d) the addresses of the premises at which a statement of the reasons for the proposed closure can be inspected, or from which a copy of that statement can be obtained, and any fees payable for copies of the statement,

(e) a statement that objections to the proposed closure may be lodged with the Regulator within such period as may be specified for the purpose in the notice (being not less than six weeks from the date of the last publication of the notice in a local newspaper),

and shall be under a duty during the interim period to secure the operation of the relevant facility or, as the case may be, the part of the relevant facility to which the proposed closure relates.

(5) Subject to subsection (2) above and without prejudice to any subsequent application of this section in relation to the relevant facility or the part of the relevant facility in question—

(a) if the final decision on the closure question is that the proposed closure will not be allowed to take effect, the Franchising Director shall be under a duty to secure the operation of the relevant facility or, as the case may be, the part of the relevant facility after the interim period; and

(b) if the final decision on the closure question is that the proposed closure will be allowed to take effect subject to compliance with conditions, the Franchising Director shall be under a duty to comply with those conditions or to secure that they are complied with.

(6) In this section—

"the area affected" means the area in which is situated the relevant facility or, as the case may be, the part of the relevant facility in question;

"the final decision on the closure question" means—

(a) in a case where the decision of the Regulator under section 43(9) below with respect to the proposed closure is not referred to the Secretary of State under section 44 below, that decision; or

(b) in a case where that decision is referred to the Secretary of State under section 44 below, the disposal of that reference by the Secretary of State;

"the interim period" means the period beginning with the date mentioned in subsection (4)(b) above and ending four weeks after the date of the final decision on the closure question;

"minor closure" has the same meaning as it has in section 41 above.

PART I

(7) The stations and light maintenance depots and the parts of stations and light maintenance depots that are to be regarded for the purposes of this section as operated on behalf of the Franchising Director are the same stations and light maintenance depots and parts of stations and light maintenance depots as are to be so regarded for the purposes of section 41 above.

(8) Any sums received by the Franchising Director under this section shall be paid into the Consolidated Fund.

Notification to, and functions of, the Regulator and the relevant consultative committees.

43.—(1) Where the Franchising Director is required by any provision of sections 37 to 42 above to publish any notice, he shall also send the following documents, that is to say—

(a) a copy of the notice,

(b) a copy of the statement of reasons to which the notice refers, and

(c) a statement of his recommendations with respect to the conditions (if any) to be attached to any consent to the closure,

to the Regulator and to every consultative committee whose area consists of or includes the whole or any part of the area affected by the proposed closure.

(2) The Regulator shall send to every consultative committee whose area consists of or includes the whole or any part of the area affected a copy of every objection to the proposed closure which is lodged with him in accordance with the terms of the statement published pursuant to paragraph (e) of whichever of sections 37(6), 38(5), 39(7), 40(5), 41(6) or 42(4) above is applicable in the case of that proposed closure.

(3) On receipt of the copy of the notice referred to in subsection (1)(a) above, a consultative committee shall—

(a) consider whether or not the proposed closure will cause any hardship;

(b) identify any reasonable means of alleviating any such hardship; and

(c) prepare, and send to the Regulator, a report of the conclusions which it has reached in the discharge of its functions under paragraphs (a) and (b) above;

and, for the purposes of paragraph (b) above, a consultative committee shall not conclude that any particular means of alleviating hardship is reasonable unless, balancing the cost to the Franchising Director (or any other public authority) of employing those means against the benefit of any alleviation thereby secured, the committee is of the opinion, on the basis of the information available to it, that the expenditure involved represents good value for money.

(4) Any consultative committee which has prepared a report under subsection (3)(c) above shall send a copy of the report to the Central Committee and may publish the report in any manner which it considers appropriate.

(5) For the purpose of facilitating the discharge of its functions under subsection (3) above, a consultative committee may, after consultation with the Regulator, hold public hearings.

PART I

(6) In deciding whether to hold a public hearing for the purposes of this section, and in conducting any such hearing, a consultative committee shall take into account such matters as may be notified to it by the Regulator.

(7) The report required by subsection (3)(c) above shall be sent to the Regulator before the expiration of the period of 12 weeks, or such longer period as the Regulator may allow in any particular case, immediately following the end of the period within which objections to the proposed closure may be lodged with the Regulator.

(8) The Regulator shall only allow a longer period for the purposes of subsection (7) above if, on an application made to him by the consultative committee in question, he considers it appropriate to do so in the circumstances of the particular case.

(9) It shall be for the Regulator to decide whether the proposed closure should, or should not, be allowed to take effect; and a decision may be given allowing the proposed closure to take effect subject to compliance with such conditions (if any) as the Regulator may see fit to impose.

(10) Before deciding whether or not to allow the proposed closure to take effect, or whether to impose any and, if so, what conditions, the Regulator shall consider—

  (a) the reasons for the proposed closure set out in the copy of the statement sent to him pursuant to subsection (1)(b) above;

  (b) any objections to the proposed closure which have been lodged with him; and

  (c) every report relating to the proposed closure which is sent to him by a consultative committee pursuant to subsection (3)(c) above.

(11) The Regulator shall make his decision with respect to the proposed closure before the expiration of the period of 26 weeks, or such longer period as the Secretary of State may at the request of the Regulator allow in any particular case, immediately following the day on which he receives the documents sent to him pursuant to subsection (1) above.

(12) When the Regulator has made a decision with respect to the proposed closure, he shall send a copy of the decision to—

  (a) the Secretary of State,

  (b) the Franchising Director,

  (c) every such consultative committee as is mentioned in subsection (1) above, and

  (d) either—

    (i) in a case falling within section 37 above, the service operator, within the meaning of that section, or

    (ii) in a case falling within section 39 or 41 above, the operator of the network, station or light maintenance depot in question who gave the notice required by subsection (1) of the section in question,

and shall publish notice of the decision at every station within the area affected.

PART I

(13) In this section, "the area affected", in relation to a proposed closure, shall be construed in accordance with the section under or by virtue of which the Franchising Director is required to publish the notice referred to in subsection (1) above.

Reference to the Secretary of State of decisions of the Regulator concerning proposed closures.

44.—(1) Any person aggrieved by a decision of the Regulator in relation to a proposed closure may refer that decision to the Secretary of State by notice in writing given to the Secretary of State not later than 4 weeks after the date of the decision.

(2) On a reference under this section, the Secretary of State may—

(a) confirm the decision given by the Regulator;

(b) in the case of a decision of the Regulator to allow a proposed closure to take effect subject to compliance with conditions, confirm the decision to allow the proposed closure to take effect but modify the conditions; or

(c) substitute his decision for that of the Regulator.

(3) Any person who refers a decision to the Secretary of State under this section shall provide, with his notice under subsection (1) above, a statement of the reasons why he is aggrieved by the decision of the Regulator.

(4) On disposing of any reference under this section, the Secretary of State shall give notice of his decision to—

(a) the Regulator,

(b) the Franchising Director,

(c) every consultative committee to which notice of the Regulator's decision was required to be given by paragraph (c) of subsection (12) of section 43 above,

(d) any person to whom notice of the Regulator's decision was required to be given by paragraph (d) of that subsection, and

(e) if not falling within paragraphs (a) to (d) above, the person who referred the Regulator's decision to the Secretary of State under subsection (1) above,

and shall publish notice of his decision on the reference at every station at which the Regulator was required by section 43(12) above to publish notice of his decision.

Closure conditions: general.

45.—(1) In this Part, "closure conditions" means the conditions subject to compliance with which consent to a closure is given.

(2) Closure conditions—

(a) may impose requirements on the Franchising Director with respect to the times at which, or stages by which, a closure is to take effect;

(b) may require the Franchising Director to secure the provision of a bus substitution service, within the meaning of sections 119 to 124 of the Transport Act 1985.

1985 c. 67.

(3) The provisions of this section are without prejudice to the generality of the closure conditions that may be imposed in any case.

46.—(1) The Regulator may from time to time vary or revoke any conditions for the time being required to be complied with in connection with a closure, other than—

(a) a condition imposed by the Secretary of State under Schedule 5 to this Act, or

(b) a condition requiring the Franchising Director to secure the provision of a bus substitution service (within the meaning of sections 119 to 124 of the Transport Act 1985),

whether or not those conditions have been imposed, modified or confirmed by the Secretary of State under section 44 above and whether the closure took place before or after the coming into force of this section.

(2) Where, in exercise of his power under subsection (1) above, the Regulator decides to vary or revoke any closure condition, he shall send a copy of his decision to—

(a) the Secretary of State,

(b) the Franchising Director,

(c) every consultative committee whose area consists of or includes the whole or any part of the area affected by the closure to which the condition relates, and

(d) either—

(i) if the closure in question is one falling within section 37 above, the service operator, within the meaning of that section, or

(ii) if the closure in question is one falling within section 39 or 41 above, the operator of the network, station or light maintenance depot in question who gave the notice required by subsection (1) of the section in question,

and shall publish notice of the decision at every station within the area affected by the closure to which the condition relates.

(3) Any person aggrieved by a decision of the Regulator under subsection (1) above may refer that decision to the Secretary of State in accordance with section 44 above; and that section shall apply in relation to the reference of any such decision to vary or revoke a condition as it applies in relation to the reference of a decision in connection with a proposed closure, but taking any reference to proposed closure as a reference to variation or revocation of a condition.

(4) In this section—

"the area affected", in relation to any closure, shall be construed in accordance with the section under or by virtue of which the Franchising Director was required to publish in connection with that closure the notice referred to in section 43(1) above;

"closure" includes any closure within the meaning of subsection (7) of section 56 of the Transport Act 1962, whether that subsection applied in relation to the closure or not.

47.—(1) There are hereby transferred to the Franchising Director (so as to be exercisable concurrently with the Board) the functions of the Board under—

(a) section 4A of the Transport Act 1962 (provision of road passenger transport services), and

PART I

1985 c. 67.

(b) sections 119 to 124 of the Transport Act 1985 (bus substitution services etc),

so far as relating to services which have been temporarily interrupted or discontinued.

(2) In their application to the Franchising Director by virtue of subsection (1) above, the sections there mentioned shall have effect—

(a) as if any reference to the Board were a reference to the Franchising Director;

(b) as if any reference to the imposition of a condition by the Secretary of State were a reference to the imposition of a closure condition under this Part by the Secretary of State or the Regulator;

(c) in the case of sections 119 to 122 of the Transport Act 1985, with the modifications set out in subsection (3) below; and

(d) in the case of section 123 of that Act, with the modifications set out in subsection (4) below.

(3) The modifications of sections 119 to 122 are that—

(a) any reference to the Secretary of State (other than a reference to the imposition of a condition by him) shall be taken as a reference to the Regulator;

1968 c. 73.

(b) any reference to section 54(5) of the Transport Act 1968 shall be taken as a reference to section 43(9) or 44(2) above;

(c) in subsection (1)(a) of section 119, the words "by the Board" shall be treated as omitted; and

(d) subsections (4) and (5) of section 122 shall be disregarded.

(4) The modifications of section 123 are that—

(a) any reference to the Secretary of State shall be taken as a reference to the Regulator;

(b) in subsection (1), for paragraphs (a) and (c) there shall be substituted respectively—

"(a) "Area Committee" means a rail users' consultative committee established under subsection (2) of section 2 of the Railways Act 1993 or, in relation to the Greater London area, within the meaning of that section, the London Regional Passengers' Committee;"; and

"(c) "the Central Committee" means the Central Rail Users' Consultative Committee;";

and the words following paragraph (c) shall be disregarded;

(c) subsection (3) shall be disregarded;

(d) in subsection (4)—

1962 c. 46.

(i) the reference to section 56(4) of the Transport Act 1962 shall be taken as a reference to section 76 or, as the case may be, section 77 below; and

(ii) the reference to the services and facilities provided by the Railways Board shall be taken as a reference to services for the carriage of passengers by railway;

(e) in subsection (10), the reference to section 119 of that Act shall be taken to include a reference to section 37 or 38 above.

(5) In sections 23 to 31 above, any reference to services for the carriage of passengers by railway includes a reference to bus substitution services required to be provided in place of any such services.

(6) Where the Board is subject to a condition requiring the securing of the provision of a bus substitution service, the duty to comply with that condition shall, without prejudice to the generality of section 85 below, be regarded as a liability that may be transferred by a scheme under that section; and where there is such a transfer, any reference to the Board in sections 119 to 124 of the Transport Act 1985 shall accordingly be taken to include a reference to the transferee.

1985 c. 67.

(7) In this section "bus substitution service" has the same meaning as it has in sections 120 to 124 of the Transport Act 1985.

48.—(1) Sections 37, 38, 43 and 44 above shall not apply in relation to any proposal to discontinue an experimental passenger service on any line or from any station.

Experimental railway passenger services.

(2) In any case where—

(a) an experimental passenger service on any line or from any station is provided in satisfaction of requirements imposed by a franchise agreement,

(b) the requirement so to provide that service comes to an end, and

(c) the operator intends to discontinue that service,

the Franchising Director shall give due notice if he proposes not to secure its continued provision.

(3) In any case where—

(a) an experimental passenger service on any line or from any station is provided otherwise than as mentioned in subsection (2)(a) above, and

(b) the operator proposes to discontinue that service,

he shall give due notice of that proposal and shall not discontinue that service before the expiry of the notice period.

(4) For the purposes of subsection (2) above, the Franchising Director shall be taken to have given due notice of a proposal if, and only if, after consultation with every consultative committee whose area consists of or includes the whole or any part of the area affected, he has, not less than six weeks before giving effect to the proposal,—

(a) published a notice giving details of the proposal in two successive weeks in a local newspaper circulating in the area affected and in two national newspapers and in such other manner as may appear to him appropriate; and

(b) sent a copy of that notice to every such consultative committee.

(5) For the purposes of subsection (3) above, the operator shall be taken to have given due notice of a proposal if, and only if, not less than six weeks before giving effect to the proposal, he has published in two successive weeks in a local newspaper circulating in the area affected and in two national newspapers, and in such other manner as may appear to him appropriate, a notice giving details of the proposal.

PART I

(6) In this Part "experimental passenger service", in relation to any line or station, means a railway passenger service on that line or from that station which is designated by the Franchising Director as experimental and which either—

(a) was so designated before its introduction; or

(b) before being designated under this section as experimental, was at some time provided on an experimental basis, within the meaning of section 56A of the Transport Act 1962.

1962 c. 46.

(7) Where the Franchising Director decides to designate a service as experimental, he shall—

(a) if the service is to be provided otherwise than in satisfaction of requirements imposed by a franchise agreement, give notice of the designation to the person who is to be the operator of the service;

(b) send a copy of that notice to the Regulator and to every consultative committee whose area consists of or includes the whole or any part of the area affected; and

(c) publish notice of the designation in two successive weeks in a local newspaper circulating in the area affected and in two national newspapers.

(8) No service may be designated as experimental for a period exceeding 5 years.

(9) Where a service is designated as experimental for a period of less than 5 years, the designation may subsequently be extended, but the aggregate of the periods for which a service is designated as experimental shall not exceed 5 years.

(10) In determining for the purposes of subsection (8) or (9) above the period or periods for which a service is designated as experimental—

(a) there shall be left out of account so much of any period when the service was designated as experimental as falls before the day on which the service was introduced; but

(b) if the service is one which has been provided on an experimental basis, within the meaning of section 56A of the Transport Act 1962, every period during which it was so provided, or during which the provisions of that section had effect in relation to it by virtue of subsection (11)(b) below, shall be counted as a period during which the service was designated as experimental.

(11) Where, immediately before the coming into force of section 49(1) below so far as relating to section 56A of the Transport Act 1962 (proposals to discontinue services provided on an experimental basis), a railway passenger service is being provided on an experimental basis within the meaning of the said section 56A—

(a) none of the following provisions, that is to say, sections 37 and 38 above, section 49(2) and (3) below and Schedule 5 to this Act, shall have effect in relation to that service until such time as a franchise agreement is entered into in respect of that service or in respect of some or all of the other railway passenger services provided in the area in which, or on the line on which, that service is provided; and

(b) the provisions of the said section 56A shall continue to have effect with respect to that service—

(i) until the time mentioned in paragraph (a) above, or

(ii) until the service becomes an experimental passenger service under this section,

whichever first occurs.

(12) In this section—

"the area affected", in relation to an experimental service on any line or from any station, means the area in which is situated the line or, as the case may be, the station in question;

"operator", in relation to any service, means—

(a) in the case of a service provided in satisfaction of requirements imposed by a franchise agreement, the franchisee; or

(b) in the case of a service provided otherwise than in satisfaction of requirements imposed by a franchise agreement, the person who provides the service.

(13) In this Part, "notice period", in relation to the duty of an operator to give due notice of a proposed discontinuance of an experimental passenger service, means the period of six weeks immediately following the fulfilment by the operator of that duty.

49.—(1) The former closure provisions, that is to say—

(a) section 56(7) to (10) and (13) of the Transport Act 1962,

(b) section 56A of that Act,

(c) section 54 of the Transport Act 1968, and

(d) any other enactment (including an enactment comprised in local legislation) to the extent that it applies the enactments specified in paragraphs (a) to (c) above, with or without modification,

shall, subject to the provisions of this Act, cease to have effect.

Abolition of former closure procedures, exemptions from new procedures and imposition of alternative procedure.
1962 c. 46.
1968 c. 73.

(2) Section 37 above shall not have effect in relation to any railway passenger services, or any railway passenger services of a class or description, which the Secretary of State may by order designate as services in relation to which that section is not to have effect.

(3) Schedule 5 to this Act (which makes similar provision to that made by section 56(7) to (10) and (13) of the Transport Act 1962) shall have effect in relation to such of the railway passenger services, or railway passenger services of a class or description, in relation to which section 37 above does not have effect as the Secretary of State may by order designate as railway passenger services in relation to which that Schedule is to have effect.

(4) Section 39 above shall not have effect with respect to any networks, or any networks of a class or description, which the Secretary of State may by order designate as networks in relation to which that section is not to have effect.

PART I

1962 c. 46.

(5) Section 41 above shall not have effect in relation to any stations or light maintenance depots, or stations or light maintenance depots of a class or description, which the Secretary of State may by order designate as stations, or (as the case may be) light maintenance depots, in relation to which that section is not to have effect.

(6) Where any enactment or instrument passed or made before the relevant date contains provision to the effect that section 56 of the Transport Act 1962 is not to apply in respect of the discontinuance of specified railway passenger services or railway passenger services of a specified class or description, that provision shall (notwithstanding anything in subsection (1) above) have effect in relation to any such discontinuance after the relevant date as if references in that provision to that section were references—

(a) to section 37 above; and

(b) to Schedule 5 to this Act;

and in this subsection "the relevant date" means the date on which the provisions mentioned in paragraphs (a) and (b) above come into force.

(7) Any reference in this section to railway passenger services, networks, stations or light maintenance depots includes a reference to part of a railway passenger service, network, station or light maintenance depot, as the case may be.

(8) For the purposes of this section, "railway" has its wider meaning.

Exclusion of liability for breach of statutory duty.

50.—(1) The obligations of the Franchising Director, imposed by or under any provision of this Part—

(a) to comply with any closure conditions,

(b) to secure compliance with any closure conditions,

(c) to secure the provision of any services, or

(d) to secure the operation of any additional railway asset,

shall not give rise to any form of duty or liability enforceable by civil proceedings for breach of statutory duty.

(2) Subject to section 57 below, the obligations of—

(a) any service operator (within the meaning of section 37 above), imposed by or under section 37(1) above, not to discontinue any railway passenger services,

(b) any operator (within the meaning of section 48 above), imposed by or under section 48(3) above, not to discontinue any experimental passenger services, or

(c) any operator of an additional railway asset, imposed by or under section 39(1) or 41(1) above, not to discontinue the operation of any additional railway asset,

shall not give rise to any form of duty or liability enforceable by civil proceedings for breach of statutory duty.

Supplementary powers of the Franchising Director etc.

Performance of the Franchising Director's duties to secure the provision of services etc.

51.—(1) Where the Franchising Director is under a duty to secure the provision of any services or the operation of any additional railway assets, or is empowered by section 30 above to secure the operation of any additional railway assets, he may perform that duty or exercise that power by entering into agreements or arrangements under which other persons (in this section referred to as "sub-contractors") are to provide the services or, as the case may be, operate the additional railway assets in question.

(2) The Franchising Director may enter into an agreement or arrangement such as is mentioned in subsection (1) above notwithstanding that the sub-contractor in question is a company which is wholly owned by the Franchising Director.

(3) Any agreement or arrangement such as is mentioned in subsection (1) above may include such provisions, including provision with respect to the fares or other charges that may be imposed by the sub-contractor in question, as the Franchising Director may think fit.

(4) Any sums required by the Franchising Director for the purpose of performing any such duty, or exercising any such power, as is mentioned in subsection (1) above shall be paid by the Secretary of State out of money provided by Parliament.

(5) Any sums received by the Franchising Director in consequence of the performance of any such duty, or the exercise of any such power, as is mentioned in subsection (1) above shall be paid into the Consolidated Fund.

52.—(1) The Franchising Director may enter into agreements with the Board or any wholly owned subsidiary of the Board for the provision by the Board or subsidiary of any railway passenger services which are not provided under a franchise agreement.

(2) Any sums required by the Franchising Director for the making of payments under any agreement entered into by virtue of this section shall be paid by the Secretary of State out of money provided by Parliament.

(3) Any sums received by the Franchising Director under any such agreement shall be paid into the Consolidated Fund.

Contracts between the Franchising Director and the Board etc. for the provision of non-franchised railway passenger services.

53.—(1) The Franchising Director may form companies for the purpose of facilitating the performance of any functions assigned or transferred to him under or by virtue of this Act.

(2) The Franchising Director may—

(a) hold interests in any company which he forms as mentioned in subsection (1) above;

(b) exercise rights conferred by the holding of interests in any such company; and

(c) provide financial or other assistance to or in respect of any such company, including assistance by way of guarantee of its obligations.

(3) The Franchising Director may (whether by exercising his powers to make a transfer scheme or otherwise and whether or not for any consideration) acquire or dispose of any property, rights or liabilities which have been, or which are intended to be,—

(a) designated as franchise assets by or under any franchise agreement,

(b) used for the purpose of providing franchised services,

Powers of the Franchising Director to form and finance companies and to acquire and dispose of assets.

PART I

(c) used for the purpose of operating any additional railway asset under a franchise agreement, or

(d) used for the purpose of providing any services, or operating any additional railway asset, in pursuance of a duty or power to secure the provision of such services or the operation of such an additional railway asset.

(4) Any sums required by the Franchising Director for making payments in consequence of the exercise of any such powers as are mentioned in this section shall be paid by the Secretary of State out of money provided by Parliament.

(5) Any sums received by the Franchising Director in consequence of the exercise of any such powers as are mentioned in this section shall be paid into the Consolidated Fund.

Exercise of functions for purpose of encouraging investment in the railways.

54.—(1) The Franchising Director or a Passenger Transport Authority or Passenger Transport Executive—

(a) in exercising or deciding whether or not to exercise any of his, or (as the case may be) their, franchising functions, may take into account the desirability of encouraging railway investment; and

(b) may exercise any such functions for the purpose of encouraging railway investment or for purposes which include that purpose.

(2) The Franchising Director may, for the purpose of encouraging railway investment, enter into agreements with any person under which the Franchising Director undertakes to exercise franchising functions of his, to refrain from exercising such functions, or to exercise such functions in a particular manner.

(3) In this section—

"franchising functions", in relation to the Franchising Director, means—

(a) any functions of his under sections 17 to 19, 23, 24, 26 to 35, 52 and 53(3) above;

(b) any power conferred on him under or by virtue of Part II below with respect to the effecting by transfer scheme of any transfer contemplated by any provision of those sections; and

(c) any other functions of his which relate to the provision of railway passenger services, or the operation of additional railway assets, under or by virtue of franchise agreements;

"franchising functions", in relation to a Passenger Transport Authority or Passenger Transport Executive, means any functions conferred or imposed on the Authority or, as the case may be, the Executive under or by virtue of section 34 above;

"railway investment" means investment in assets for use in the provision of railway services.

Enforcement by the Regulator and the Franchising Director

55.—(1) Subject to subsections (2) to (5) and section 56 below, where the appropriate officer is satisfied that a relevant operator is contravening, or is likely to contravene, any relevant condition or requirement, he shall by a final order make such provision as is requisite for the purpose of securing compliance with that condition or requirement.

Orders for securing compliance.

(2) Subject to subsection (5) below, where it appears to the appropriate officer—

    (a) that a relevant operator is contravening, or is likely to contravene, any relevant condition or requirement, and

    (b) that it is requisite that a provisional order be made,

he shall (instead of taking steps towards the making of a final order) by a provisional order make such provision as appears to him requisite for the purpose of securing compliance with that condition or requirement.

(3) In determining for the purposes of subsection (2)(b) above whether it is requisite that a provisional order be made, the appropriate officer shall have regard, in particular, to the extent to which any person is likely to sustain loss or damage in consequence of anything which, in contravention of the relevant condition or requirement, is likely to be done, or omitted to be done, before a final order may be made.

(4) Subject to subsection (5) and section 56 below, the appropriate officer shall confirm a provisional order, with or without modifications, if—

    (a) he is satisfied that the relevant operator to whom the order relates is contravening, or is likely to contravene, any relevant condition or requirement; and

    (b) the provision made by the order (with any modifications) is requisite for the purpose of securing compliance with that condition or requirement.

(5) The appropriate officer shall not make a final order, or make or confirm a provisional order, in relation to a relevant operator if he is satisfied—

    (a) that the duties imposed on him by section 4 or, as the case may be, section 5 above preclude the making or, as the case may be, the confirmation of the order;

    (b) that the relevant operator has agreed to take, and is taking, all such steps as it appears to the appropriate officer for the time being to be appropriate for the relevant operator to take for the purpose of securing or facilitating compliance with the condition or requirement in question; or

    (c) that the contraventions were, or the apprehended contraventions are, of a trivial nature.

(6) Where the appropriate officer is satisfied as mentioned in subsection (5) above, he shall—

    (a) serve notice that he is so satisfied on the relevant operator; and

    (b) publish the notice in such manner as he considers appropriate for the purpose of bringing the matters to which the notice relates to the attention of persons likely to be affected by them.

PART I

(7) A final or provisional order—

(a) shall require the relevant operator to whom it relates (according to the circumstances of the case) to do, or not to do, such things as are specified in the order or are of a description so specified;

(b) shall take effect at such time, being the earliest practicable time, as is determined by or under the order; and

(c) may be revoked at any time by the appropriate officer.

(8) Without prejudice to the generality of the power conferred by subsection (1) above, the provision that may be made in a final order includes, in particular, the imposition by the appropriate officer on the relevant operator to whom the order relates of a requirement to pay to the appropriate officer a monetary penalty of such amount as may be appropriate, in all the circumstances of the case, in respect of the contravention in question.

(9) Without prejudice to section 50 above, nothing in this section or in sections 56 to 58 below shall exclude the availability of any remedy in respect of any contravention or apprehended contravention of a relevant condition or requirement.

(10) In this Part—

"the appropriate officer" means—

(a) in relation to any relevant condition or requirement in the case of a licence holder or a person under closure restrictions, the Regulator;

(b) in relation to any relevant condition or requirement in the case of a franchisee or a franchise operator, the Franchising Director;

"final order" means an order under this section, other than a provisional order;

"provisional order" means an order under this section which, if not previously confirmed in accordance with subsection (4) above, will cease to have effect at the end of such period (not exceeding three months) as is determined by or under the order;

"relevant condition or requirement" means—

(a) in the case of a licence holder, any condition of his licence;

(b) in the case of a franchisee, or any franchise operator who is a party to the franchise agreement, any term of the franchise agreement;

(c) in the case of a person under closure restrictions—

(i) the duty under section 37(1), 39(1) or 41(1) above not to discontinue a railway passenger service, or the operation of the whole or any part of a network, station or light maintenance depot, before the date stated by him in accordance with section 37(3), 39(4) or 41(3) above; and

(ii) the duty under section 48(3) above not to discontinue an experimental passenger service before the expiry of the notice period;

"relevant operator" means any licence holder, franchisee, franchise operator who is a party to the franchise agreement or person under closure restrictions.

(11) In subsection (10) above, "person under closure restrictions" means a person—

(a) who proposes a closure in circumstances such that he is required by any provision of this Part to give notice of the proposal to the Franchising Director; or

(b) who proposes to discontinue an experimental passenger service in circumstances such that he is required by section 48 above to give due notice of the proposal.

(12) Any sums received by the appropriate officer by way of monetary penalty under this section shall be paid into the Consolidated Fund.

56.—(1) Before he makes a final order or confirms a provisional order, the appropriate officer shall give notice—

(a) stating that he proposes to make or confirm the order and setting out its effect,

(b) setting out—

(i) the relevant condition or requirement for the purpose of securing compliance with which the order is to be made or confirmed,

(ii) the acts or omissions which, in his opinion, constitute or would constitute contraventions of that condition or requirement, and

(iii) the other facts which, in his opinion, justify the making or confirmation of the order, and

(c) specifying the period (not being less than 28 days from the date of publication of the notice) within which representations or objections with respect to the proposed order or proposed confirmation may be made,

and shall consider any representations or objections which are duly made and not withdrawn.

(2) A notice under subsection (1) above shall be given—

(a) by publishing the notice in such manner as the appropriate officer considers appropriate for the purpose of bringing the matters to which the notice relates to the attention of persons likely to be affected by them; and

(b) by serving a copy of the notice, and a copy of the proposed order or of the order proposed to be confirmed, on the relevant operator to whom the order relates.

(3) The appropriate officer shall not make a final order with modifications, or confirm a provisional order with modifications, except—

(a) with the consent to the modifications of the relevant operator to whom the order relates; or

(b) after complying with the requirements of subsection (4) below.

Procedural requirements.

Part I

(4) The requirements mentioned in subsection (3) above are that the appropriate officer shall—

(a) serve on the relevant operator to whom the order relates such notice as appears to him requisite of his proposal to make or confirm the order with modifications;

(b) in that notice specify the period (not being less than 28 days from the date of service of the notice) within which representations or objections with respect to the proposed modifications may be made; and

(c) consider any representations or objections which are duly made and not withdrawn.

(5) As soon as practicable after making a final order or making or confirming a provisional order, the appropriate officer shall—

(a) serve a copy of the order on the relevant operator to whom the order relates; and

(b) publish the order in such manner as he considers appropriate for the purpose of bringing it to the attention of persons likely to be affected by it.

(6) Before revoking a final order or a provisional order which has been confirmed, the appropriate officer shall give notice—

(a) stating that he proposes to revoke the order and setting out the effect of its revocation, and

(b) specifying the period (not being less than 28 days from the date of publication of the notice) within which representations or objections with respect to the proposed revocation may be made,

and shall consider any representations or objections which are duly made and not withdrawn.

(7) If, after giving notice under subsection (6) above, the appropriate officer decides not to revoke the order to which the notice relates, he shall give notice of his decision.

(8) A notice under subsection (6) or (7) above shall be given—

(a) by publishing the notice in such manner as the appropriate officer considers appropriate for the purpose of bringing the matters to which the notice relates to the attention of persons likely to be affected by them; and

(b) by serving a copy of the notice on the relevant operator to whom the order relates.

Validity and effect of orders.

57.—(1) If the relevant operator to whom a final or provisional order relates is aggrieved by the order and desires to question its validity on the ground—

(a) that its making or confirmation was not within the powers of section 55 above, or

(b) that any of the requirements of section 56 above have not been complied with in relation to it,

he may, within 42 days from the date of service on him of a copy of the order, make an application to the court under this section.

(2) On any such application the court, if satisfied that the making or confirmation of the order was not within those powers or that the interests of the relevant operator have been substantially prejudiced by a failure to comply with those requirements—

    (a) may quash the order or any provision of the order; or

    (b) if and to the extent that the application related to so much of an order as imposes a monetary penalty, may substitute a monetary penalty of such lesser amount as the court considers appropriate in all the circumstances of the case.

(3) Except as provided by this section, the validity of a final or provisional order shall not be questioned by any legal proceedings whatever.

(4) The obligation to comply with a final or provisional order shall be a duty owed to any person who may be affected by a contravention of the order.

(5) Where a duty is owed by virtue of subsection (4) above to any person, any breach of the duty which causes that person to sustain loss or damage shall be actionable at the suit or instance of that person.

(6) In any proceedings brought against a relevant operator in pursuance of subsection (5) above, it shall be a defence for him to prove that he took all reasonable steps and exercised all due diligence to avoid contravening the order.

(7) Without prejudice to any right which any person may have by virtue of subsection (5) above to bring civil proceedings in respect of any contravention or apprehended contravention of a final or provisional order, compliance with any such order shall be enforceable by civil proceedings by the appropriate officer for an injunction or for interdict or for any other appropriate relief or remedy.

(8) Where a relevant operator to whom a final or provisional order relates has made an application pursuant to subsection (1) above questioning the validity of that order, the making of that application shall not affect—

    (a) his obligation to comply with the order, or

    (b) the right which any person may have to bring civil proceedings against him in pursuance of subsection (5) or (7) above.

(9) In this section and section 58 below "the court" means the High Court in relation to England and Wales and the Court of Session in relation to Scotland.

Power to require information etc.

58.—(1) Where it appears to the appropriate officer that a relevant operator may be contravening, or may have contravened, any relevant condition or requirement, the appropriate officer may, for any purpose connected with such of his functions under section 55 above as are exercisable in relation to that matter, serve a notice under subsection (2) below on any person.

Part I

(2) A notice under this subsection is a notice signed by the appropriate officer and—

(a) requiring the person on whom it is served to produce, at a time and place specified in the notice, to the appropriate officer or to any person appointed by the appropriate officer for the purpose, any documents which are specified or described in the notice and are in that person's custody or under his control; or

(b) requiring that person, if he is carrying on a business, to furnish, at a time and place and in the form and manner specified in the notice, to the appropriate officer such information as may be specified or described in the notice.

(3) No person shall be required under this section to produce any documents which he could not be compelled to produce in civil proceedings in the court or, in complying with any requirement for the furnishing of information, to give any information which he could not be compelled to give in evidence in any such proceedings.

(4) A person who without reasonable excuse fails to do anything required of him by notice under subsection (2) above is guilty of an offence and shall be liable on summary conviction to a fine not exceeding level 5 on the standard scale.

(5) A person who intentionally alters, suppresses or destroys any document which he has been required by any notice under subsection (2) above to produce is guilty of an offence and shall be liable—

(a) on summary conviction, to a fine not exceeding the statutory maximum;

(b) on conviction on indictment, to a fine.

(6) If a person makes default in complying with a notice under subsection (2) above, the court may, on the application of the appropriate officer, make such order as the court thinks fit for requiring the default to be made good; and any such order may provide that all the costs or expenses of and incidental to the application shall be borne by the person in default or by any officers of a company or other association who are responsible for its default.

(7) Any reference in this section to the production of a document includes a reference to the production of a legible and intelligible copy of information recorded otherwise than in legible form; and the reference to suppressing a document includes a reference to destroying the means of reproducing information recorded otherwise than in legible form.

Railway administration orders, winding up and insolvency

Meaning and effect of railway administration order.

59.—(1) A "railway administration order" is an order of the court made in accordance with section 60, 61 or 62 below in relation to a protected railway company and directing that, during the period for which the order is in force, the affairs, business and property of the company shall be managed, by a person appointed by the court,—

(a) for the achievement of the purposes of such an order; and

(b) in a manner which protects the respective interests of the members and creditors of the company.

(2) The purposes of a railway administration order made in relation to any company shall be—

(a) the transfer to another company, or (as respects different parts of its undertaking) to two or more different companies, as a going concern, of so much of the company's undertaking as it is necessary to transfer in order to ensure that the relevant activities may be properly carried on; and

(b) the carrying on of those relevant activities pending the making of the transfer.

(3) Schedule 6 to this Act shall have effect for applying provisions of the Insolvency Act 1986 where a railway administration order is made.

1986 c. 45.

(4) Schedule 7 to this Act shall have effect for enabling provision to be made with respect to cases in which, in pursuance of a railway administration order, another company is to carry on all or any of the relevant activities of a protected railway company in place of that company.

(5) Without prejudice to paragraph 20 of Schedule 6 to this Act, the power conferred by section 411 of the Insolvency Act 1986 to make rules shall apply for the purpose of giving effect to the railway administration order provisions of this Act as it applies for the purpose of giving effect to Parts I to VII of that Act, but taking any reference in that section to those Parts as a reference to those provisions.

(6) For the purposes of this Part—

(a) "protected railway company" means a company which is both a private sector operator and the holder of—

(i) a passenger licence; or

(ii) a network licence, a station licence or a light maintenance depot licence; and

(b) the "relevant activities", in relation to a protected railway company, are—

(i) in the case of a company which is the holder of a passenger licence, the carriage of passengers by railway; or

(ii) in the case of a company which is the holder of a network licence, a station licence or a light maintenance depot licence, the management of a network, a station or a light maintenance depot, according to the description of licence in question.

(7) In this section—

"business" and "property" have the same meaning as they have in the Insolvency Act 1986;

"the court", in the case of any protected railway company, means the court having jurisdiction to wind up the company;

"the railway administration order provisions of this Act" means this section, sections 60 to 65 below and Schedules 6 and 7 to this Act.

60.—(1) If, on an application made to the court by petition presented—

(a) by the Secretary of State, or

Railway administration orders made on special petitions.

(b) if the petition relates to a protected railway company which is the holder of a passenger licence, by the Franchising Director with the consent of the Secretary of State,

the court is satisfied that either or both of the grounds specified in subsection (2) below is satisfied in relation to that protected railway company, the court may make a railway administration order in relation to that company.

(2) The grounds mentioned in subsection (1) above are, in relation to any company,—

(a) that the company is or is likely to be unable to pay its debts;

(b) that, in a case in which the Secretary of State has certified that it would be appropriate for him to petition for the winding up of the company under section 124A of the 1986 Act (petition by the Secretary of State following inspectors' report etc), it would be just and equitable, as mentioned in that section, for the company to be wound up.

(3) Notice of any petition under this section for a railway administration order shall be given forthwith to such persons and in such manner as may be prescribed by rules made under section 411 of the 1986 Act; and no such petition shall be withdrawn except with the leave of the court.

(4) Subsections (4) and (5) of section 9 of the 1986 Act (powers on application for administration order) shall apply on the hearing of the petition for a railway administration order in relation to any company as they apply on the hearing of a petition for an administration order.

(5) Subsections (1), (2), (4) and (5) of section 10 of the 1986 Act (effect of petition) shall apply in the case of a petition for a railway administration order in relation to any company as if—

(a) the reference in subsection (1) to an administration order were a reference to a railway administration order;

(b) paragraph (b) of that subsection did require the leave of the court for the taking of any of the steps mentioned in paragraphs (b) and (c) of subsection (2) (appointment of, and exercise of functions by, administrative receiver); and

(c) the reference in paragraph (c) of subsection (1) to proceedings included a reference to any proceedings under or for the purposes of section 55 above.

(6) For the purposes of this section a company is unable to pay its debts if—

(a) it is a company which is deemed to be so unable under section 123 of the 1986 Act (definition of inability to pay debts); or

(b) it is an unregistered company, within the meaning of Part V of the 1986 Act, which is deemed, by virtue of any of sections 222 to 224 of that Act, to be so unable for the purposes of section 221 of that Act (winding up of unregistered companies).

(7) In this section—

"the 1986 Act" means the Insolvency Act 1986;

"the court" has the same meaning as in section 59 above.

PART I
Restriction on making winding-up order in respect of protected railway company.

61.—(1) Where a petition for the winding up of a protected railway company is presented by a person other than the Secretary of State, the court shall not make a winding-up order in relation to that company on that petition unless—

(a) notice of the petition has been served on—

(i) the Secretary of State; and

(ii) the Franchising Director, if the protected railway company is the holder of a passenger licence; and

(b) a period of at least fourteen days has elapsed since the service of that notice.

(2) Where a petition for the winding up of a protected railway company has been presented—

(a) the Secretary of State, or

(b) if the company is the holder of a passenger licence, the Franchising Director with the consent of the Secretary of State,

may, at any time before a winding-up order is made on the petition, make an application to the court for a railway administration order in relation to that company; and where such an application is made the court may, if it is satisfied as mentioned in section 60(1) above, make a railway administration order instead of a winding-up order.

(3) Where, on a petition for the winding up of a protected railway company, the court makes, or proposes to make, a railway administration order by virtue of subsection (2) above, subsections (4) and (5) of section 9 of the Insolvency Act 1986 (powers on application for administration order) shall apply on the hearing of that petition as they apply on the hearing of a petition for an administration order.

1986 c. 45.

(4) In this section "the court" has the same meaning as in section 59 above.

Restrictions on voluntary winding up and insolvency proceedings in the case of protected railway companies.

62.—(1) No resolution for voluntary winding up shall be passed by a protected railway company without leave of the court granted on an application made for the purpose by the company.

(2) No such leave shall be granted unless—

(a) notice of the application has been served on—

(i) the Secretary of State; and

(ii) the Franchising Director, if the protected railway company is the holder of a passenger licence; and

(b) a period of at least fourteen days has elapsed since the service of that notice.

(3) Where an application for leave under subsection (1) above has been made by a protected railway company—

(a) the Secretary of State, or

(b) if the company is the holder of a passenger licence, the Franchising Director with the consent of the Secretary of State,

may, at any time before leave has been granted under subsection (1) above, make an application to the court for a railway administration order in relation to that company; and where such an application is made

PART I

the court may, if it is satisfied as mentioned in section 60(1) above, make a railway administration order instead of granting leave under subsection (1) above.

(4) Where, on an application for leave under subsection (1) above, the court makes, or proposes to make, a railway administration order by virtue of subsection (3) above, subsections (4) and (5) of section 9 of the Insolvency Act 1986 (powers on application for administration order) shall apply on the hearing of that application as they apply on the hearing of a petition for an administration order.

1986 c. 45.

(5) No administration order under Part II of the Insolvency Act 1986 shall be made in relation to a protected railway company unless—

(a) notice of the application for the order has been served on—

(i) the Secretary of State; and

(ii) the Franchising Director, if the protected railway company is the holder of a passenger licence; and

(b) a period of at least fourteen days has elapsed since the service of that notice.

(6) Where an application for an administration order under Part II of the Insolvency Act 1986 has been made in the case of a protected railway company—

(a) the Secretary of State, or

(b) if the company is the holder of a passenger licence, the Franchising Director with the consent of the Secretary of State,

may, at any time before such an order has been made on that application, make an application to the court for a railway administration order in relation to that company; and where such an application is made the court may, if it is satisfied as mentioned in section 60(1) above, make a railway administration order instead of an administration order under Part II of the Insolvency Act 1986.

(7) No step shall be taken by any person to enforce any security over a protected railway company's property, except where that person has served fourteen days' notice of his intention to take that step on—

(a) the Secretary of State; and

(b) the Franchising Director, if the company is the holder of a passenger licence.

(8) In this section—

"the court" has the same meaning as in section 59 above;

"resolution for voluntary winding up" has the same meaning as in the Insolvency Act 1986;

"security" and "property" have the same meaning as in the Insolvency Act 1986.

Government financial assistance where railway administration orders made.

63.—(1) Where a railway administration order is for the time being in force in relation to a company, the Secretary of State may, with the consent of the Treasury—

(a) make to the company grants or loans of such sums as appear to him to be appropriate for the purpose of facilitating the achievement of the purposes of the order;

(b) agree to indemnify the person appointed to achieve the purposes of the order in respect of liabilities incurred and loss or damage sustained by that person in connection with the carrying out of his functions under the order.

(2) The Secretary of State may, with the consent of the Treasury, guarantee, in such manner and on such conditions as he may think fit, the repayment of the principal of, the payment of interest on and the discharge of any other financial obligation in connection with any sum which is borrowed from any person by a company in relation to which a railway administration order is in force at the time when the guarantee is given.

(3) Without prejudice to any provision applied in relation to the company by Schedule 6 to this Act—

(a) the terms and conditions on which a grant is made to any company under this section may require the whole or a part of the grant to be repaid to the Secretary of State if there is a contravention of the other terms and conditions on which the grant is made; and

(b) any loans which the Secretary of State makes to a company under this section shall be repaid to him at such times and by such methods, and interest on the loans shall be paid to him at such rates and at such times, as he may, with the consent of the Treasury, from time to time direct.

(4) Any grant or loan made under this section and any sums required to be paid by the Secretary of State in respect of an indemnity given under this section shall be paid out of money provided by Parliament.

(5) Any sums received under subsection (3) above by the Secretary of State shall be paid into the Consolidated Fund.

64.—(1) This section applies in relation to any guarantee given by the Secretary of State under section 63 above.

Guarantees under section 63.

(2) Immediately after a guarantee to which this section applies is given, the Secretary of State shall lay a statement of the guarantee before each House of Parliament.

(3) Where any sum is paid out for fulfilling a guarantee to which this section applies, the Secretary of State shall, as soon as possible after the end of each financial year (beginning with that in which the sum is paid out and ending with that in which all liability in respect of the principal of the sum and in respect of the interest thereon is finally discharged), lay before each House of Parliament a statement relating to that sum.

(4) Any sums required by the Secretary of State for fulfilling a guarantee to which this section applies shall be paid out of money provided by Parliament.

(5) Without prejudice to any provision applied in relation to the relevant company by Schedule 6 to this Act, if any sums are paid out in fulfilment of a guarantee to which this section applies, the relevant company shall make to the Secretary of State, at such times and in such manner as the Secretary of State may from time to time direct—

(a) payments of such amounts as the Secretary of State may so direct in or towards repayment of the sums so paid out; and

Part I

(b) payments of interest, at such rate as the Secretary of State may so direct, on what is outstanding for the time being in respect of sums so paid out;

and the consent of the Treasury shall be required for the giving of a direction under this subsection.

(6) Any sums received by the Secretary of State under subsection (5) above shall be paid into the Consolidated Fund.

(7) In subsection (5) above "the relevant company" in relation to a guarantee, means the company which borrowed the sums in respect of which the guarantee was given.

Meaning of "company" and application of provisions to unregistered, foreign and other companies.
1985 c. 6.

65.—(1) In the railway administration order provisions of this Act—

"company" means—

(a) any company formed and registered under the Companies Act 1985 or any existing company within the meaning given in section 735(1) of that Act; and

(b) any unregistered company; and

"unregistered company" has the meaning given in Part V of the 1986 Act.

(2) In the application of section 59(1) above in a case where the protected railway company there mentioned is a foreign company, the reference to the affairs, business and property of the company shall be taken as a reference to the affairs and business of the company, so far as carried on in Great Britain, and the property of the company within Great Britain.

(3) In the application of section 9(5) of the 1986 Act by virtue of subsection (4) of section 60 above or subsection (3) of section 61 above where the petition mentioned in the subsection in question relates to a company which is a foreign company, the reference to restricting the exercise of any powers of the directors or of the company shall be taken as a reference to restricting—

(a) the exercise within Great Britain of the powers of the directors or of the company; or

(b) any exercise of those powers so far as relating to the affairs, business or property of the company in Great Britain.

(4) In the application of provisions in section 10 of the 1986 Act by virtue of subsection (5) of section 60 above where the company mentioned in that subsection is a foreign company—

(a) paragraph (a) of subsection (1) shall be omitted;

(b) any reference in paragraph (b) or (c) of that subsection to property or goods shall be taken as a reference to property or (as the case may be) goods for the time being situated within Great Britain;

(c) in paragraph (c) of that subsection—

(i) the reference to the commencement or continuation of proceedings shall be taken as a reference to the commencement or continuation of proceedings in Great Britain; and

(ii) the reference to the levying of distress against the company shall be taken as a reference to the levying of distress against the foreign company to the extent of its property in England and Wales; and

(d) any reference in subsection (2) to an administrative receiver shall be taken to include a reference to any person performing, in relation to the foreign company, functions equivalent to those of an administrative receiver, within the meaning of section 251 of the 1986 Act.

(5) Subsections (1) to (4) of section 62 above shall not have effect in relation to a protected railway company which is a foreign company.

(6) In the application of subsection (7) of that section where the protected railway company there mentioned is a foreign company, the reference to the company's property shall be taken as a reference to such of its property as is for the time being situated in Great Britain.

(7) In this section—

"the 1986 Act" means the Insolvency Act 1986;

"foreign company" means a company incorporated outside Great Britain;

"the railway administration order provisions of this Act" means sections 59 to 64 above, this section and Schedules 6 and 7 to this Act.

Consumer protection

66.—(1) In section 50 of the 1973 Act, at the beginning of subsection (2) (which prohibits the making of a monopoly reference by the Director General of Fair Trading in connection with monopoly situations arising in relation to the supply of certain goods and services, including the supply of railway services) there shall be inserted the words "Subject to subsection (2A) of this section" and after that subsection there shall be inserted—

"(2A) Subsection (2) of this section shall not preclude the making of a monopoly reference by the Director with respect to the existence or possible existence of a monopoly situation in relation to the supply of such services as are specified in paragraph 5 of Schedule 5 to this Act in Great Britain, except in relation to the supply of any such services by—

(a) a body corporate to which section 16 of this Act applies;

(b) a subsidiary, within the meaning of section 736 of the Companies Act 1985, of any such body corporate; or

(c) a publicly owned railway company, within the meaning of the Railways Act 1993."

(2) In section 51 of that Act, in subsection (3) (which specifies those Ministers the consent of one or more of whom is required before the Secretary of State for Trade and Industry may make a monopoly reference under that section in connection with monopoly situations arising in relation to the supply of certain goods and services, including the supply of railway services) after the words "the Secretary of State for the Environment," there shall be inserted the words "the Secretary of State for Transport,".

Part I

(3) For the purposes of sections 64 to 77 of that Act (merger references), where a person enters into a franchise agreement as a franchisee, there shall be taken to be brought under his control an enterprise, within the meaning of section 63(2) of that Act, engaged in the supply of the railway services to which the agreement relates.

(4) In section 137 of the 1973 Act, in subsection (3) (meaning of the expression "the supply of services"), after paragraph (f) there shall be inserted the words "and

> (g) includes the supply of network services and station services, within the meaning of Part I of the Railways Act 1993;".

(5) In Schedule 5 to the 1973 Act (goods and services in respect of which the making of a monopoly reference is prohibited or made subject to special restrictions) for paragraph 5 (which relates to the carriage of goods or passengers by railway) there shall be substituted—

1987 c. 53.

> "5. Services for the carriage of passengers, or of goods, by railway, network services and station services, within the meaning of Part I of the Railways Act 1993, but excluding the carriage of passengers or goods on shuttle services (within the meaning of the Channel Tunnel Act 1987)."

(6) Expressions used in this section and in the 1973 or 1980 Act have the same meaning in this section as they have in that Act.

Respective functions of the Regulator and the Director General of Fair Trading, and functions of the Monopolies Commission.

67.—(1) If and to the extent that he is requested by the Director General of Fair Trading (in this Part referred to as "the Director") to do so, it shall be the duty of the Regulator to exercise the functions of the Director under Part III of the 1973 Act so far as relating to courses of conduct which are or may be detrimental to the interests of consumers of railway services, whether those interests are economic or interests in respect of health, safety or other matters; and references in that Part to the Director shall be construed accordingly.

(2) There are hereby transferred to the Regulator (so as to be exercisable concurrently with the Director)—

(a) the functions of the Director under sections 44 and 45 of the 1973 Act, and

(b) the functions of the Director under sections 50, 52, 53, 86 and 88 of that Act,

so far as relating to monopoly situations which exist or may exist in relation to the supply of railway services; and references in Part IV and sections 86, 88 and 133 of that Act to the Director shall be construed accordingly.

(3) There are hereby transferred to the Regulator (so as to be exercisable concurrently with the Director) the functions of the Director under sections 2 to 10 and 16 of the 1980 Act so far as relating to courses of conduct which have or are intended to have or are likely to have the effect of restricting, distorting, or preventing competition in connection with the supply of railway services; and references in those sections and in section 19 of that Act to the Director shall be construed accordingly.

(4) Before either relevant authority (that is to say, the Regulator or the Director) first exercises in relation to any matter functions transferred by any of the following provisions, namely—

(a) paragraph (a) of subsection (2) above,

(b) paragraph (b) of that subsection, and

(c) subsection (3) above,

he shall consult the other relevant authority; and neither relevant authority shall exercise in relation to any matter functions transferred by any of those provisions if functions transferred by that provision have been exercised in relation to that matter by the other relevant authority.

(5) It shall be the duty of the Regulator, for the purpose of assisting the Monopolies Commission in carrying out an investigation on a reference falling within subsection (6) below, to give to the Commission—

(a) any information which is in his possession and which relates to matters falling within the scope of the investigation and—

(i) is requested by the Commission for that purpose; or

(ii) is information which in his opinion it would be appropriate for that purpose to give to the Commission without any such request; and

(b) any other assistance which the Commission may require and which it is within his power to give, in relation to any such matters;

and the Commission shall, for the purposes of carrying out any such investigation, take into account any information given to them for that purpose under this subsection.

(6) The references which fall within this subsection are—

(a) any reference made to the Monopolies Commission by the Regulator by virtue of subsection (2) or (3) above; and

(b) any reference made to the Commission by the Secretary of State under section 11 of the 1980 Act, if the person who is the subject of the reference is—

(i) the Board or a wholly owned subsidiary of the Board, or

(ii) a publicly owned railway company which supplies network services or station services.

(7) A copy of any report of the Monopolies Commission on a monopoly reference which relates to the supply of railway services may be transmitted by the Commission to the Regulator, notwithstanding that the reference was made by a person other than the Regulator or that it could not have been made by him.

(8) If any question arises as to whether subsection (2) or (3) above applies to any particular case, that question shall be referred to and determined by the Secretary of State; and no objection shall be taken to anything done under—

(a) Part IV or section 86 or 88 of the 1973 Act, or

(b) sections 2 to 10 of the 1980 Act,

by or in relation to the Regulator on the ground that it should have been done by or in relation to the Director.

(9) Section 93B of the 1973 Act (offences of supplying false or misleading information to the Secretary of State, the Director General of Fair Trading or the Monopolies Commission in connection with their functions under Parts IV, V, VI or VIII of the 1973 Act or under the 1980 Act) shall have effect, so far as relating to functions exercisable by the

PART I

Regulator by virtue of subsection (2) or (3) above, as if the reference in subsection (1)(a) of that section to the Director included a reference to the Regulator.

(10) Expressions used in this section and in the 1973 or 1980 Act have the same meaning in this section as they have in that Act.

Other functions of the Regulator

Investigatory functions.

68.—(1) Subject to subsection (2) below, it shall be the duty of the Regulator to investigate any alleged or apprehended contravention of—

(a) a condition of a licence, or

(b) a condition of a closure consent,

if the alleged or apprehended contravention is the subject of a representation (other than one appearing to him to be frivolous or vexatious) made to him by or on behalf of a person who appears to the Regulator to have an interest in the matter.

(2) The Regulator may, if he thinks fit, require a consultative committee to investigate and report to him on any matter falling within subsection (1) above which relates to—

(a) the provision of services for the carriage of passengers by railway, or

(b) the provision of station services,

and which it would otherwise have been his duty to investigate.

General functions.

69.—(1) It shall be the duty of the Regulator, so far as it appears to him practicable from time to time to do so—

(a) to keep under review the provision, both in Great Britain and elsewhere, of railway services; and

(b) to collect information with respect to the provision of those services, with a view to facilitating the exercise of his functions under this Part.

(2) The Secretary of State may give general directions indicating—

(a) considerations to which the Regulator should have particular regard in determining the order of priority in which matters are to be brought under review in performing his duty under subsection (1)(a) or (b) above; and

(b) considerations to which, in cases where it appears to the Regulator that any of his functions under this Part are exercisable, he should have particular regard in determining whether to exercise those functions.

(3) It shall be the duty of the Regulator, where either he considers it expedient or he is requested by the Secretary of State or the Director to do so, to give information, advice and assistance to the Secretary of State or the Director with respect to any matter in respect of which any function of the Regulator under this Part is exercisable.

(4) If the Regulator—

(a) is requested to do so by the Franchising Director, or

(b) considers it appropriate to do so,

he may provide the Franchising Director with any information which he has which relates to the functions of the Franchising Director.

70.—(1) The Regulator shall—

(a) prepare and from time to time revise, and

(b) publish and otherwise encourage the adoption and implementation of,

a code of practice for protecting the interests of users of railway passenger services or station services who are disabled.

Code of practice for protection of interests of rail users who are disabled.

(2) In preparing or revising the code of practice, the Regulator shall consult the Disabled Persons Transport Advisory Committee, established under section 125 of the Transport Act 1985.

1985 c. 67.

71.—(1) The Regulator may arrange for the publication, in such form and in such manner as he considers appropriate, of such information and advice as it may appear to him expedient to give to users or potential users of railway services in Great Britain.

Publication of information and advice.

(2) In arranging for the publication of any such information or advice the Regulator shall have regard to the need for excluding, so far as that is practicable—

(a) any matter which relates to the affairs of an individual, where publication of that matter would or might, in the opinion of the Regulator, seriously and prejudicially affect the interests of that individual; and

(b) any matter which relates specifically to the affairs of a particular body of persons, whether corporate or unincorporate, where publication of that matter would or might, in the opinion of the Regulator, seriously and prejudicially affect the interests of that body.

(3) The Director shall consult the Regulator before publishing under section 124 of the 1973 Act any information or advice which may be published by the Regulator under this section.

Registers and reports of the Regulator and the Franchising Director

72.—(1) The Regulator shall, at such premises and in such form as he may determine, maintain a register for the purposes of this Part.

Keeping of register by the Regulator.

(2) Subject to subsection (3) and to any direction given under subsection (4) below, the Regulator shall cause to be entered in the register—

(a) in relation to licences, the provisions of—

(i) every licence and every licence exemption;

(ii) every assignment of a licence of which notice is received by the Regulator;

(iii) every modification or revocation of a licence;

(iv) every revocation of a licence exemption;

(v) every requirement imposed, or consent or approval given, by the Regulator under a licence;

(vi) every requirement imposed, or consent or approval given, under a licence by any person (other than the Regulator) who is a qualified person, within the meaning of section 9(3) above, for the purpose in question, being a requirement, consent or approval whose provisions have been notified to the Regulator pursuant to a condition of the licence;

(vii) every final or provisional order which relates to a licence, every revocation of such an order and every notice given by the Regulator under section 55(6) above that he is satisfied that he does not need to make such an order;

and notice of every surrender of a licence;

(b) in relation to access agreements, access contracts and installation access contracts, the provisions of—

(i) every facility exemption granted under section 20(3) above;

(ii) every direction to enter into an access contract or an installation access contract;

(iii) every access agreement;

(iv) every amendment (however described) of an access agreement;

(v) every general approval given under section 22(3) above which is for the time being in force;

(vi) every document issued or made by the Regulator under an access agreement;

(c) in relation to closures, the provisions of—

(i) every closure consent and every closure condition; and

(ii) every final or provisional order made by the Regulator which relates to any closure or proposed closure or to any closure consent or closure condition, every revocation of such an order and every notice given by the Regulator under section 55(6) above that he is satisfied that he does not need to make such an order;

(d) in relation to experimental passenger services, within the meaning of section 48 above, the provisions of—

(i) every notice under section 48(7) above designating a service as experimental;

(ii) every notice under section 48(2) or (3) above of a proposal to discontinue a service designated as experimental;

(iii) every final or provisional order made by the Regulator which relates to the provision or discontinuance of any such service, every revocation of such an order and every notice given by the Regulator under section 55(6) above that he is satisfied that he does not need to make such an order; and

(e) the provisions of every railway administration order and of every discharge of such an order.

(3) In entering any provision in the register, the Regulator shall have regard to the need for excluding, so far as that is practicable, the matters specified in section 71(2)(a) and (b) above.

(4) If it appears to the Secretary of State that the entry of any provision in the register would be against the public interest or the commercial interests of any person, he may direct the Regulator not to enter that provision in the register.

(5) Where an access agreement is entered into or amended, the facility owner or installation owner concerned shall send a copy of the access agreement or amendment to the Regulator not later than 14 days after the date on which the access agreement is entered into or the amendment is made, as the case may be.

(6) A person who fails to comply with subsection (5) above is guilty of an offence and shall be liable on summary conviction to a fine not exceeding level 3 on the standard scale.

(7) The contents of the register shall be available for inspection by the public during such hours and subject to the payment of such fee as may be specified in an order made by the Secretary of State.

(8) Any person may, on the payment of such fee as may be specified in an order so made, require the Regulator to supply him with a copy of, or extract from, any part of the register, being a copy or extract which is certified by the Regulator to be a true copy or extract.

(9) The contents of the register shall be available for inspection at any time by the Franchising Director, without payment of any fee; and the Franchising Director may require the Regulator, without payment of any fee, to supply him with a copy of, or extract from, any part of the register, being a copy or extract which is certified by the Regulator to be a true copy or extract.

(10) Any reference in this section to "assignment" shall be construed in Scotland as a reference to assignation.

(11) Any sums received by the Regulator under this section shall be paid into the Consolidated Fund.

73.—(1) The Franchising Director shall, at such premises and in such form as he may determine, maintain a register for the purposes of this Part.

Keeping of register by the Franchising Director.

(2) Subject to subsection (3) and to any direction given under subsection (4) below, the Franchising Director shall cause to be entered in the register the provisions of—

(a) every franchise exemption;

(b) every franchise agreement;

(c) every notice of a determination under section 25(4) above;

(d) every amendment (however described) of a franchise agreement;

(e) every final or provisional order which relates to a franchise agreement, every revocation of such an order and every notice given by the Franchising Director under section 55(6) above that he is satisfied that he does not need to make such an order;

and, without prejudice to the generality of paragraph (d) above, "amendment" in that paragraph includes any variation of the property, rights and liabilities which from time to time constitute the franchise assets in relation to the franchise agreement in question, whether the variation is effected in accordance with the terms of, or by an amendment made to, the franchise agreement.

Part I

(3) In entering any provision in the register, the Franchising Director shall have regard to the need for excluding, so far as that is practicable, the matters specified in paragraphs (a) and (b) of section 71(2) above, for this purpose taking references in those paragraphs to the Regulator as references to the Franchising Director.

(4) If it appears to the Secretary of State that the entry of any provision in the register would be against the public interest or the commercial interests of any person, he may direct the Franchising Director not to enter that provision in the register.

(5) The contents of the register shall be available for inspection by the public during such hours and subject to the payment of such fee as may be specified in an order made by the Secretary of State.

(6) Any person may, on the payment of such fee as may be specified in an order so made, require the Franchising Director to supply him with a copy of, or extract from, any part of the register, being a copy or extract which is certified by the Franchising Director to be a true copy or extract.

(7) The contents of the register shall be available for inspection at any time by the Regulator, without payment of any fee; and the Regulator may require the Franchising Director, without payment of any fee, to supply him with a copy of, or extract from, any part of the register, being a copy or extract which is certified by the Franchising Director to be a true copy or extract.

(8) Any sums received by the Franchising Director under this section shall be paid into the Consolidated Fund.

Annual and other reports of the Regulator.

74.—(1) The Regulator shall, as soon as practicable after the end of the first relevant financial year and of each subsequent financial year, make to the Secretary of State a report on—

(a) his activities during that year; and

(b) the Monopolies Commission's activities during that year, so far as relating to references made by the Regulator.

(2) Every such report shall include—

(a) a general survey of developments, during the year to which it relates, in respect of matters falling within the scope of the Regulator's functions;

(b) general surveys of any developments during that year which relate to—

(i) the provision of railway passenger services or station services for, or the use of such services by, persons who are disabled; or

(ii) the employment by licence holders of persons who are disabled;

(c) a statement setting out any general directions given to the Regulator during that year under section 69(2) above; and

(d) a general survey of the activities during that year of the Central Committee and the consultative committees and a summary of any reports made to him by the Central Committee or any consultative committee.

(3) The Secretary of State shall lay a copy of every report made by the Regulator under subsection (1) above before each House of Parliament and shall arrange for copies of every such report to be published in such manner as he may consider appropriate.

(4) The Regulator may also prepare such other reports as he thinks fit with respect to any matter falling within the scope of his functions.

(5) The Regulator may arrange for copies of any report prepared under subsection (4) above to be published in such manner as he may consider appropriate.

(6) In making or preparing any report under this section, the Regulator shall have regard to the need for excluding, so far as that is practicable, the matters specified in section 71(2)(a) and (b) above.

(7) Section 125(1) of the 1973 Act (annual and other reports) shall not apply to activities of the Monopolies Commission on which the Regulator is required to report by this section.

(8) In this section—

"financial year" means a period of twelve months ending with 31st March; and

"first relevant financial year" means the financial year in which is made the first appointment of a person as the Regulator.

75.—(1) The Franchising Director shall, as soon as practicable after the end of the first relevant financial year, and of each subsequent financial year, make to the Secretary of State a report on—

Annual reports of the Franchising Director.

(a) his activities during that year; and

(b) the general performance of franchisees during that year in carrying out their functions under their franchise agreements.

(2) The Secretary of State shall lay a copy of every report made by the Franchising Director under subsection (1) above before each House of Parliament and shall arrange for copies of every such report to be published in such manner as he may consider appropriate.

(3) In making or preparing any report under this section, the Franchising Director shall have regard to the need for excluding, so far as that is practicable, the matters specified in paragraphs (a) and (b) of section 71(2) above, for this purpose taking references in those paragraphs to the Regulator as references to the Franchising Director.

(4) In this section—

"financial year" means a period of twelve months ending with 31st March; and

"first relevant financial year" means the financial year in which is made the first appointment of a person as the Franchising Director.

The Central Committee and the consultative committees

76.—(1) It shall be the duty of the Central Committee to investigate any matter which relates—

General duties of the Central Committee.

(a) to the provision of railway passenger services—

(i) by the Board or any subsidiary of the Board,

(ii) under a franchise agreement, or

(iii) on behalf of the Franchising Director, or

(b) to the provision of station services by any person in a case where the operator of the station in question is authorised by a licence to be the operator of that station,

if the condition specified in subsection (2) below is satisfied in relation to the matter in question.

(2) The condition mentioned in subsection (1) above is satisfied if—

(a) the matter is the subject of a representation made to the Committee by a user or potential user of railway passenger services and does not appear to the Committee to be frivolous or vexatious;

(b) the matter is referred to the Committee by the Regulator; or

(c) the matter appears to the Committee to be one which it ought to investigate.

(3) If any matter falling within paragraph (a) of subsection (2) above appears to the Central Committee to relate only to the provision of railway passenger services, or of station services, within the area of one consultative committee, the Committee shall refer that matter to the consultative committee for that area.

(4) If, on investigating any matter, the Central Committee considers it appropriate to do so, the Committee shall make representations to the person providing the service in question and—

(a) in the case of a service provided under a franchise agreement, to the franchisee, or

(b) in the case of a service provided on behalf of the Franchising Director, to the Franchising Director,

about the matter, or any matter to which it relates or which appears to the Committee to be relevant to the subject of the matter investigated.

(5) Where the Central Committee—

(a) having made representations under subsection (4) above, is of the opinion that it is unable to achieve a satisfactory resolution of the matter by that means, or

(b) on investigating any matter, has reason to believe that the holder of a passenger licence or a station licence is contravening, or is likely to contravene, any condition of the licence,

the Committee shall refer the matter to the Regulator, with a view to his exercising such of his powers as he considers appropriate in the circumstances of the case.

(6) Where the Central Committee investigates any matter—

(a) it may prepare, and send to the Secretary of State and the Regulator, a report of its findings; and

(b) it may publish any such report, unless the matter in question is one which was referred to the Central Committee by the Regulator as mentioned in subsection (2)(b) above.

(7) Where the Central Committee has investigated any matter under this section, it shall neither—

(a) include in any report or representations a proposal for any steps to be taken by any person in relation to that matter, nor

(b) refer the matter to the Regulator under subsection (5)(a) above by reason only of the failure of any person to take any steps in relation to that matter,

unless, balancing the cost of taking those steps against the benefits which the Committee considers will be enjoyed by any person in consequence of the taking of those steps, the Committee is of the opinion, on the basis of the information available to it, that the expenditure involved represents good value for money.

(8) The services which are to be regarded for the purposes of this section as provided on behalf of the Franchising Director are the same services as are to be so regarded for the purposes of section 37 above.

(9) In this section, any reference to railway passenger services includes a reference to bus substitution services required to be provided in place of any such services; and in this subsection, "bus substitution services" has the same meaning as it has in sections 120 to 124 of the Transport Act 1985.

1985 c. 67.

77.—(1) It shall be the duty of each consultative committee to investigate any matter which relates—

(a) to the provision of railway passenger services—

(i) by the Board or any subsidiary of the Board,

(ii) under a franchise agreement, or

(iii) on behalf of the Franchising Director, or

(b) to the provision of station services by any person in a case where the operator of the station in question is authorised by a licence to be the operator of that station,

if the condition specified in subsection (2) below is satisfied in relation to the matter in question.

General duties of consultative committees.

(2) The condition mentioned in subsection (1) above is satisfied if the matter—

(a) is the subject of a representation made to the committee by a user or potential user of railway passenger services and does not appear to the committee to be frivolous or vexatious;

(b) is referred to the committee—

(i) by the Regulator under section 68(2) above; or

(ii) by the Central Committee under section 76(3) above; or

(c) appears to the committee to be one which it ought to investigate.

(3) If, on investigating any matter, a consultative committee considers it appropriate to do so, the committee shall make representations to the person providing the service in question and—

(a) in the case of a service provided under a franchise agreement, to the franchisee, or

(b) in the case of a service provided on behalf of the Franchising Director, to the Franchising Director,

about the matter, or any matter to which it relates or which appears to the committee to be relevant to the subject of the matter investigated.

(4) Where a consultative committee—

(a) having made representations under subsection (3) above, is of the opinion that it is unable to achieve a satisfactory resolution of the matter by that means, or

(b) on investigating any matter, has reason to believe that the holder of a passenger licence or a station licence is contravening, or is likely to contravene, any condition of the licence,

the committee shall refer the matter to the Regulator (or, in the case of a matter that was referred to the committee by the Regulator, refer it back to the Regulator) with a view to his exercising such of his powers as he considers appropriate in the circumstances of the case.

(5) Where a consultative committee investigates any matter pursuant to subsections (1) to (3) above—

(a) it may prepare, and send to the Central Committee, a report of its findings; and

(b) it may publish any such report, unless the matter in question is one which was referred to the consultative committee by the Regulator as mentioned in subsection (2)(b)(i) above.

(6) At the request of the Regulator, a consultative committee shall make a report to him on such matters relating to the quality of the railway passenger services, and the station services, provided in the committee's area as may be specified in the request.

(7) The Regulator may arrange for the publication of any report under subsection (6) above in such manner as he may consider appropriate.

(8) If the Franchising Director, after consultation with the Regulator, so requests, a consultative committee shall assist the Franchising Director, to such extent and in such respects as may be specified in the request, in ascertaining whether, in the case of any franchise agreement, the franchise operator is attaining the standards set for the provision of the franchised services.

(9) Where a consultative committee has investigated any matter pursuant to subsections (1) to (3) or subsection (6) above, it shall neither—

(a) include in any report or representations a proposal for any steps to be taken by any person in relation to that matter, nor

(b) refer the matter to the Regulator under subsection (4)(a) above by reason only of the failure of any person to take any steps in relation to that matter,

unless, balancing the cost of taking those steps against the benefits which the committee considers will be enjoyed by any person in consequence of the taking of those steps, the committee is of the opinion, on the basis of the information available to it, that the expenditure involved represents good value for money.

(10) The services which are to be regarded for the purposes of this section as provided on behalf of the Franchising Director are the same services as are to be so regarded for the purposes of section 37 above.

(11) In this section, any reference to railway passenger services includes a reference to bus substitution services required to be provided in place of any such services; and in this subsection, "bus substitution services" has the same meaning as it has in sections 120 to 124 of the Transport Act 1985.

1985 c. 67.

78.—(1) In consequence of sections 76 and 77 above, subsections (4) to (6) of section 56 of the Transport Act 1962 (which make provision with respect to the functions of the former Central Committee and Area Committees with respect to services and facilities provided by certain Boards and, as applied or amended, by certain other persons) shall not have effect in relation to matters affecting the services or facilities which are for the time being provided by the Board or a subsidiary of the Board or under a franchise agreement.

Functions under section 56 of the Transport Act 1962.
1962 c. 46.

(2) In section 56 of that Act, in subsection (5), the words from the beginning to "section; and" (which preclude committees from considering charges for services and questions relating to the discontinuance or reduction of railway services) shall be omitted.

(3) Subject to subsections (1) and (2) above—

(a) the functions of the former Central Committee under subsections (4) to (6A) of section 56 of that Act are hereby transferred to the Central Committee; and

(b) the functions of the former Area Committees under those subsections are hereby transferred to the consultative committees.

(4) In consequence of subsection (3) above—

(a) any reference in those subsections to the former Central Committee shall be taken as a reference to the Central Committee; and

(b) for the words "each Area Committee", "any Area Committee", "Area Committees", "an Area Committee" and "An Area Committee", wherever occurring in those subsections, there shall be substituted respectively the words "each consultative committee", "any consultative committee", "consultative committees", "a consultative committee" and "A consultative committee".

(5) After subsection (6) of that section there shall be inserted—

"(6ZA) If the Secretary of State so directs in the case of any consultative committee, subsections (4) to (6) of this section shall have effect in relation to that committee and the Central Committee as if the reference in subsection (4) of this section to services and facilities provided by any of the Boards included a reference to any such ferry service as may be specified in the direction, whether provided by a Board or by some other person; and, in the application of subsections (4) to (6) of this section in relation to any such ferry service, any reference in those subsections to a Board shall be taken to include a reference to the person providing the ferry service."

Part I

(6) At the end of that section there shall be added—

"(20) In this section—

"the Central Committee" means the Central Rail Users' Consultative Committee, constituted under the Railways Act 1993;

"consultative committee" means—

(a) a Rail Users' Consultative Committee established under the Railways Act 1993; or

(b) so far as relating to the Greater London area, within the meaning of section 2 of that Act, the London Regional Passengers' Committee."

(7) In this section—

"former Area Committees" means Area Transport Users Consultative Committees, established under section 56 of the Transport Act 1962;

1962 c. 46.

"the former Central Committee" means the Central Transport Consultative Committee for Great Britain, established under that section.

Annual reports by the Central Committee and the consultative committees.

79.—(1) Each committee shall, as soon as practicable after the end of the first relevant financial year and of each subsequent financial year—

(a) make a report to the Regulator on the committee's activities during that year; and

(b) in the case of the Central Committee and the consultative committees for Scotland and for Wales, send a copy of that report to the Secretary of State;

and the Secretary of State shall lay before each House of Parliament a copy of the reports sent to him pursuant to paragraph (b) above.

(2) Each committee may arrange for any report which it makes under subsection (1) above to be published in such manner as the committee considers appropriate.

(3) In arranging for the publication of any report under this section, a committee shall have regard to the need for excluding, so far as that is practicable, the matters specified in paragraphs (a) and (b) of section 71(2) above, for this purpose taking references in those paragraphs to the Regulator as references to the committee.

(4) In this section—

"committee" means the Central Committee or a consultative committee;

"financial year" means a period of twelve months ending with 31st March; and

"first relevant financial year", in relation to a committee, means the financial year in which the committee is established.

Information

Duty of certain persons to furnish information to the Franchising Director on request.

80.—(1) Any of the following persons, that is to say—

(a) the Board,

(b) any wholly owned subsidiary of the Board, or

(c) any person who is the holder of a network licence or a station licence,

shall be under a duty to furnish to the Franchising Director in such form and manner as he may by notice request such information as he may so request, being information which the Franchising Director considers necessary for the purpose of facilitating the performance of any function of his under this Part.

(2) A request under subsection (1) above must be complied with within such time (being not less than 28 days from the making of the request) as may be specified in the request.

(3) If any such request is not complied with, the Franchising Director may serve a notice under subsection (4) below on the person from whom the information was requested under subsection (1) above.

(4) A notice under this subsection is a notice signed by the Franchising Director and—

(a) requiring the person on whom it is served to produce, at a time and place specified in the notice, to the Franchising Director or to any person appointed by the Franchising Director for the purpose, any documents which are specified or described in the notice and are in that person's custody or under his control; or

(b) requiring that person to furnish, at a time and place and in the form and manner specified in the notice, to the Franchising Director such information as may be specified or described in the notice.

(5) No person shall be required under this section to produce any documents which he could not be compelled to produce in civil proceedings in the court or, in complying with any requirement for the furnishing of information, to give any information which he could not be compelled to give in evidence in any such proceedings.

(6) A person who without reasonable excuse fails to do anything required of him by notice under subsection (4) above is guilty of an offence and shall be liable on summary conviction to a fine not exceeding level 5 on the standard scale.

(7) A person who intentionally alters, suppresses or destroys any document which he has been required by any notice under subsection (4) above to produce is guilty of an offence and shall be liable—

(a) on summary conviction, to a fine not exceeding the statutory maximum;

(b) on conviction on indictment, to a fine.

(8) If a person makes default in complying with a notice under subsection (4) above, the court may, on the application of the Franchising Director, make such order as the court thinks fit for requiring the default to be made good; and any such order may provide that all the costs or expenses of and incidental to the application shall be borne by the person in default or by any officers of a company or other association who are responsible for its default.

Part I

(9) Any reference in this section to the production of a document includes a reference to the production of a legible and intelligible copy of information recorded otherwise than in legible form; and the reference to suppressing a document includes a reference to destroying the means of reproducing information recorded otherwise than in legible form.

(10) In this section "the court" means the High Court, in relation to England and Wales, and the Court of Session, in relation to Scotland.

Interpretation

Meaning of "railway".
1992 c. 42.

81.—(1) Subject to subsection (2) below, the definition of "railway" in section 67(1) of the Transport and Works Act 1992 shall have effect for the purposes of this Part as it has effect for the purposes of that Act, and cognate expressions shall be construed accordingly.

(2) Where it is stated for the purposes of any provision of this Part that railway has its wider meaning, "railway" shall be taken, for the purposes of that provision, to mean—

(a) a railway,

(b) a tramway, or

(c) a transport system which uses another mode of guided transport but which is not a trolley vehicle system,

and cognate expressions shall be construed accordingly.

(3) In paragraphs (a) to (c) of subsection (2) above "guided transport", "railway", "tramway" and "trolley vehicle system" have the meaning given by section 67(1) of the Transport and Works Act 1992.

Meaning of "railway services" etc.

82.—(1) In this Part, "railway services" means services of any of the following descriptions, that is to say—

(a) services for the carriage of passengers by railway;

(b) services for the carriage of goods by railway;

(c) light maintenance services;

(d) station services;

(e) network services.

(2) In this Part—

"light maintenance services" means services of any of the following descriptions, that is to say—

(a) the refuelling, or the cleaning of the exterior, of locomotives or other rolling stock;

(b) the carrying out to locomotives or other rolling stock of maintenance work of a kind which is normally carried out at regular intervals of twelve months or less to prepare the locomotives or other rolling stock for service;

"network services" means any service which consists of, or is comprised in, the provision or operation of a network (or of any of the track or other installations comprised in a network), but does not include any service which falls within paragraphs (a) to (d) of subsection (1) above;

"services for the carriage of passengers by railway" includes services for and in connection with the carriage of luggage, parcels or mail on trains which at the time are available, and primarily intended, for use by passengers; and references to carrying, or to the carriage of, passengers by railway shall be construed accordingly;

"station services" means any service which consists of, or is comprised in, the provision or operation of a station;

and, for the purposes of the above definitions of "network services" and "station services", where a person permits another to use any land or other property comprised in a network or station he shall be regarded as providing a service which falls within the meaning of "network services" or "station services", as the case may be.

(3) Without prejudice to the generality of the definition in subsection (2) above, "network services" includes services of any of the following descriptions, that is to say—

(a) the construction, maintenance, re-alignment, re-configuration or renewal of track,

(b) the installation, operation, maintenance or renewal of a railway signalling system or of any other railway communication equipment,

(c) the construction, control, maintenance or renewal of electrical conductor rails or overhead lines, of any supports for such rails or lines, and of any electrical substations or power connections used or to be used in connection therewith, and the provision of electrical power by means thereof,

(d) the provision and operation of services for the recovery or repair of locomotives or other rolling stock in connection with any accident, malfunction or mechanical or electrical failure,

(e) the provision and operation of services for keeping track free from, or serviceable notwithstanding, obstruction (whether by snow, ice, water, fallen leaves or any other natural or artificial obstacle or hindrance) or for removing any such obstruction,

(f) the provision, operation, maintenance and renewal of any plant, equipment or machinery used in carrying on any of the activities specified in paragraphs (a) to (e) above,

(g) the exercise of day to day control over train movements over or along any track comprised in the network,

(h) the preparation of a timetable for the purposes of such control as is referred to in paragraph (g) above,

and it is immaterial for the purposes of this subsection and that subsection whether or not the person who provides the service in question also provides or operates a network, or any of the track or other installations comprised in a network, or provides the service on behalf of a person who does so.

(4) In determining whether any service is a station service, it is immaterial whether or not the person who provides the service also provides or operates a station, or any part of a station, or provides the service on behalf of a person who does so.

(5) In this section, "maintenance" includes the detection and rectification of any faults.

PART I

(6) "Railway" has its wider meaning in the application of this section in relation to any provision of this Part for the purposes of which "railway" has that meaning.

Interpretation of Part I.
1973 c. 41.
1980 c. 21.

83.—(1) In this Part, unless the context otherwise requires—

"the 1973 Act" means the Fair Trading Act 1973;

"the 1980 Act" means the Competition Act 1980;

"access agreement" means—

(a) an access contract entered into pursuant to directions under section 17 or 18 above; or

(b) an installation access contract entered into pursuant to directions under section 19 above;

"access contract" has the meaning given by section 17(6) above;

"access option" shall be construed in accordance with section 17(6) above;

"additional railway asset" has the meaning given by section 29(8) above;

"ancillary service" means any service which is necessary or expedient for giving full effect to any permission or right which a person may have to use any track, station or light maintenance depot;

"appropriate officer" has the meaning given by section 55(10) above;

"the Central Committee" means the Central Rail Users' Consultative Committee;

"closure" shall be construed in accordance with section 37(1), 38(1), 39(1), 40(1), 41(1) or 42(1) above, as the case may be, and "proposed closure" shall be construed accordingly;

"closure conditions" has the meaning given by section 45 above;

"closure consent" means any decision required by section 43 or 44 above before a proposed closure may take effect;

"consultative committee" means a Rail Users' Consultative Committee, established under subsection (2) of section 2 above (but this definition is subject to subsection (4) of that section);

"the Director" means the Director General of Fair Trading;

"exempt facility" shall be construed in accordance with section 20(13) above;

"experimental passenger service" has the meaning given by section 48(6) above;

"facility exemption" has the meaning given by section 20(13) above;

"facility owner" has the meaning given by section 17(6) above;

"final order" and "provisional order" have the meaning given by section 55(10) above;

"franchise agreement" has the meaning given by section 23(3) above;

"franchise assets" has the meaning given by section 27(11) above;

"franchise exemption" has the meaning given by section 24(13) above;

"franchise operator" has the meaning given by section 23(3) above;

"franchise period" has the meaning given by section 23(3) above;

"franchise term" has the meaning given by section 23(3) above;

"franchised services" has the meaning given by section 23(3) above;

"franchisee" has the meaning given by section 23(3) above;

"goods" includes mail, parcels, animals, plants and any other creature, substance or thing capable of being transported, but does not include passengers;

"information" includes accounts, estimates, records and returns;

"installation access contract" has the meaning given by section 19(9) above;

"installation owner" has the meaning given by section 19(9) above;

"licence" means a licence under section 8 above and "licence holder" shall be construed accordingly;

"licence exemption" has the meaning given by section 7(13) above;

"light maintenance" (without more) means—

    (a) the refuelling, or the cleaning of the exterior, of locomotives or other rolling stock; or

    (b) the carrying out to locomotives or other rolling stock of maintenance work of a kind which is normally carried out at regular intervals of twelve months or less to prepare the locomotives or other rolling stock for service;

and, for the purposes of paragraph (b) above, "maintenance work" includes the detection and rectification of any faults;

"light maintenance depot" means any land or other property which is normally used for or in connection with the provision of light maintenance services, whether or not it is also used for other purposes;

"light maintenance depot licence" means a licence authorising a person—

    (a) to be the operator of a light maintenance depot; and

    (b) to be the operator of a train being used on a network for a purpose preparatory or incidental to, or consequential on, the provision of light maintenance services;

"light maintenance services" has the meaning given by section 82 above;

"locomotive" means any railway vehicle which has the capacity for self-propulsion (whether or not the power by which it operates is derived from a source external to the vehicle);

"network" means—

    (a) any railway line, or combination of two or more railway lines, and

    (b) any installations associated with any of the track comprised in that line or those lines,

together constituting a system of track and other installations which is used for and in connection with the support, guidance and operation of trains;

"network licence" means a licence authorising a person—

    (a) to be the operator of a network;

Part I

(b) to be the operator of a train being used on a network for any purpose comprised in the operation of that network; and

(c) to be the operator of a train being used on a network for a purpose preparatory or incidental to, or consequential on, using a train as mentioned in paragraph (b) above;

"network services" has the meaning given by section 82 above;

"notice period" has the meaning given by section 48(13) above;

"operator", in relation to a railway asset, has the meaning given by section 6(2) above;

"passenger licence" means a licence authorising a person—

(a) to be the operator of a train being used on a network for the purpose of carrying passengers by railway; and

(b) to be the operator of a train being used on a network for a purpose preparatory or incidental to, or consequential on, using a train as mentioned in paragraph (a) above;

"passenger service operator" means a person who provides services for the carriage of passengers by railway;

"premises" includes any land, building or structure;

"prescribed" means prescribed by regulations made by the Secretary of State;

"private sector operator" means any body or person other than a public sector operator;

"protected railway company" has the meaning given by section 59(6)(a) above;

"public sector operator" has the meaning given by section 25 above;

"railway" shall be construed in accordance with section 81 above;

"railway asset" has the meaning given by section 6(2) above;

"railway facility" means any track, station or light maintenance depot;

"railway passenger service" means any service for the carriage of passengers by railway;

"railway services" has the meaning given by section 82 above;

"railway vehicle" includes anything which, whether or not it is constructed or adapted to carry any person or load, is constructed or adapted to run on flanged wheels over or along track;

"records" includes computer records and any other records kept otherwise than in a document;

"relevant activities", in relation to a protected railway company, has the meaning given by section 59(6)(b) above;

"relevant condition or requirement" has the meaning given by section 55(10) above;

"relevant operator" has the meaning given by section 55(10) above;

"rolling stock" means any carriage, wagon or other vehicle used on track and includes a locomotive;

"station" means any land or other property which consists of premises used as, or for the purposes of, or otherwise in connection with, a railway passenger station or railway passenger terminal (including any approaches, forecourt, cycle store or car park), whether or not the land or other property is, or the premises are, also used for other purposes;

"station licence" means a licence authorising a person to be the operator of a station;

"station services" has the meaning given by section 82 above;

"track" means any land or other property comprising the permanent way of any railway, taken together with the ballast, sleepers and metals laid thereon, whether or not the land or other property is also used for other purposes; and any reference to track includes a reference to—

    (a) any level crossings, bridges, viaducts, tunnels, culverts, retaining walls, or other structures used or to be used for the support of, or otherwise in connection with, track; and

    (b) any walls, fences or other structures bounding the railway or bounding any adjacent or adjoining property;

"train" means—

    (a) two or more items of rolling stock coupled together, at least one of which is a locomotive; or

    (b) a locomotive not coupled to any other rolling stock;

"vehicle" includes railway vehicle.

(2) For the purposes of this Part, a person shall be regarded as providing or operating services for the carriage of goods by railway notwithstanding that he provides or operates the services solely for the carriage of his own goods or otherwise for his own benefit.

Part II

Re-organisation of the Railways

New companies, transfer schemes and disposals

84.—(1) The Board shall have power to form, or take part in forming, companies—

    (a) for the purposes of the Board's business;

    (b) for the purpose of facilitating the disposal of—

        (i) the whole or any part of the undertaking, or any property, rights or liabilities, of the Board or of any wholly owned subsidiary of the Board; or

        (ii) without prejudice to the generality of sub-paragraph (i) above, any securities of any subsidiary of the Board;

    (c) for the purpose of facilitating the performance by the Franchising Director of his functions under sections 23 to 36 above;

    (d) for such other purposes as may be specified by the Secretary of State in a direction to the Board.

[margin note: Powers of the Board to form companies.]

PART II

(2) The Secretary of State may, after consultation with the Board, direct the Board to exercise any power conferred by paragraph (a), (b), (c) or (d) of subsection (1) above; and, if he so directs, he may also give the Board directions with respect to—

(a) the nature and objects of the company which is to be formed;

(b) the manner in which, and time within which, it is to be formed.

(3) The Board shall not exercise any power conferred by subsection (1) above, except—

(a) in the case of the power conferred by paragraph (a), with the consent of, or pursuant to a direction given under subsection (2) above by, the Secretary of State; or

(b) in any other case, pursuant to such a direction.

(4) Each of the powers conferred on the Board by this section—

(a) is in addition to, and not in derogation from, any other powers of the Board; and

(b) relates only to the capacity of the Board as a statutory corporation;

and nothing in this section shall be construed as authorising the disregard by the Board of any enactment or rule of law.

Powers of the Board to make transfer schemes.

85.—(1) The Board shall have power to make schemes for the transfer of the whole or any part of the undertaking, or any property, rights or liabilities, of—

(a) the Board,

(b) any wholly owned subsidiary of the Board,

(c) any publicly owned railway company,

(d) the Franchising Director, or

(e) any company which is wholly owned by the Franchising Director,

to any other person falling within paragraphs (a) to (e) above or to a franchise company.

(2) In relation to the transfer or disposal (or the proposed transfer or disposal) of the whole or any part of an undertaking, any reference in this Part to property, rights or liabilities includes a reference to the undertaking or part (and, accordingly, to the property, rights and liabilities comprised in that undertaking or part).

(3) The powers conferred on the Board by subsection (1) above shall only be exercisable—

(a) for the purposes of the Board's business, or to facilitate a disposal in the ordinary course of that business;

(b) for the purpose of effecting or facilitating the disposal of such property, rights or liabilities as the Secretary of State may direct; or

(c) for the purpose of facilitating the performance by the Franchising Director of his functions under sections 23 to 36 above,

and paragraph (a) above accordingly applies only in relation to transfers between the Board and any of its wholly owned subsidiaries or between two or more of its wholly owned subsidiaries.

(4) The Secretary of State may, after consultation with the Board, direct the Board to exercise any power conferred by subsection (1) above; and, if he does so, he may also give the Board directions with respect to—

(a) the manner in which, and time within which, the power is to be exercised;

(b) the property, rights or liabilities to be transferred;

(c) the person to whom the transfer is to be made.

(5) The Board shall not exercise the power conferred by subsection (1) above—

(a) for a purpose falling within paragraph (a) of subsection (3) above, except with the consent of, or pursuant to a direction given under subsection (4) above by, the Secretary of State; or

(b) for a purpose specified in paragraph (b) or (c) of subsection (3) above, except pursuant to such a direction.

(6) Subject to the following provisions of this Part, on the day on which a scheme under subsection (1) above comes into force (in this Part referred to as the "transfer date") the property, rights and liabilities affected by the scheme shall, subject to section 97 below, be transferred and vest by virtue of, and in accordance with, the scheme.

(7) Each of the powers conferred on the Board by this section—

(a) is in addition to, and not in derogation from, the other powers so conferred and the other powers of the Board; and

(b) relates only to the capacity of the Board as a statutory corporation;

and nothing in this section shall be construed as authorising the disregard by the Board of any enactment or rule of law.

(8) In this Part, "franchise company" means any body corporate which is, or is to be, the franchisee or the franchise operator under a franchise agreement.

(9) Expressions used in subsection (8) above and in Part I above have the same meaning in that subsection as they have in that Part.

86.—(1) The Franchising Director shall have power to make schemes for the transfer, at or after the end of the franchise period, of property, rights and liabilities which, immediately before the end of that period, are for the time being designated as franchise assets for the purposes of the franchise agreement in question to—

(a) the Franchising Director;

(b) a company which is wholly owned by the Franchising Director; or

(c) a franchise company.

Powers of the Franchising Director to make transfer schemes.

(2) In the following provisions of this section—

(a) the "transferor" means the person from whom any such property, rights or liabilities as are mentioned in subsection (1) above are transferred by a scheme under this section; and

(b) the "transferee" means the person to whom any such property, rights or liabilities are so transferred.

(3) Subject to any contrary agreement or arrangements which may be made between the transferor and the transferee, where any property, rights or liabilities are transferred by a scheme under this section, there shall be paid by the transferee to the transferor or, as the case may require, by the transferor to the transferee, on the day on which the scheme comes into force such sums as may be specified in, or determined in accordance with, the franchise agreement mentioned in subsection (1) above.

(4) Subject to the following provisions of this Part, on the day on which a scheme under this section comes into force, the property, rights and liabilities affected by the scheme shall, subject to section 97 below, be transferred and vest by virtue of and in accordance with the scheme.

(5) Except as otherwise provided by this Act—

(a) any reference in this Act to a "transfer scheme" shall be taken as including a reference to a scheme under this section;

(b) in the application of any provision of this Act in relation to a scheme under this section, any reference to the "transfer date" shall be taken as a reference to the date on which the scheme comes into force.

(6) In this section "franchise agreement", "franchise period" and "designated as franchise assets" have the same meaning as they have in Part I above.

(7) Any sums required by the Franchising Director for the purpose of making payments in respect of property, rights or liabilities transferred by a scheme under this section shall be paid by the Secretary of State out of money provided by Parliament.

(8) Any sums received by the Franchising Director in respect of property, rights or liabilities so transferred shall be paid into the Consolidated Fund.

Transfer to the Secretary of State or the Franchising Director of the Board's function of making transfer schemes.

87.—(1) The Secretary of State may by order transfer any functions of the Board under section 85 above to himself or to the Franchising Director.

(2) An order under this section may provide for the transfer of the function in question for all purposes or for such purposes as may be specified in the order.

(3) Where any function is transferred to the Franchising Director under this section, the Secretary of State may, after consultation with the Franchising Director, direct the Franchising Director to exercise the function by making a scheme for the transfer of an undertaking or part of an undertaking, or any property, rights or liabilities, to a publicly owned railway company, a company wholly owned by the Franchising Director or a franchise company; and, if the Secretary of State gives such a direction, he may also—

(a) give the Franchising Director directions with respect to any matter specified in paragraph (a), (b) or (c) of section 85(4) above; or

(b) if the transfer is directed to be made to a publicly owned railway company which has not yet been formed, direct the Franchising Director to form, or take part in forming, a company for the purpose.

(4) In relation to any function transferred to the Franchising Director under this section, subsection (3) above shall have effect in substitution for subsection (4) of section 85 above and any reference in this Act to a direction under the said subsection (4) shall be construed accordingly.

(5) An order under this section may make such modifications of this Part as may be consequential upon, or incidental or supplemental to, the transfer effected by the order.

88.—(1) Where the Secretary of State gives the Board directions—

(a) under section 84 above, with respect to the formation of a wholly owned subsidiary of the Board, and

(b) under section 85 above, with respect to the making of a scheme for the transfer of anything to that wholly owned subsidiary,

the wholly owned subsidiary of the Board shall remain such until the transfer under the scheme has taken effect.

(2) Where the Secretary of State gives the Board directions under section 85 above with respect to the making of a scheme for the transfer of anything to a company which is wholly owned by the Crown, that company shall remain wholly owned by the Crown until the transfer under the scheme has taken effect.

(3) Where the Secretary of State gives the Franchising Director directions under or by virtue of section 87 above with respect to the making of a scheme for the transfer of anything to a publicly owned railway company, that company shall remain a publicly owned railway company until the transfer under the scheme has taken effect.

(4) Where a wholly owned subsidiary of the Board is formed pursuant to a direction under section 84 above, none of the following persons, that is to say, the Board, any wholly owned subsidiary of the Board or any person acting on behalf of the Board or its wholly owned subsidiaries, shall dispose of any interests in that subsidiary except—

(a) with the consent of the Secretary of State and subject to compliance with such conditions (if any) as he may impose in connection with that consent; or

(b) pursuant to a direction of the Secretary of State under subsection (6) below or section 89 below.

(5) None of the following persons, that is to say, the Franchising Director, any company which is wholly owned by the Franchising Director or any person acting on behalf of the Franchising Director or any such company, shall dispose of any interests in a company which is wholly owned by the Franchising Director except—

(a) with the consent of the Secretary of State and subject to compliance with such conditions (if any) as he may impose in connection with that consent; or

Transfers of interests in certain companies: provisions supplemental to sections 84 to 87.

PART II

(b) pursuant to a direction of the Secretary of State under subsection (7) below.

(6) The Secretary of State may at any time direct the Board to transfer, or arrange for there to be transferred, to him or such other person as may be specified in the direction any interests in a company so specified, being a wholly owned subsidiary of the Board formed pursuant to a direction under section 84 above, which are for the time being held by or on behalf of the Board.

(7) The Secretary of State may at any time direct the Franchising Director to transfer, or arrange for there to be transferred, to the Secretary of State or such other person as may be specified in the direction any interests in any company so specified which are for the time being held by the Franchising Director, any company which is wholly owned by the Franchising Director or any person acting on behalf of the Franchising Director or any such company.

(8) Where the Secretary of State gives a direction under subsection (6) or (7) above, it shall be the duty of the Board or, as the case may be, the Franchising Director to secure that the interests in question are transferred in accordance with the terms of the direction in such manner, and on or before such date, as may be specified for the purpose in the direction, and notwithstanding any duty imposed upon the Board by section 3(1) of the Transport Act 1962.

1962 c. 46.

Disposals by the Board and its subsidiaries.

89.—(1) If the Secretary of State, after consultation with the Board, so directs, the Board shall dispose or secure the disposal (whether by way of sale, lease or exchange and, if by way of sale or lease, whether for nominal or valuable consideration) of—

(a) the whole or any part of the undertaking, or any property, rights or liabilities, of the Board or of any wholly owned subsidiary of the Board; or

(b) without prejudice to paragraph (a) above, any securities of any subsidiary of the Board which are held by or on behalf of the Board or any other subsidiary of the Board.

(2) The directions that may be given under this section by the Secretary of State include directions specifying—

(a) the manner in which, and time within which, the disposal is to be effected;

(b) that which is to be disposed of;

(c) the person to whom the disposal is to be made.

(3) No disposal shall be made by the Board, or by any subsidiary of the Board, in pursuance of a direction under this section except with the consent of the Secretary of State and subject to compliance with such conditions (if any) as he may impose in connection with that consent.

(4) The powers of disposal conferred on the Board by virtue of this section are in addition and without prejudice to those conferred by section 14(1)(e) of the Transport Act 1962 (power to dispose of any part of the Board's undertaking, or any property, no longer required for the purposes of the Board's business) which shall accordingly also continue to be exercisable by the Board.

(5) In section 27 of the Transport Act 1962, in subsection (4) (which provides that the Secretary of State may direct the Board and the British Waterways Board to discontinue any of their activities, dispose of any part of their undertaking, dispose of any assets held by them, call in any loan made by them or exercise any power they may possess to revoke any guarantees given by them) the words "dispose of any part of their undertaking, dispose of any assets held by them" shall cease to have effect in so far as relating to the Board.

90.—(1) The Secretary of State may, after consultation with the Board, give directions to the Board with respect to the exercise of any rights conferred on the Board by the holding of interests in companies.

(2) A direction under subsection (1) above may be general in character or may relate to the manner in which such rights as are mentioned in that subsection are to be exercised in a particular case.

(3) In section 27 of the Transport Act 1962, in subsection (1) (which provides that the Secretary of State may give general directions to the Board as to the exercise and performance of their functions in relation to matters appearing to him to affect the national interest, including the exercise of rights conferred by the holding of interests in companies) the words "(including the exercise of rights conferred by the holding of interests in companies)" shall cease to have effect so far as relating to the Board.

(4) Subsection (5) of that section (which provides that the Secretary of State may, after consultation with the Board, direct the Board to exercise control over a subsidiary of the Board so as to require the subsidiary to discontinue any of their activities, dispose of any part of their undertaking, dispose of any assets held by them, call in any loan made by them or exercise any power they may possess to revoke any guarantees given by them) shall cease to have effect so far as relating to the Board.

Transfer schemes: supplemental provision

91.—(1) A transfer scheme may—
- (a) define the property, rights and liabilities to be transferred to the transferee—
    - (i) by specifying or describing the property, rights and liabilities in question;
    - (ii) by referring to all (or all but so much as may be excepted) of the property, rights and liabilities comprised in a specified part of the transferor's undertaking; or
    - (iii) partly in the one way and partly in the other;
- (b) provide that any rights or liabilities specified or described in the scheme shall be enforceable either by or against the transferor or transferee (or both of them);
- (c) impose on the transferor or transferee an obligation to enter into such written agreements with, or execute such other instruments in favour of, the transferor or transferee or such other person as may be specified in the scheme;
- (d) make such supplemental, incidental, consequential or transitional provision as the maker of the scheme considers appropriate.

PART II

(2) An obligation imposed by a provision included in a transfer scheme by virtue of paragraph (c) of subsection (1) above shall be enforceable by civil proceedings by the transferor or transferee or other person mentioned in that paragraph for an injunction or for interdict or for any other appropriate relief or remedy.

(3) A transaction of any description which is effected in pursuance of such a provision as is mentioned in subsection (2) above—

(a) shall have effect subject to the provisions of any enactment which provides for transactions of that description to be registered in any statutory register; but

(b) subject to that, shall be binding on all other persons, notwithstanding that it would, apart from this subsection, have required the consent or concurrence of any other person.

(4) No right of reverter (or corresponding right in Scotland), right of pre-emption, right of forfeiture, right of re-entry, right of irritancy, option or similar right affecting land shall operate or become exercisable as a result of any transfer of land—

(a) by virtue of a transfer scheme;

(b) by or under an agreement or instrument made or executed pursuant to any provision of Schedule 8 to this Act or pursuant to any directions given, or requirement imposed, under that Schedule; or

(c) pursuant to an obligation imposed by a provision included in a transfer scheme by virtue of paragraph (c) of subsection (1) above;

and, without prejudice to paragraph 8 of Schedule 8 to this Act, any such right or option shall accordingly have effect in the case of any such transfer as if the transferee in relation to that transfer were the same person in law as the transferor and as if no transfer of the land had taken place.

(5) Subsection (4) above shall have effect in relation to—

(a) the grant or creation of an estate or interest in, or right over, land, or

(b) the doing of any other thing in relation to land,

as it has effect in relation to a transfer of land; and any reference in that subsection or in the following provisions of this section to the transferor or the transferee shall be construed accordingly.

(6) In any case where—

(a) any such right or option as is mentioned in subsection (4) above would, apart from that subsection, have operated in favour of, or become exercisable by, a person, but

(b) the circumstances are such that, in consequence of the operation of that subsection, the right or option cannot subsequently operate in favour of that person or, as the case may be, become exercisable by him,

such compensation as may be just shall be paid to him by the transferor or the transferee (or by both) in respect of the extinguishment of the right or option.

(7) Any dispute as to whether any, and (if so) how much, compensation is payable under subsection (6) above, or as to the person to or by whom it shall be paid, shall be referred to and determined by—

(a) an arbitrator appointed by the President for the time being of the Royal Institution of Chartered Surveyors; or

(b) where the proceedings are to be held in Scotland, an arbiter appointed by the Lord President of the Court of Session; or

(c) where the proceedings are to be held in Northern Ireland, an arbitrator appointed by the Lord Chancellor.

(8) If it appears to the transferor that a person is or may be entitled to compensation under subsection (6) above, he shall—

(a) notify that person that he is or may be so entitled, and

(b) invite him to make such representations as he wishes to the transferor not later than fourteen days after the date of issue of the document containing the notification required by paragraph (a) above,

or, if the transferor is not aware of the name and address of the person concerned, shall publish, in such manner as he considers appropriate, a notice containing information about the interest affected and inviting any person who thinks that he is or may be entitled to compensation to make such representations to the transferor within such period (being not less than 28 days from the date of publication of the notice) as may be specified in the notice.

92.—(1) A transfer scheme may provide that any functions of the transferor under a statutory provision— [Functions under local or private legislation etc.]

(a) shall be transferred to the transferee;

(b) shall be concurrently exercisable by two or more transferees; or

(c) shall be concurrently exercisable by the transferor and one or more transferees.

(2) Subsection (1) above applies in relation to any function under a statutory provision if and to the extent that the statutory provision—

(a) relates to any part of the transferor's undertaking, or to any property, which is to be transferred by the scheme; or

(b) authorises the carrying out of works designed to be used in connection with any such part of the transferor's undertaking or the acquisition of land for the purpose of carrying out any such works.

(3) Subsection (1) above does not apply to any function of the Board or of any of the Board's subsidiaries under any provision of this Act or of—

(a) the Transport Act 1962; [1962 c. 46.]

(b) the Transport Act 1968; [1968 c. 73.]

(c) section 4 of the Railways Act 1974; or [1974 c. 48.]

(d) sections 119 to 124 of the Transport Act 1985. [1985 c. 67.]

(4) A transfer scheme may define any functions of the transferor to be transferred or made concurrently exercisable by the scheme in accordance with subsection (1) above—

Part II

(a) by specifying the statutory provisions in question;

(b) by referring to all the statutory provisions (except those specified in subsection (3) above) which—

(i) relate to any part of the transferor's undertaking, or to any property, which is to be transferred by the scheme, or

(ii) authorise the carrying out of works designed to be used in connection with any such part of the transferor's undertaking or the acquisition of land for the purpose of carrying out any such works; or

(c) by referring to all the statutory provisions within paragraph (b) above, but specifying certain excepted provisions.

(5) In this section "statutory provision" means a provision whether of a general or of a special nature contained in, or in any document made or issued under, any Act, whether of a general or a special nature.

Assignment of employees to particular parts of undertakings.

93.—(1) Schemes may be made—

(a) assigning such qualifying employees, or qualifying employees of such a class or description, as may be specified in the scheme to such part of their employer's undertaking as may be so specified;

(b) modifying the terms and conditions of employment of those employees; and

(c) providing for the payment of compensation to any of those employees by his employer in respect of any overall detriment incurred by the employee in consequence of any modifications made by the scheme to his terms and conditions of employment.

(2) A scheme shall be made only for the purpose of facilitating, or otherwise in contemplation of, or in connection with,—

(a) the disposal of the undertaking, or part of the undertaking, of the Board or of a wholly owned subsidiary of the Board;

(b) the transfer, by virtue of a transfer scheme, of any property, rights or liabilities—

(i) from the Board or a wholly owned subsidiary of the Board to any such subsidiary or to a publicly owned railway company or a company wholly owned by the Franchising Director; or

(ii) from a company wholly owned by the Franchising Director to another such company;

(c) the provision of railway passenger services, or the operation of additional railway assets, under a franchise agreement, in circumstances where a previous franchise agreement relating to the provision of those services or the operation of those assets comes, or has come, to an end;

(d) the performance of any duty imposed on the Franchising Director by any provision of Part I above to secure—

(i) the provision of any railway passenger services;

(ii) the operation of any network or part of a network;

(iii) the operation of any station or light maintenance depot, or any part of a station or light maintenance depot; or

(e) the exercise of the power conferred on the Franchising Director by section 30 above to secure the operation of any additional railway assets.

(3) The power to make a scheme shall be exercisable—

(a) by the Board, in respect of employees of the Board or of any wholly owned subsidiary of the Board; or

(b) by the Franchising Director, in respect of employees of any company which is wholly owned by the Franchising Director.

(4) Where a scheme modifies the terms and conditions of employment of any person, the person's terms and conditions of employment after the modification takes effect must overall, and taking account of the amount or value of any compensation payable to him by virtue of subsection (1)(c) above in respect of any such detriment as is there mentioned, be no less favourable to him than his terms and conditions of employment before the modification takes effect.

(5) The duty imposed on an employer by section 4 of the Employment Protection (Consolidation) Act 1978 (requirement for written statement in respect of certain changes relating to an employee's employment) shall extend to all of the modifications made by a scheme to a qualifying employee's terms and conditions of employment, as if those modifications were changes required to be dealt with in a written statement under that section.

1978 c. 44.

(6) If any qualifying employee whose terms and conditions of employment are modified by a scheme is aggrieved—

(a) at the provisions made by the scheme with respect to the payment of compensation, so far as applicable in his case, or

(b) at the fact that the scheme does not make any such provision,

he may make a written complaint to the maker of the scheme not later than twelve weeks after the date of issue of the written statement required by section 4 of the Employment Protection (Consolidation) Act 1978 in consequence of the modifications made by the scheme in the qualifying employee's terms and conditions of employment.

(7) Any complaint under subsection (6) above shall be referred to, and determined by, such arbitrator as may be agreed by the qualifying employee and the person to whom the complaint was made or, at the request of either of them, by a panel of three arbitrators appointed by the Secretary of State and consisting of—

(a) a person who appears to the Secretary of State to be representative of employers in the railway industry;

(b) a person who appears to the Secretary of State to be representative of employees in the railway industry; and

(c) an independent chairman.

(8) A scheme may make such incidental, consequential, supplemental or transitional provision as appears necessary or expedient to the person making the scheme.

(9) A scheme may make different provision for different qualifying employees or for qualifying employees of different classes or descriptions.

PART II

(10) A scheme shall not come into force unless it has been approved by the Secretary of State or until such date as the Secretary of State may, after consultation with the maker of the scheme, specify for the purpose in giving his approval.

(11) In the application of this section in relation to Scotland, any reference to an arbitrator shall be taken as a reference to an arbiter.

1978 c. 44.
1965 c. 19 (N.I.).

(12) In the application of this section to Northern Ireland, for any reference to section 4 of the Employment Protection (Consolidation) Act 1978 there shall be substituted a reference to section 4(4) to (6B) of the Contracts of Employment and Redundancy Payments Act (Northern Ireland) 1965.

(13) In this section—

"qualifying employee", in the case of any scheme, means a person who, immediately before the coming into force of that scheme—

(a) is an employee of—

(i) the Board;

(ii) a wholly owned subsidiary of the Board; or

(iii) a company which is wholly owned by the Franchising Director; and

(b) is not assigned solely to duties in that part of his employer's undertaking to which he is, or is to be, assigned by that scheme;

"scheme" means a scheme under this section;

and expressions used in this section and in Part I above have the same meaning in this section as they have in that Part.

Accounting provisions.

94.—(1) This section applies where any property, rights or liabilities are transferred by virtue of a transfer scheme between—

(a) the Board and any company which, at the time of the transfer, is either—

(i) a wholly owned subsidiary of the Board; or

(ii) wholly owned by the Crown; or

(b) any two companies which, at the time of the transfer, fall within paragraph (a) above.

(2) Where this section applies, the transfer scheme may state—

(a) the value at which any asset transferred to the transferee by virtue of the scheme is to be entered in the opening accounts of the transferee; or

(b) the amount at which any liability so transferred is to be entered in those accounts.

(3) The value or amount (if any) stated by virtue of subsection (2) above shall be—

(a) in a case where the whole of the asset or liability in question is transferred by the transfer scheme, the value or amount at which the asset or liability appeared in the last full accounts of the transferor, or

(b) in a case where part only of the asset or liability is so transferred, such part of the value or amount at which the asset or liability appeared in the last full accounts of the transferor as may be determined by or in accordance with the transfer scheme,

unless the maker of the transfer scheme considers that some other amount or value is appropriate in all the circumstances of the case, in which case the amount or value stated by virtue of subsection (2) above shall be that other amount or value.

(4) Where this section applies, the transfer scheme may provide that the amount to be included in the opening accounts of the transferee in respect of any item shall be determined as if so much of anything done (or treated as done) by the transferor (whether by way of acquiring, revaluing or disposing of any asset or incurring, revaluing or discharging any liability, or by carrying any amount to any provision or reserve, or otherwise) as may be determined by or in accordance with the transfer scheme had been done by the transferee.

(5) Without prejudice to the generality of the preceding provisions of this section, where this section applies, the transfer scheme may provide—

(a) that the amount to be included from time to time in any reserves of the transferee as representing its accumulated realised profits shall be determined as if such proportion of any profits realised and retained by the transferor as may be determined by or in accordance with the transfer scheme, had been realised and retained by the transferee;

(b) that the amount to be included from time to time in the opening accounts and any subsequent statutory accounts of the transferee as representing its accumulated realised losses shall be determined as if such proportion of any accumulated realised losses of the transferor as may be determined by or in accordance with the transfer scheme had been losses realised by the transferee.

(6) In this section—

"accounting year" means—

(a) in the case of the Board, the period of twelve months ending with 31st March in any year; and

(b) in the case of any company, its financial year, within the meaning of the Companies Act 1985;

1985 c. 6.

"the last full accounts", in connection with any transfer scheme, means—

(a) where the Board is the transferor, the annual accounts prepared by the Board in accordance with section 24 of the Transport Act 1962 for the accounting year last ended before the making of the transfer scheme; and

1962 c. 46.

(b) where any other person is the transferor, the statutory accounts of that person for the accounting year last ended before the making of the transfer scheme;

"the opening accounts of the transferee" means any statutory accounts prepared by the transferee for the accounting year next ending after the transfer date;

PART II

1985 c. 6.

"statutory accounts" means any accounts prepared by a company for the purpose of any provision of the Companies Act 1985 (including group accounts).

Power of the Secretary of State or the Franchising Director to require provision of information in connection with transfer schemes.

95.—(1) Where, in exercise of any functions conferred on him by section 86 above or transferred to him by an order under section 87 above, the Franchising Director or the Secretary of State (in this section referred to as "the relevant authority") proposes to make a transfer scheme, he may direct any person to whom this section applies—

(a) to furnish him with such information as the relevant authority considers necessary to enable him to make the scheme; and

(b) to do so within such time (being not less than 28 days from the giving of the direction) as may be specified in the direction;

and the persons to whom this section applies are the Regulator, the Board, any wholly owned subsidiary of the Board, any publicly owned railway company, any franchise company and any company which is wholly owned by the Franchising Director.

(2) If a person fails to comply with a direction under subsection (1) above, the relevant authority may serve a notice under subsection (3) below on that person.

(3) A notice under this subsection is a notice signed by the relevant authority and—

(a) requiring the person on whom it is served to produce, at a time and place specified in the notice, to the relevant authority or to any person appointed by the relevant authority for the purpose, any documents which are specified or described in the notice and are in that person's custody or under his control; or

(b) requiring that person to furnish, at a time and place and in the form and manner specified in the notice, to the relevant authority such information as may be specified or described in the notice.

(4) No person shall be required under this section to produce any documents which he could not be compelled to produce in civil proceedings in the court or, in complying with any requirement for the furnishing of information, to give any information which he could not be compelled to give in evidence in any such proceedings.

(5) A person who without reasonable excuse fails to do anything required of him by notice under subsection (3) above is guilty of an offence and shall be liable on summary conviction to a fine not exceeding level 5 on the standard scale.

(6) A person who intentionally alters, suppresses or destroys any document which he has been required by any notice under subsection (3) above to produce is guilty of an offence and shall be liable—

(a) on summary conviction, to a fine not exceeding the statutory maximum;

(b) on conviction on indictment, to a fine.

(7) If a person makes default in complying with a notice under subsection (3) above, the court may, on the application of the relevant authority, make such order as the court thinks fit for requiring the default to be made good; and any such order may provide that all the costs or

expenses of and incidental to the application shall be borne by the person in default or by any officers of a company or other association who are responsible for its default.

(8) Any reference in this section to the production of a document includes a reference to the production of a legible and intelligible copy of information recorded otherwise than in legible form; and the reference to suppressing a document includes a reference to destroying the means of reproducing information recorded otherwise than in legible form.

(9) In this section "the court" means the High Court, in relation to England and Wales, and the Court of Session, in relation to Scotland.

96.—(1) A transfer scheme made by the Board or the Franchising Director, otherwise than under section 86 above, shall not come into force unless it has been approved by the Secretary of State or until such date as the Secretary of State may specify for the purpose in giving his approval.

(2) The Secretary of State shall not make a transfer scheme except after consultation with the transferor.

(3) Before approving a transfer scheme made by the Franchising Director or the Board, the Secretary of State, after consultation with the transferor and, in the case of a scheme made by the Franchising Director, with the Franchising Director, may modify the scheme.

(4) It shall be the duty of the transferor to provide the Secretary of State with all such information and other assistance as he may require for the purposes of or in connection with the exercise, in relation to a transfer scheme, of any power conferred on him by this section.

Functions of the Secretary of State in relation to transfer schemes.

97. The provisions of Schedule 8 to this Act shall apply to any transfer by virtue of a transfer scheme; and sections 85(6) and 86(4) above shall have effect subject to the provisions of that Schedule.

Supplementary provisions as to transfers by transfer scheme.

Ownership of successor companies

98.—(1) This section applies where any property, rights or liabilities are vested in accordance with a transfer scheme in a successor company which at the time of the vesting is either—

    (a) a wholly owned subsidiary of the Board; or

    (b) Government owned.

(2) Where this section applies, the successor company shall, as a consequence of the vesting referred to in subsection (1) above, issue to the appropriate person such securities of that company as may from time to time be directed—

    (a) by the Secretary of State, if the transfer scheme was made in pursuance of a direction given by him; or

    (b) in any other case, by the Board with the consent of the Secretary of State.

(3) The "appropriate person" for the purposes of subsection (2) above is—

    (a) the Board, in a case where the direction under that subsection is given at a time when the successor company is a wholly owned subsidiary of the Board; or

Initial share holding in successor companies.

PART II

(b) the Secretary of State, in a case where the direction under that subsection is given at a time when the successor company is Government owned.

(4) No direction shall be given under subsection (2) above to the successor company at any time after that company—

(a) has ceased to be Government owned, or

(b) has ceased to be a wholly owned subsidiary of the Board,

unless, in a case where paragraph (b) above would otherwise apply, the cessation mentioned in that paragraph occurs in consequence of the successor company's becoming Government owned pursuant to a direction under section 88(6) above, in which case directions under subsection (2) above may continue to be given until the company ceases to be Government owned.

(5) Securities required to be issued in pursuance of a direction under subsection (2) above shall be issued or allotted at such time or times, and on such terms, as may be specified in the direction.

(6) Shares of the successor company which are issued in pursuance of a direction under subsection (2) above—

(a) shall be of such nominal value as the Secretary of State may direct; and

1985 c. 6.
(b) shall be issued as fully paid and treated for the purposes of the Companies Act 1985 as if they had been paid up by virtue of the payment to that company of their nominal value in cash.

(7) Any dividends or other sums received by the Treasury or the Secretary of State in right of, or on the disposal of, any securities acquired by virtue of this section shall be paid into the Consolidated Fund.

(8) In this section, "Government owned", in relation to any successor company, means wholly owned by the Crown, but not wholly owned by the Franchising Director.

Government investment in securities of successor companies.

99.—(1) The Treasury or, with the approval of the Treasury, the Secretary of State may at any time acquire securities of a successor company which at that time is—

(a) a wholly owned subsidiary of the Board; or

(b) wholly owned by the Crown.

(2) The Secretary of State shall not dispose of any securities acquired under this section without the approval of the Treasury.

(3) Any expenses incurred by the Treasury or the Secretary of State in consequence of the provisions of this section shall be paid out of money provided by Parliament.

(4) Any dividends or other sums received by the Treasury or the Secretary of State in right of, or on the disposal of, any securities acquired under this section shall be paid into the Consolidated Fund.

Exercise of functions through nominees.

100.—(1) The Treasury or, with the approval of the Treasury, the Secretary of State may, for the purposes of section 98 or 99 above or section 106 below, appoint any person to act as the nominee, or one of the nominees, of the Treasury or the Secretary of State; and—

(a) securities of a successor company may be issued under section 98 above or section 106 below to any nominee of the Treasury or the Secretary of State appointed for the purposes of that section, and

(b) any such nominee appointed for the purposes of section 99 above may acquire securities under that section,

in accordance with directions given from time to time by the Treasury or, with the consent of the Treasury, by the Secretary of State.

(2) Any person holding any securities as a nominee of the Treasury or the Secretary of State by virtue of subsection (1) above shall hold and deal with them (or any of them) on such terms and in such manner as the Treasury or, with the consent of the Treasury, the Secretary of State may direct.

101.—(1) As soon as he considers expedient and, in any case, not later than six months after any operating company ceases to be a public sector railway company, the Secretary of State shall by order fix a target investment limit in relation to the shares for the time being held in that company by virtue of any provision of this Part by the Treasury and their nominees and by the Secretary of State and his nominees (in this section referred to as "the Government shareholding"). *Target investment limit for Government shareholding in certain successor companies.*

(2) The target investment limit for the Government shareholding in an operating company shall be expressed as a proportion of the voting rights which are exercisable in all circumstances at general meetings of the company (in this section referred to as "the ordinary voting rights").

(3) The first target investment limit fixed under this section for the Government shareholding in a particular company shall not exceed, by more than 0.5 per cent. of the ordinary voting rights, the proportion of those rights which is in fact carried by the Government shareholding in that company at the time when the order fixing the limit is made.

(4) The Secretary of State may from time to time by order fix a new target investment limit for the Government shareholding in an operating company in place of the one previously in force under this section; but—

(a) any new limit must be lower than the one it replaces; and

(b) an order under this section may only be revoked by an order fixing a new limit.

(5) It shall be the duty of the Treasury and of the Secretary of State so to exercise—

(a) their powers under section 99 above and any power to dispose of any shares held by virtue of any provision of this Part, and

(b) their power to give directions to their respective nominees,

as to secure in relation to each operating company that the Government shareholding in that company does not carry a proportion of the ordinary voting rights exceeding any target investment limit for the time being in force under this section in relation to that company.

(6) Notwithstanding subsection (5) above but subject to subsection (7) below, the Treasury or the Secretary of State may take up, or direct any nominee of the Treasury or of the Secretary of State to take up, any rights which are for the time being available to them or him, or to the nominee, either—

PART II

(a) as an existing holder of shares or other securities of an operating company; or

(b) by reason of the rescission of any contracts for the sale of such shares or securities.

(7) If, as a result of anything done under subsection (6) above, the proportion of the ordinary voting rights carried by the Government shareholding in an operating company at any time exceeds the target investment limit for the time being in force under this section in relation to that company, it shall be the duty of the Treasury or, as the case may be, the Secretary of State to comply with subsection (5) above as soon after that time as is reasonably practicable.

(8) For the purposes of this section the temporary suspension of any of the ordinary voting rights shall be disregarded.

(9) The Secretary of State shall not exercise any power conferred on him by this section except with the consent of the Treasury.

(10) In this section—

"operating company" means a successor company—

1985 c. 6.
(a) which is a company limited by shares and formed and registered under the Companies Act 1985 (or the former Companies Acts, as defined in section 735(1)(c) of that Act);

(b) which was a public sector railway company at the time when any property, rights or liabilities of another public sector railway company were vested in it by a transfer scheme;

(c) which has since ceased to be a public sector railway company; and

(d) which at the time of the vesting referred to in paragraph (b) above was not, and at no time since has been, a franchise company;

"public sector railway company" means—

(a) the Board;

(b) any wholly owned subsidiary of the Board; or

(c) any publicly owned railway company.

Finances of successor companies

Temporary restrictions on borrowings etc.
102.—(1) If articles of association of a successor company confer on the Secretary of State powers exercisable with the consent of the Treasury for, or in connection with, restricting the sums of money which may be borrowed or raised by the group during any period, those powers shall be exercisable in the national interest notwithstanding any rule of law and the provisions of any enactment.

(2) For the purposes of this section an alteration of the articles of association of a successor company shall be disregarded if the alteration—

(a) has the effect of conferring or extending any such power as is mentioned in subsection (1) above; and

(b) is made at a time when that company is neither a wholly owned subsidiary of the Board nor wholly owned by the Crown.

(3) In this section "group", in relation to a company, means that company and all of its subsidiaries taken together.

103.—(1) The Secretary of State may, with the approval of the Treasury, make loans of such amounts as he thinks fit to any successor company which is for the time being wholly owned by the Crown.

(2) Any loans which the Secretary of State makes under this section shall be repaid to him at such times and by such methods, and interest on any such loans shall be paid to him at such rates and at such times, as he may, with the approval of the Treasury, from time to time direct.

(3) The Treasury may issue out of the National Loans Fund to the Secretary of State such sums as are required by him for making loans under this section.

(4) Any sums received under subsection (2) above by the Secretary of State shall be paid into the National Loans Fund.

(5) It shall be the duty of the Secretary of State as respects each financial year—

(a) to prepare, in such form as the Treasury may direct, an account of sums issued to him in pursuance of subsection (3) above and of sums received by him under subsection (2) above and of the disposal by him of the sums so issued or received; and

(b) to send the account to the Comptroller and Auditor General not later than the end of the month of August in the following financial year;

and the Comptroller and Auditor General shall examine, certify and report on the account and shall lay copies of it and of his report before each House of Parliament.

PART II
Government lending to certain successor companies.

104.—(1) The Treasury may guarantee, in such manner and on such terms as they may think fit, the repayment of the principal of, the payment of interest on, and the discharge of any other financial obligation in connection with, any sums which are borrowed from a person other than the Secretary of State by any successor company which is for the time being wholly owned by the Crown.

(2) Immediately after a guarantee is given under this section, the Treasury shall lay a statement of the guarantee before each House of Parliament; and immediately after any sum is issued for fulfilling a guarantee so given, the Treasury shall so lay a statement relating to that sum.

(3) Any sums required by the Treasury for fulfilling a guarantee under this section shall be charged on and issued out of the Consolidated Fund.

(4) If any sums are issued in fulfilment of a guarantee given under this section, the company whose obligations are so fulfilled shall make to the Treasury, at such times and in such manner as the Treasury may from time to time direct—

(a) payments of such amounts as the Treasury may so direct in or towards repayment of the sums so issued; and

(b) payments of interest on what is outstanding for the time being in respect of sums so issued at such rate as the Treasury may so direct.

(5) Any sums received under subsection (4) above by the Treasury shall be paid into the Consolidated Fund.

Treasury guarantees for loans made to certain successor companies.

PART II
Grants to certain successor companies.

105.—(1) The Secretary of State may, with the approval of the Treasury, make to any successor company which is for the time being wholly owned by the Crown grants of such amounts, at such times and in such manner, as he may with the approval of the Treasury determine, towards the expenditure of that company.

(2) Grants under this section may be made subject to such conditions as the Secretary of State with the approval of the Treasury may determine.

(3) Any sums required by the Secretary of State for making grants under this section shall be paid out of money provided by Parliament.

Extinguishment of certain liabilities of successor companies.

106.—(1) The Secretary of State may by order extinguish all or any of the liabilities of a successor company which is for the time being—

(a) a wholly owned subsidiary of the Board, or

(b) wholly owned by the Crown,

in respect of the principal of such relevant loans as may be specified in the order; and the assets of the National Loans Fund shall accordingly be reduced by amounts corresponding to any liabilities so extinguished.

(2) Where the Secretary of State has made an order under subsection (1) above and he considers it appropriate to do so, he may from time to time give a direction under this subsection to the company whose liabilities are extinguished by the order, or to a company or companies wholly owning the company whose liabilities are so extinguished; and a company to which such a direction is given shall, as a consequence of the making of the order, issue such securities of the company as may be specified or described in the direction—

(a) to the Treasury or the Secretary of State; or

(b) if it is the company whose liabilities are extinguished by the order, to a company or companies wholly owning that company.

(3) For the purposes of any statutory accounts of a company to whom securities are issued by virtue of subsection (2)(b) above, the value at the time of its issue of any such security shall be taken—

(a) in the case of a share, to have been equal to its nominal value; and

(b) in the case of a debenture, to have been equal to the principal sum payable under the debenture,

and such nominal value or principal sum shall be taken in those accounts to be accumulated realised profits.

(4) In subsection (3) above "statutory accounts of a company" means any accounts prepared by the company for the purpose of any provision of the Companies Act 1985 (including group accounts).

1985 c. 6.

(5) The Secretary of State—

(a) shall not give a direction under subsection (2) above for the issue of securities except at a time when the company whose liability is extinguished by the order or, as the case may be, the company which is directed to issue securities satisfies the condition in subsection (6) below; and

(b) shall not give a direction under paragraph (b) of subsection (2) above except at a time when the company, or each of the companies, to whom the securities are to be issued satisfies that condition.

(6) The condition referred to in subsection (5) above is that the company is for the time being—

(a) a wholly owned subsidiary of the Board; or

(b) wholly owned by the Crown.

(7) Unless the Secretary of State otherwise determines in any particular case, where a company is directed to issue debentures in pursuance of this section—

(a) the aggregate of the principal sums payable under the debentures to which the direction relates shall be equal to the aggregate of the sums the liability to repay which is extinguished by the order; and

(b) the terms as to the payment of the principal sums payable on the debentures to which the direction relates, and as to the payment of interest on those principal sums, shall be the same as the corresponding terms of the loans specified in the order.

(8) For the purposes of subsection (7) above, any express or implied terms of a loan shall be disregarded in so far as they relate to the early discharge of liabilities to make repayments of principal and payments of interest.

(9) Subsections (5) to (7) of section 98 above shall apply for the purposes of this section as they apply for the purposes of that section.

(10) The Secretary of State shall not exercise any power conferred on him by this section except with the consent of the Treasury.

(11) In this section "relevant loan", in relation to a successor company, means any loan made to the Board under section 20 of the Transport Act 1962, if and to the extent that the liability to repay that loan is transferred to and vested in that company by virtue of a transfer scheme.

1962 c. 46.

(12) For the purposes of this section the company or companies wholly owning another company are—

(a) any company of which that other is a wholly owned subsidiary, or

(b) any two or more companies which between them hold all the issued securities of that other.

Provisions with respect to flotation

107.—(1) In any case where—

(a) the same document contains listing particulars for securities of two or more licensed successor companies, and

Responsibility for composite listing particulars of certain licensed successor companies.

Part II

(b) any person's responsibility for any information included in the document is stated in the document to be confined to its inclusion as part of the listing particulars for securities of any one of those companies,

that person shall not be treated as responsible for that information in so far as it is stated in the document to form part of the listing particulars for securities of any other of those companies.

(2) Sections 150 and 154 of the 1986 Act (advertisements etc in connection with listing applications) shall have effect in relation to any information issued for purposes connected with any securities of a licensed successor company as if any reference to a person's incurring civil liability included a reference to any other person being entitled, as against that person, to be granted a civil remedy or to rescind or repudiate any contract.

(3) Subsections (1) and (2) above have effect only in relation to licensed successor companies—

(a) which are wholly owned subsidiaries of the Board; or

(b) which are wholly owned by the Crown.

(4) In this section—

1986 c. 60.

"the 1986 Act" means the Financial Services Act 1986;

"licensed successor company" means a successor company which is the holder of a licence under section 8 above;

"listing particulars" means any listing particulars or supplementary listing particulars within the meaning of the 1986 Act;

"responsible" means responsible for the purposes of Part IV of the 1986 Act and "responsibility" shall be construed accordingly.

Application of Trustee Investments Act 1961 in relation to investment in certain licensed successor companies.
1961 c. 62.

108.—(1) Subsection (2) below shall have effect for the purpose of applying paragraph 3(b) of Part IV of Schedule 1 to the Trustee Investments Act 1961 (which provides that shares and debentures of a company shall not count as wider-range and narrower-range investments respectively within the meaning of that Act unless the company has paid dividends in each of the five years immediately preceding that in which the investment is made) in relation to investment, during the first investment year or any following year, in shares or debentures of a licensed successor company—

(a) whose shares or debentures are included in the Official List, within the meaning of Part IV of the Financial Services Act 1986, in pursuance of that Part; and

(b) which, immediately before its shares or debentures were admitted to that Official List, was—

(i) a wholly owned subsidiary of the Board; or

(ii) a company wholly owned by the Crown.

(2) The licensed successor company shall be deemed to have paid a dividend as mentioned in the said paragraph 3(b)—

(a) in every year preceding the first investment year which is included in the relevant five years; and

(b) in the first investment year, if that year is included in the relevant five years and that company does not in fact pay such a dividend in that year.

(3) In this section—

"the first investment year", in relation to a licensed successor company means the calendar year in which shares in that company are first issued in pursuance of section 98(2) above;

"licensed successor company" has the same meaning as it has in section 107 above;

"the relevant five years" means the five years immediately preceding the year in which the investment in question is made or proposed to be made.

Other financial provisions

109. After section 21 of the Transport Act 1962 (Treasury guarantees) there shall be inserted—

Grants to the Board.
1962 c. 46.

"Grants to the Railways Board.

21A.—(1) The Secretary of State may, with the approval of the Treasury, make to the Railways Board grants of such amounts, at such times and in such manner, as he may with the approval of the Treasury determine—

(a) towards the expenditure of that Board; or

(b) without prejudice to paragraph (a) of this subsection, for the purpose of enabling that Board to make any payment (whether by way of repayment of principal or payment of interest or of any other description) in respect of any loan made to them under section twenty of this Act.

(2) Grants under this section may be made subject to such conditions as the Secretary of State may with the approval of the Treasury determine.

(3) Any sums required by the Secretary of State for making grants under this section shall be paid out of money provided by Parliament.

(4) This section is without prejudice to any other power to make grants to the Railways Board.".

110.—(1) If the Secretary of State by order so provides, sections 19 to 21A of the Transport Act 1962 (which, among other things, make provision for and in connection with—

Application of sections 19 to 21A of the Transport Act 1962 to wholly owned subsidiaries of the Board.

(a) the borrowing powers of the Board,

(b) the making by the Secretary of State of loans to the Board,

(c) the giving by the Treasury of guarantees in respect of sums borrowed by the Board from persons other than the Secretary of State, and

(d) the making by the Secretary of State of grants to the Board),

shall apply in relation to any wholly owned subsidiary of the Board designated in the order as they apply in relation to the Board, but with such modifications as may be specified in the order.

132 c. 43 Railways Act 1993

PART II

1962 c. 46.

(2) Without prejudice to the generality of the modifications of those sections that may be specified in an order under this section, any such order may include provision imposing limits on the amounts that may be outstanding at any time in respect of the principal of any money borrowed by wholly owned subsidiaries of the Board under section 19 of the Transport Act 1962 in its application by virtue of this section.

Financial limits on loans.
1968 c. 73.

111. In section 42 of the Transport Act 1968, in subsection (6) (limit on aggregate amount outstanding in respect of the principal of any money borrowed by the Board under section 19 of the Transport Act 1962 and the Board's commencing capital debt), paragraph (b) (which relates to the Board's commencing capital debt, and which is spent) shall be omitted and after that paragraph there shall be inserted—

> "(c) the principal of any money borrowed by wholly owned subsidiaries of the Board under that section in its application by virtue of section 110 of the Railways Act 1993,".

Stamp duty and stamp duty reserve tax

Stamp duty and stamp duty reserve tax.

112. Schedule 9 to this Act (which makes provision about stamp duty and stamp duty reserve tax in relation to or in connection with the other provisions of this Part) shall have effect.

Supplemental

Objectives of the Secretary of State and corresponding duties of the Board.

113.—(1) It shall be the principal objective of the Secretary of State in exercising the powers conferred on him by or under sections 84 to 97 above to secure as soon as, in his opinion, is reasonably practicable the result that the function of providing railway services in Great Britain is performed by private sector operators.

(2) In pursuing that principal objective, the Secretary of State shall have regard to the desirability of—

(a) encouraging competition between those who provide railway services;

(b) maintaining efficiency, economy and safety of operation in the provision of railway services in Great Britain;

(c) providing opportunities for persons employed in railway undertakings to acquire (whether alone or jointly with others) an interest in the ownership of the undertakings in which they are employed; and

(d) securing that the disposal takes place on the most favourable financial terms that can reasonably be obtained in all the circumstances of the case;

and for the purposes of paragraph (d) above, financial terms may be regarded as "favourable" notwithstanding that any expenses incurred in procuring or effecting the disposal are not exceeded by any proceeds of sale arising from it.

(3) The Secretary of State may give the Board directions, whether of a general or specific character, requiring such steps as may be specified or otherwise described in the directions to be taken by the Board with a view to—

(a) facilitating the attainment by the Secretary of State of the principal objective specified in subsection (1) above;

(b) identifying methods of accomplishing any of the matters specified in paragraphs (a) to (d) of subsection (2) above; or

(c) generally assisting in securing the prompt and effective implementation of any proposals made by the Secretary of State for the exercise of any power conferred on him by or under this Act.

(4) Expressions used in this section and in Part I above have the same meaning in this section as they have in that Part.

114.—(1) None of the following persons, that is to say—

(a) the Secretary of State,

(b) the Franchising Director,

(c) the Board,

shall be regarded for any purpose of the Companies Act 1985 or the Companies (Northern Ireland) Order 1986 as a shadow director, within the meaning of that Act or Order, of any body falling within subsection (2) below.

The Secretary of State, the Franchising Director and the Board not to be regarded as shadow directors of certain railway companies etc.
1985 c. 6.
S.I. 1986/1032 (N.I. 6).

(2) Those bodies are—

(a) any publicly owned railway company;

(b) any company which is wholly owned by the Franchising Director;

(c) any subsidiary of the Board;

(d) any franchise company;

(e) any company concerning which a direction (whether of a general or specific character) has been given under section 90 above to the Board with respect to the exercise by the Board of the rights conferred by their holding of interests in that company.

115. In Part III of Schedule 1 to the House of Commons Disqualification Act 1975, the following entry shall be inserted at the appropriate place—

Parliamentary disqualification.
1975 c. 24.

"Director of a company—

(a) which, within the meaning of Part II of the Railways Act 1993, is a successor company wholly owned by the Crown, or

(b) which, within the meaning of that Act, is wholly owned by the Director of Passenger Rail Franchising,

being a director nominated or appointed by a Minister of the Crown, the Director of Passenger Rail Franchising or any other person acting on behalf of the Crown".

116.—(1) In this Part, unless the context otherwise requires—

Interpretation of Part II.

"dispose", in relation to any land, includes the making of any disposition and "disposal" shall be construed accordingly;

"franchise company" has the meaning given by section 85(8) above;

PART II

"property", "rights" and "liabilities" shall be construed in accordance with section 85(2) above and subsection (2) below;

"successor company" means a company in which any property, rights or liabilities are vested by virtue of and in accordance with a transfer scheme;

"transfer date" has the meaning given by section 85(6) or, as the case may be, 86(5)(b) above;

"transferee" and "transferor", in relation to any transfer of property, rights or liabilities effected or proposed to be effected by virtue of a transfer scheme, mean respectively the person to whom and the person from whom they are, or are to be, so transferred.

(2) Any reference in this Part to property, rights or liabilities is a reference to property or (as the case may be) rights or liabilities—

(a) whether or not capable of being transferred or assigned otherwise than under or by virtue of this Act;

(b) whether situate or subsisting in the United Kingdom or elsewhere; and

(c) whether the person entitled to the property or rights or, as the case may be, subject to the liabilities is so entitled or subject—

(i) under the law of the United Kingdom or of any part of the United Kingdom; or

(ii) under the law of any country or territory outside the United Kingdom;

and references to an undertaking or part of an undertaking shall be construed accordingly.

PART III

MISCELLANEOUS, GENERAL AND SUPPLEMENTAL PROVISIONS

Safety, emergencies, security etc.

Safety of railways and other guided transport systems.
1974 c. 37.

117.—(1) Part I of the Health and Safety at Work etc. Act 1974 ("the 1974 Act") shall have effect as if the provisions mentioned in subsection (4) below (which relate to the proper construction and safe operation of certain transport systems, and of the vehicles used on those systems, and the protection of railway employees or the general public from personal injury and other risks arising therefrom)—

(a) were existing statutory provisions, within the meaning of that Part; and

(b) in the case of the enactments mentioned in paragraphs (a) to (m) of that subsection, were specified in the third column of Schedule 1 to that Act.

(2) If to any extent they would not do so apart from this subsection, the general purposes of Part I of the 1974 Act shall include—

(a) securing the proper construction and safe operation of transport systems to which this section applies, and of any locomotives, rolling stock or other vehicles used, or to be used, on those systems; and

(b) protecting the public (whether passengers or not) from personal injury and other risks arising from the construction and operation of transport systems to which this section applies.

(3) Without prejudice to the generality of subsection (1) of section 15 of the 1974 Act (health and safety regulations), regulations under that section may—

(a) repeal or modify any of the provisions mentioned in subsection (4) below; and

(b) make any provision which, but for any such repeal or modification, could be made by regulations or orders made under any enactment there mentioned.

(4) The provisions referred to in subsections (1) and (3) above are—

(a)	the Highway (Railway Crossings) Act 1839;	1839 c. 45.
(b)	sections 9 and 10 of the Railway Regulation Act 1842;	1842 c. 55.
(c)	section 22 of the Regulation of Railways Act 1868;	1868 c. 119.
(d)	the Regulation of Railways Act 1871;	1871 c. 78.
(e)	sections 1 and 4 of the Regulation of Railways Act 1889;	1889 c. 57.
(f)	the Railway Employment (Prevention of Accidents) Act 1900;	1900 c. 27.
(g)	section 42 of the Road and Rail Traffic Act 1933;	1933 c. 53.
(h)	section 40 of the British Transport Commission Act 1954;	1954 c. lv.
(j)	section 66 of the British Transport Commission Act 1957;	1957 c. xxxiii.
(k)	sections 124 and 125 of the Transport Act 1968;	1968 c. 73.
(l)	the Level Crossings Act 1983;	1983 c. 16.
(m)	sections 41 to 45 of the Transport and Works Act 1992;	1992 c. 42.
(n)	any regulations made under section 2 of the European Communities Act 1972 for the purpose of implementing the Council Directive of 29th July 1991 on the development of the Community's railways, so far as the regulations are made for safety purposes.	1972 c. 68. 91/440/EEC.

(5) In consequence of subsection (1) above and the resulting application of sections 38 and 50 of the 1974 Act (consent to prosecutions, and procedural requirements for making regulations)—

(a) in section 57 of the Transport and Works Act 1992 (duty to consult before making regulations under, among other provisions, section 38(2), 41 or 43 of that Act) for the words "38(2), 41 or 43" there shall be substituted the words "or 38(2)"; and

(b) in section 58 of that Act (which requires the consent of the Secretary of State or the Director of Public Prosecutions to a prosecution for an offence under Part II of that Act) after the words "offence under this Part" there shall be inserted the words ", other than an offence under section 41 or 43 above,".

(6) This section applies to the following transport systems, that is to say—

(a) any railway, tramway or trolley vehicle system; or

(b) any transport system using any other mode of guided transport.

PART III

1992 c. 42.

(7) The definitions of "guided transport", "railway", "tramway", "trolley vehicle system" and "vehicle" in section 67(1) of the Transport and Works Act 1992 shall have effect for the purposes of this section as they have effect for the purposes of that Act, but disregarding for the purposes of this section paragraph (b) of the definition of "railway" (which includes a condition as to the minimum gauge of the track).

Control of railways in time of hostilities, severe international tension or great national emergency.

118.—(1) In time of hostilities, whether actual or imminent, severe international tension or great national emergency, the Secretary of State may give directions under this subsection to such of the following persons as he may consider appropriate, that is to say—

(a) the Regulator;

(b) the Franchising Director;

(c) any person who is the owner or operator of a relevant asset;

(d) any person who provides railway services.

(2) The Secretary of State may at any time give directions under this subsection to any person falling within paragraphs (a) to (d) of subsection (1) above whom he may consider appropriate, requiring that person to participate in the planning of steps that might be taken in time of actual or imminent hostilities, severe international tension or great national emergency.

(3) The power to give directions under subsection (1) above to the Regulator or the Franchising Director includes power to direct him to carry out his functions in such manner or for such purposes as may be specified in the direction.

(4) The power to give directions under subsection (1) above to a person who is the owner or operator of a relevant asset or who provides railway services includes power—

(a) in the case of a person who is the owner of a relevant asset, to direct that person to permit the use of, or to exercise his rights over, the relevant asset in such manner or for such purposes as may be specified in the direction;

(b) in the case of a person who is the operator of a relevant asset, to direct that person to exercise his powers of management over the relevant asset in such manner or for such purposes as may be so specified; and

(c) in the case of a person who provides railway services, to direct that person to do so in such manner or for such purposes as may be so specified.

(5) The Regulator and the Franchising Director shall each be under a duty to comply with a direction given to him under this section, notwithstanding the requirements of any other enactment or instrument relating to him.

(6) A person who is the owner or operator of a relevant asset or who provides railway services shall be under a duty to comply with a direction given to him under this section, notwithstanding the requirements of any other enactment or instrument relating to him or to—

(a) the use of, or the exercise of rights over, the relevant asset,

(b) the management of the relevant asset, or

(c) the railway services,

as the case may be, and notwithstanding any other duty or obligation to which he may be subject.

(7) Any person who, without reasonable excuse, contravenes or fails to comply with a direction given to him under this section is guilty of an offence and shall be liable—

(a) on summary conviction, to a fine not exceeding the statutory maximum; or

(b) on conviction on indictment, to a fine or imprisonment for a term not exceeding two years or both.

(8) No proceedings shall be instituted in England and Wales in respect of an offence under this section except by or with the consent of the Secretary of State or the Director of Public Prosecutions.

(9) Any person (other than the Regulator and the Franchising Director) who suffers direct injury or loss arising from compliance with a direction under subsection (1) above shall be entitled to receive compensation from the Secretary of State of such amount as may be agreed by that person and the Secretary of State or, in default of agreement, of such amount as may be determined—

(a) where the proceedings are to be held in England and Wales, by an arbitrator appointed by the President for the time being of the Royal Institution of Chartered Surveyors, or

(b) where the proceedings are to be held in Scotland, by an arbiter appointed by the Lord President of the Court of Session.

(10) Any sums required by the Secretary of State for paying compensation under this section shall be paid out of money provided by Parliament.

(11) In this section—

"great national emergency" means any natural disaster or other emergency which, in the opinion of the Secretary of State, is or may be likely to give rise to such disruption of the means of transport that the population, or a substantial part of the population, of Great Britain is or may be likely to be deprived of essential goods or services;

"operator", in relation to a relevant asset, means the person having the management of the relevant asset for the time being;

"owner", in relation to a relevant asset, means any person—

(a) who is the owner of, or who has any right over or interest in, the relevant asset; and

(b) whose consent is needed to the use of the relevant asset by any other person;

"relevant asset" means a network, a station, a light maintenance depot or any track or rolling stock;

and, subject to that, expressions used in this section and in Part I or II above have the same meaning in this section as they have in that Part.

(12) In consequence of this section, section 27(6) of the Transport Act 1962 (directions to Boards in the interests of national defence) shall cease to have effect so far as relating to the Board.

1962 c. 46.

PART III

Security: power of Secretary of State to give instructions.

119.—(1) The Secretary of State may from time to time give—

    (a) to any person who is the owner or operator of a relevant asset, or

    (b) to any person who provides railway services,

such instructions as the Secretary of State considers appropriate for the purpose of ensuring that relevant assets within Great Britain, or persons or property on or in any such relevant asset, are protected against acts of violence.

(2) An instruction may be given to any person who appears to the Secretary of State to be about to become such a person as is mentioned in paragraph (a) or (b) of subsection (1) above, but an instruction given to a person by virtue of this subsection shall not take effect until he becomes such a person and, in relation to an instruction so given, the provisions of this section shall apply with the necessary modifications.

(3) Without prejudice to the generality of subsection (1) above, an instruction may, in particular, require the person to whom it is given ("the recipient")—

    (a) not to cause or permit any persons, or any designated persons, or more than a specified number of persons or designated persons, to enter any relevant asset or any designated relevant asset, or not to cause or permit them to do so unless they submit to a search or unless or until some other specified condition is complied with;

    (b) not to cause or permit any goods, or any designated goods, or more than a specified quantity of goods or designated goods, to be brought or loaded on to or into any relevant asset or any designated relevant asset, or not to do so unless the goods in question are subjected to a search or unless or until some other specified condition is complied with;

    (c) to run no trains, or to restrict the running of trains, or to run no train unless it is subjected to a search, or unless or until some other specified condition is complied with;

    (d) to secure the carrying out of a search of—

        (i) any designated relevant assets, or

        (ii) any persons or designated persons who, or any goods or designated goods which, are on or in any such assets;

    (e) to furnish to the Secretary of State such information as he may require for the purpose mentioned in subsection (1) above;

    (f) to prepare plans specifying action to be taken by the recipient and his servants or agents—

        (i) in the event that an act of violence of a specified description occurs, or

        (ii) in times when there is an increased likelihood of such acts occurring,

and to conduct, at specified intervals, exercises in connection with the implementation of such plans;

    (g) to employ specified numbers of suitably trained staff for the purpose of preventing the occurrence of acts of violence;

    (h) to meet specified requirements with respect to the construction of, or to make specified modifications to—

(i) any relevant assets, or any designated relevant assets, of which the recipient is the owner or operator, or

(ii) any apparatus or equipment, or any designated apparatus or equipment, on or in any such assets.

(4) Where an instruction requires the carrying out of a search, it may also specify—

(a) the kind of search which is to be carried out;

(b) the manner in which the search is to be carried out; and

(c) the persons, or the class or description of persons, who are to carry out the search.

(5) Where any person refuses to submit himself or any goods in his possession to a search required by an instruction, any person authorised to carry out that search may take any steps that are necessary, including the use of reasonable force—

(a) to prevent the person concerned from entering the relevant asset in relation to which the search is being carried out; or

(b) to eject him, and any goods in his possession, from that asset;

but this subsection is without prejudice to any other powers of the person carrying out the search.

(6) An instruction—

(a) shall be in writing;

(b) shall specify the time at which, or the period within which, it is to be complied with, and the period during which it is to have effect;

(c) may be varied or revoked by the Secretary of State.

(7) No instruction shall have effect in relation to any rolling stock which is for the time being in use in police service or in the service of the armed forces of the Crown.

(8) A person who is the owner or operator of a relevant asset or who provides railway services shall be under a duty to comply with an instruction given to him under this section, notwithstanding the requirements of any other enactment or instrument relating to him or to—

(a) the use of, or the exercise of rights over, the relevant asset,

(b) the management of the relevant asset, or

(c) the railway services,

as the case may be, and notwithstanding any other duty or obligation to which he may be subject.

(9) A person who without reasonable excuse fails to do anything required of him by an instruction is guilty of an offence and shall be liable—

(a) on summary conviction, to a fine not exceeding the statutory maximum; or

(b) on conviction on indictment, to a fine or to a term of imprisonment not exceeding two years, or to both.

PART III

(10) No proceedings shall be instituted in England and Wales in respect of an offence under subsection (9) above except by or with the consent of the Secretary of State or the Director of Public Prosecutions.

(11) In this section—

"act of violence" means—

(a) any act which constitutes, or

(b) any potential act which, if carried out, would constitute,

the offence of murder, attempted murder, manslaughter, culpable homicide, assault, real injury or malicious mischief, or an offence under section 18, 20, 21, 22, 23, 24, 28 or 29 of the Offences against the Person Act 1861, under section 2 of the Explosive Substances Act 1883 or under section 1 of the Criminal Damage Act 1971;

1861 c. 100.
1883 c. 3.
1971 c. 48.

"designated" means specified in an instruction, or of a class or description so specified;

"instruction" means an instruction given under this section, and any reference to an instruction includes a reference to an instruction as varied under subsection (6)(c) above;

"operator" and "owner" have the same meaning as in section 118 above;

"relevant asset" has the same meaning as in section 118 above, and any reference to such an asset includes a reference to any part of any such asset;

"specified" means specified in an instruction;

and, subject to that, expressions used in this section and in Part I above have the same meaning in this section as they have in that Part.

Security: enforcement notices.

120.—(1) Where it appears to the Secretary of State that a person upon whom an instruction has been served has failed, is failing or is likely to fail to comply with that instruction, he may serve on that person a notice (in this section referred to as an "enforcement notice") containing such provision as the Secretary of State may consider requisite for the purpose of ensuring that the person complies with the instruction and specifying, in particular—

(a) the things, or the description of things, which the person is required to do, or refrain from doing, in order to comply with the instruction;

(b) the time within which, or after which, the person must do, or refrain from doing, those things; and

(c) the period during which the person is to do, or refrain from doing, those things.

(2) The Secretary of State may vary or revoke an enforcement notice, and any reference in this section to an enforcement notice includes a reference to such a notice as varied under this subsection.

(3) Where the Secretary of State varies or revokes an enforcement notice under subsection (2) above he shall serve notice of the variation or revocation on the person on whom the enforcement notice in question was served.

(4) A person who without reasonable excuse fails to do anything required of him by an enforcement notice is guilty of an offence and shall be liable—

(a) on summary conviction, to a fine not exceeding the statutory maximum; or

(b) on conviction on indictment, to a fine or to a term of imprisonment not exceeding two years, or to both.

(5) No proceedings shall be instituted in England and Wales in respect of an offence under subsection (4) above except by or with the consent of the Secretary of State or the Director of Public Prosecutions.

(6) Section 119(8) above shall have effect in relation to an enforcement notice as it has effect in relation to an instruction.

(7) Expressions used in this section and in section 119 above have the same meaning in this section as they have in that section.

121.—(1) For the purpose of enabling the Secretary of State to determine whether to give an instruction to any person, or of ascertaining whether any instruction or enforcement notice is being or has been complied with, a person authorised for the purpose by the Secretary of State in writing (in this section referred to as "an authorised person") shall have power, on production (if required) of his credentials, to inspect any relevant asset.

Security: inspections.

(2) An authorised person inspecting a relevant asset under subsection (1) above shall have power—

(a) to subject any property found by him on or in the relevant asset, or any apparatus or equipment installed in the relevant asset, to such tests as he considers necessary for the purpose for which the inspection is carried out;

(b) to take such steps as he considers necessary for that purpose—

(i) to ascertain what practices or procedures are being followed in relation to security; or

(ii) to test the effectiveness of any practice or procedure relating to security; or

(c) to require the owner or operator of the relevant asset to furnish to him such information as the authorised person considers necessary for that purpose;

but nothing in paragraph (a) above shall entitle an authorised person to subject any rolling stock, or any part of any rolling stock, to any test.

(3) An authorised person, for the purpose of exercising any power conferred on him by subsection (1) or (2) above in relation to any relevant asset, shall have power—

(a) to board any rolling stock and to take all such steps as are necessary to ensure that it is not moved; or

(b) to enter any land or other property comprised either in any track or in a network, station or light maintenance depot;

but nothing in this subsection authorises any use of force.

(4) A person is guilty of an offence if he—

(a) intentionally obstructs an authorised person acting in the exercise of any power conferred on him by this section;

Part III

(b) fails, without reasonable excuse, to comply with a requirement imposed on him under paragraph (c) of subsection (2) above to furnish information to an authorised person; or

(c) in furnishing any information required under that paragraph, makes a statement which he knows to be false in a material particular, or recklessly makes a statement which is false in a material particular.

(5) A person guilty of an offence under subsection (4) above shall be liable—

(a) on summary conviction, to a fine not exceeding the statutory maximum;

(b) on conviction on indictment, to a fine or to imprisonment for a term not exceeding two years, or to both.

(6) No proceedings shall be instituted in England and Wales in respect of an offence under subsection (4) above except by or with the consent of the Secretary of State or the Director of Public Prosecutions.

(7) Expressions used in this section and in section 119 or 120 above have the same meaning in this section as they have in that section.

Statutory authority

Statutory authority as a defence to actions in nuisance etc.

122.—(1) Subject to the following provisions of this section—

(a) any person shall have authority—

(i) to use, or to cause or permit any agent or independent contractor of his to use, rolling stock on any track, or

(ii) to use, or to cause or permit any agent or independent contractor of his to use, any land comprised in a network, station or light maintenance depot for or in connection with the provision of network services, station services or light maintenance services, and

(b) any person who is the owner or occupier of any land shall have authority to authorise, consent to or acquiesce in—

(i) the use by another of rolling stock on any track comprised in that land, or

(ii) the use by another of that land for or in connection with the provision of network services, station services or light maintenance services,

if and so long as the qualifying conditions are satisfied in the particular case.

(2) For the purposes of this section, the "qualifying conditions" are—

(a) in relation to any use of rolling stock on track—

(i) that the track is comprised in a network, station or light maintenance depot, and

(ii) that the operator of that network, station or light maintenance depot is the holder of an appropriate licence or has the benefit of an appropriate licence exemption; and

(b) in relation to any use of land for or in connection with the provision of network services, station services or light maintenance services, that the operator of the network, station or light maintenance depot in question is the holder of an appropriate licence or has the benefit of an appropriate licence exemption.

(3) The authority conferred by this section is conferred only for the purpose of providing a defence of statutory authority—

(a) in England and Wales—

(i) in any proceedings, whether civil or criminal, in nuisance; or

(ii) in any civil proceedings, other than proceedings for breach of statutory duty, in respect of the escape of things from land;

(b) in Scotland, in any civil proceedings on the ground of nuisance where the rule of strict liability applies, other than proceedings for breach of statutory duty.

(4) Nothing in this section shall be construed as excluding a defence of statutory authority otherwise available under or by virtue of any enactment.

(5) The owner or occupier of any land shall be regarded for the purposes of this section as "acquiescing" in—

(a) any use by another of rolling stock on track comprised in that land, or

(b) any use of that land by another for or in connection with the provision of network services, station services or light maintenance services,

notwithstanding that it is not within his power to put an end to that use by that other.

(6) For the purposes of this section—

(a) any reference to the use of rolling stock on track includes a reference to the carriage of any passengers or other persons, or any goods, of any class or description for any purpose on or by means of that rolling stock on that track; and

(b) rolling stock shall be regarded as "used" on any track at any time when it is present on that track, irrespective of whether the rolling stock is comprised in a train or not, whether the rolling stock is moving or stationary and, if moving, irrespective of the means by which the motion is caused.

(7) In this section—

"appropriate licence", in relation to the operator of a network, station or light maintenance depot, means a licence which authorises him to be the operator of that network, station or light maintenance depot;

"appropriate licence exemption", in relation to the operator of a network, station or light maintenance depot, means any such licence exemption as exempts him from the requirement to hold the licence that would otherwise be the appropriate licence in his case;

and expressions used in this section and in Part I above have the same meaning in this section as they have in that Part.

PART III

Miscellaneous and general

No person to be common carrier by railway.

123. No person shall be regarded as a common carrier by railway.

Carriage of mail by railway.
1953 c. 36.

124. Sections 33 to 42 of the Post Office Act 1953 (which make provision for and in connection with the power of the Post Office to compel railway undertakers to convey mail-bags on their trains) shall cease to have effect.

Railway heritage.

125.—(1) A publicly owned railway company, the Board or any wholly owned subsidiary of the Board may dispose of any historical record or artefact which it owns and which is in its possession, but only if the disposal is in accordance with any directions given to the company or, as the case may be, the Board or the subsidiary under subsection (2) below by a committee ("the committee") established under a scheme made under this section.

(2) It shall be the function of the committee—

(a) to designate those classes or descriptions of record or artefact which, in the opinion of the committee, are of sufficient interest to warrant preservation and to notify publicly owned railway companies, the Board or any wholly owned subsidiary of the Board of the classes or descriptions so designated;

(b) to give directions to publicly owned railway companies, the Board or any wholly owned subsidiary of the Board—

(i) specifying the person or persons or the classes or descriptions of person to whom the companies or, as the case may be, the Board or subsidiary must offer any historical record or artefact; and

(ii) where there are two or more such persons, specifying the order in which the offers are to be made; and

(c) to give directions to publicly owned railway companies, the Board or any wholly owned subsidiary of the Board with respect to the terms (including any terms relating to payment) on which the companies or, as the case may be, the Board or subsidiary must offer any historical record or artefact to any such person.

(3) Directions under paragraph (b) or (c) of subsection (2) above may be of a general or specific character and may make different provision in relation to different classes or descriptions of record or artefact or different records or artefacts of the same class or description.

(4) A scheme under this section—

(a) shall provide for the committee to consist of a chairman, and not less than six other members, appointed by the Board with the approval of the Secretary of State;

(b) may make provision requiring the Board—

(i) to provide the committee with such administrative and secretarial assistance as the committee may reasonably require;

(ii) to reimburse any out-of-pocket expenses duly incurred by the chairman and other members of the committee in the performance of their functions; and

(c) may contain such supplemental and incidental provision as the Secretary of State may consider necessary or expedient.

(5) The power to make a scheme under this section shall be exercisable by order made by the Secretary of State after consultation with—

(a) the Board; and

(b) such other persons as the Secretary of State may consider appropriate.

(6) Subject to paragraph 7 of Schedule 1 to the Public Records Act 1958 and any Orders in Council made under that paragraph, nothing in that Schedule shall cause any records disposed of under or by virtue of subsection (1) above to become, by reason of that or any subsequent disposal, public records within the meaning of that Act; but any records disposed of under or by virtue of that subsection which at any time are for the time being in the custody of the Secretary of State for Scotland may be treated for the purposes of section 5(1) of the Public Records (Scotland) Act 1937 as records belonging to Her Majesty.

1958 c. 51.

1937 c. 43.

(7) Nothing in subsection (1) above, and no provision of any scheme made under this section, shall apply to any disposal made in accordance with a transfer scheme under Part II above.

(8) Without prejudice to the continuing operation of section 144 of the Transport Act 1968 in relation to the transfer or other disposal of any such historical records and relics, or other documents or objects, as are mentioned in that section—

1968 c. 73.

(a) by any body or person which is a relevant authority, within the meaning of that section, or

(b) by any such subsidiary or former subsidiary as is mentioned in subsection (7A) of that section,

that section shall, in consequence of this section, cease to have effect in relation to transfers or other disposals of any such historical records or relics, or other objects or documents, by the Board as from such date as the Secretary of State may by order appoint.

(9) In this section (except subsection (8) above), "historical record or artefact" means any record or artefact of a class or description designated by the committee pursuant to subsection (2)(a) above.

126.—(1) In section 3 of the Transport Act 1962, at the beginning of subsection (1) (duty of the Board to provide railway services in Great Britain) there shall be inserted the words "Subject to subsection (1A) of this section," and after that subsection there shall be inserted—

General duties and powers of the Board.
1962 c. 46.

"(1A) The Board shall be discharged from the duty imposed by subsection (1) of this section with respect to the provision of railway services in Great Britain if and to the extent that such services are, or have at any time since the coming into force of this subsection been,—

(a) provided by the Board, or a subsidiary of the Board, pursuant to any agreements or arrangements falling within subsection (1B) of this section; or

PART III

(b) provided (whether under or by virtue of the Railways Act 1993 or otherwise) by persons other than the Board and their subsidiaries;

but, notwithstanding anything in this subsection, it shall be the duty of the Board to have, as respects any railway services provided as mentioned in paragraph (a) of this subsection (and any other services or facilities provided in connection therewith) due regard to efficiency, economy and safety of operation.

(1B) The agreements or arrangements mentioned in subsection (1A)(a) of this section are as follows, namely—

(a) an agreement or arrangement made pursuant to the Railways Act 1993, to which the Franchising Director and the Board, or a subsidiary of the Board, are parties;

(b) an agreement made between—

(i) the Board or a subsidiary of the Board, and

(ii) a person who is the owner or operator of a railway asset or track,

being an agreement under which the Board or a subsidiary of the Board operates that railway asset or track or uses it to provide network, station or light maintenance services.

(1C) For the purposes of subsection (1B) above and this subsection—

(a) any reference to a railway asset includes a reference to any part of a railway asset;

(b) "operator", in relation to a railway asset or track, means the person having the management of that railway asset or track for the time being;

(c) "owner", in relation to a railway asset or track, means any person—

(i) who has an estate or interest in, or right over, the railway asset or track in question; and

(ii) whose permission to use that railway asset or track is needed by another before that other may use it;

and, subject to that, expressions used in either subsection and in Part I of the Railways Act 1993 have the same meaning in that subsection as they have in that Part."

(2) At the end of that section there shall be added—

"(5) Subject to subsection (6) of this section, section 82 of the Railways Act 1993 (meaning of "railway services") shall apply for the purposes of this section as it applies for the purposes of Part I of that Act.

(6) If it appears to the Secretary of State that the Board—

(a) have ceased to provide railway services of a description falling within any paragraph ("the relevant paragraph") of subsection (1) of that section, or

(b) have ceased to provide such services otherwise than as mentioned in subsection (1A)(a) of this section,

he shall by order provide that, as from the date on which the order comes into force, subsection (1) of that section shall, in its application for the purposes of this section, have effect as if the relevant paragraph (which shall be specified in the order) were omitted therefrom.

(7) An order under subsection (6) of this section may make such consequential amendments or repeals of or in this section or any other enactment as may appear to the Secretary of State to be necessary or expedient for the purposes of, or in connection with, the order.

(8) The power to make an order under subsection (6) of this section shall be exercisable by statutory instrument; and a statutory instrument containing any such order shall be subject to annulment in pursuance of a resolution of either House of Parliament."

127.—(1) The Board shall have power to provide business support services for—

(a) the Regulator;

(b) any person who provides, or secures the provision of, railway services; or

(c) any person carrying on any undertaking which was, immediately before 1st April 1993, carried on by the Board or any wholly owned subsidiary of the Board.

Power of the Board to provide business support services for other operators.

(2) Without prejudice to the generality of the expression, the provision of "business support services" includes for the purposes of this section—

(a) the provision of any service or facility for or in relation to—

(i) information technology;

(ii) property management;

(iii) marketing;

(iv) the issuing of tickets;

(v) research; or

(vi) engineering; and

(b) the provision of technical or specialist advice.

(3) If the Secretary of State is of the opinion—

(a) that the Board has ceased to provide business support services of any class or description, or

(b) that it is no longer necessary, or no longer desirable, for the Board to have power to provide any business support services, or business support services of any class or description,

he may by order provide that, as from the date on which the order comes into force, the Board shall cease to have power to provide the business support services in question.

(4) The power of the Secretary of State to make an order under subsection (3) above is exercisable in relation to any power of the Board to provide business support services, whether under this section or otherwise.

PART III

(5) An order under subsection (3) above may make such consequential amendments or repeals in any enactment as may appear to the Secretary of State to be necessary or expedient for the purposes of, or in connection with, the order.

(6) In this section "railway services" has the same meaning as in Part I above.

Amendment of section 13 of the Transport Act 1962.
1962 c. 46.

128.—(1) Section 13 of the Transport Act 1962 (which confers on the British Waterways Board and the Board powers to manufacture and produce items for business purposes) shall be amended in accordance with the following provisions of this section.

(2) After subsection (1) (which confers on the Boards power to undertake activities for the purposes of any business falling within paragraphs (a) to (c) of that subsection), there shall be inserted—

"(1A) Subsection (1) of this section shall have effect, in relation to the Railways Board, with the insertion after paragraph (c) of the following—

"(d) of the Rail Regulator,

(e) of any person who provides, or secures the provision of, railway services, within the meaning of Part I of the Railways Act 1993, or

(f) of any person carrying on any undertaking which was, immediately before 1st April 1993, carried on by the Railways Board or any wholly owned subsidiary of that Board,",

and with the omission of the word "or" immediately preceding that paragraph."

(3) At the end of that section, there shall be added—

"(9) If the Secretary of State is of the opinion that it is no longer necessary, or no longer desirable, for the Railways Board to conduct any of the activities mentioned in subsection (1) of this section for the purposes of the business of any persons, or of persons of any class or description, mentioned in that subsection, he may by order provide that, as from the date on which the order comes into force, that Board shall cease to have power to conduct the activity in question in relation to the person in question.

(10) An order under subsection (9) of this section may make such consequential amendments or repeals in any enactment as may appear to the Secretary of State to be necessary or expedient for the purposes of, or in connection with, the order.

(11) Any order made under subsection (9) of this section shall be made by statutory instrument, and any such statutory instrument shall be subject to annulment in pursuance of a resolution of either House of Parliament.

(12) Any reference in this section to "business" includes, in the case of the Rail Regulator, a reference to the carrying on of any activity in the exercise of his powers or the performance of his duties."

PART III

Bye-laws.

129.—(1) An independent railway operator may make bye-laws regulating—

(a) the use and working of, and travel on or by means of, any relevant assets;

(b) the maintenance of order on any relevant assets; and

(c) the conduct of all persons while on any relevant assets.

(2) Without prejudice to the generality of subsection (1) above, an independent railway operator may, in particular, make bye-laws—

(a) with respect to tickets issued for entry upon relevant assets or travel by railway and the evasion of payment of fares or other charges;

(b) with respect to interference with, or obstruction of, the working of any railway or any relevant asset or the provision of any railway service;

(c) with respect to the smoking of tobacco in railway carriages and elsewhere and the prevention of nuisance;

(d) with respect to the receipt and delivery of goods; and

(e) for regulating the passage of bicycles and other vehicles on footways and other premises controlled by him and intended for the use of those on foot.

(3) In section 67 of the Transport Act 1962, after subsection (9) (confirmation of bye-laws by the Minister) there shall be inserted—

1962 c. 46.

"(9A) The Minister may charge the Board such fees in respect of any bylaws submitted for confirmation under this section as he may consider appropriate for the purpose of defraying any administrative expenses incurred by him in connection therewith."

(4) Subsections (3) and (5) to (12) of section 67 of the Transport Act 1962 (procedure for making bye-laws) shall apply in relation to bye-laws under this section as they apply in relation to bye-laws under subsection (1) of that section, but with the substitution for any reference to the Board of a reference to the independent railway operator in question.

(5) Subsection (4) of that section shall apply in relation to bye-laws under this section as it applies in relation to bye-laws under subsection (1) of that section, but—

(a) taking the reference to "a Board" as including a reference to an independent railway operator (and construing the reference to "the Board in question" accordingly); and

(b) taking the reference to "their railway" as including, in the case of that independent railway operator, a reference to any relevant asset.

(6) If and to the extent that, immediately before the coming into force of a transfer scheme, any bye-laws—

(a) made by the Board under section 67 of the Transport Act 1962, or having effect as if so made, or

PART III

    (b) made by an independent railway operator under this section, or having effect as if so made,

have effect in relation to an undertaking, or part of an undertaking, transferred by the scheme, those bye-laws shall, as from the coming into force of the transfer scheme in relation to that undertaking or, as the case may be, that part of the undertaking, have effect in relation to the undertaking or part (as the case may be) as bye-laws made under this section by the transferee.

(7) In this section "independent railway operator" means any person, other than the Board, who is authorised by a licence to be the operator of a railway asset or of railway assets of a class or description.

(8) The exclusion of the Board from being an independent railway operator is without prejudice to the Board's subsidiaries and wholly owned subsidiaries.

(9) For the purposes of this section "relevant assets", in the case of any independent railway operator, means—

    (a) any railway assets in relation to which he is the operator; and

    (b) any rolling stock not falling within paragraph (a) above of which he has the management for the time being.

(10) Expressions used in this section and in Part I or II above have the same meaning in this section as they have in that Part.

1962 c. 46.

(11) Apart from the amendment made by subsection (3) above, this section is without prejudice to section 84(3) of the Transport Act 1962.

(12) Any sums received by the Secretary of State under or by virtue of this section shall be paid into the Consolidated Fund.

Penalty fares.

130.—(1) The Secretary of State may by regulations make provision for and in connection with—

    (a) the imposition of requirements on persons travelling by, present on, or leaving trains or stations to produce, if required to do so in accordance with the regulations, a ticket or other authority authorising them to travel by, be present on, or leave the train or station in question; and

    (b) the charging of persons in breach of such requirements to financial penalties (in this section referred to as "penalty fares") in such circumstances, and subject to compliance with such conditions (if any), as may be prescribed;

and in this section any reference to a ticket or other authority of any description includes a reference to any other document which, under the regulations, is required to be produced in conjunction with any such ticket or other authority, for the purpose of demonstrating that the ticket or other authority produced by a person is valid in his case.

(2) Regulations may make provision for or with respect to—

    (a) the persons who may be charged penalty fares;

    (b) the persons by or on behalf of whom penalty fares may be charged;

    (c) the trains and stations by reference to which penalty fares may be charged;

(d) the amount, or the greatest amount, which a person may be charged by way of penalty fare, whether a specified amount or one determined in a prescribed manner;

(e) the authorising of persons to be collectors;

(f) the manner in which charges to penalty fares may be imposed by collectors, including any requirements to be complied with by or in relation to collectors;

(g) the authorising of collectors in prescribed circumstances to require persons on trains or stations to furnish prescribed information;

(h) the display of prescribed notices in places of a prescribed description;

(j) the manner in which, and the period within which, any penalty fare charged to a person is to be paid;

(k) the issue of prescribed documents to persons who are charged, or who have paid, penalty fares;

(l) the recovery of any unpaid penalty fare as a civil debt, including provision—

(i) for or with respect to defences that are to be available in proceedings for the recovery of an unpaid penalty fare; or

(ii) for presumptions of fact to operate, in such proceedings, in favour of the person charged with the penalty fare, but subject to compliance with prescribed procedural requirements;

(m) the retention, by persons by or on behalf of whom charges to penalty fares are imposed, of sums paid by way of penalty fare;

(n) the remission of liability to pay penalty fares and the repayment of sums paid by way of penalty fare;

(o) the prevention of a person's being liable both to payment of a penalty fare and to prosecution for a prescribed offence;

(p) the imposition of prohibitions on the charging of penalty fares by or on behalf of persons who are suspected by the Secretary of State or the Regulator, on reasonable grounds, of failing to comply with such requirements imposed by or under the regulations as may be prescribed.

(3) The documents mentioned in subsection (2)(k) above include any document which consists of or includes—

(a) notice of the imposition of a charge to a penalty fare;

(b) a receipt for the payment of a penalty fare; or

(c) a ticket or other authority to travel by, be present on, or leave a train or station.

(4) Regulations may impose, or make provision for and in connection with the imposition or enforcement of, prescribed requirements in prescribed circumstances on or against a holder of a passenger licence or station licence or a passenger service operator (whether or not one by or on behalf of whom penalty fares are or are to be charged); and, without prejudice to the generality of the foregoing, any such regulations may make provision with respect to—

(a) the display of notices relating to penalty fares;

PART III

(b) the provision of facilities for the issue of tickets or other authorities to travel by, be present on, or leave trains or stations;

(c) the provision of information to prescribed persons or persons of a prescribed class or description.

(5) The functions which may be conferred on the Regulator by regulations include—

(a) functions which involve the exercise by him of judgement or a discretion; and

(b) functions which empower him in prescribed circumstances to impose such conditions or requirements as he may think fit on prescribed persons or on persons of a prescribed class or description.

(6) Regulations may confer power on the Regulator to make by rules any provision which could be made by the Secretary of State by regulations, other than provision for or with respect to any matter specified in—

(a) paragraph (d), (l) or (o) of subsection (2) above; or

(b) subsection (7) below;

and any such rules shall have effect, to such extent as may be prescribed, as if they were regulations.

(7) Regulations may provide that where information is required to be furnished pursuant to the regulations—

(a) a refusal to furnish any such information, or

(b) the furnishing of information which is false in a material particular,

shall, in prescribed circumstances, be an offence punishable on summary conviction by a fine not exceeding level 2 on the standard scale.

(8) Apart from subsection (7) above, nothing in this section creates, or authorises the creation of, any offence.

(9) Regulations may make provision for any area within Great Britain and may make different provision for or in relation to different areas.

(10) Any power of the Regulator to make rules under or by virtue of this section includes power to revoke, amend or re-enact any rules so made; and—

(a) any such rules may make different provision for different cases; and

(b) without prejudice to paragraph (a) above, subsection (9) above shall apply in relation to any such rules as it applies in relation to regulations.

(11) Subsections (2) to (5) above are without prejudice to the generality of subsection (1) above.

(12) In this section—

"collectors" means the individuals who perform the function (whether as servants or agents or otherwise) of imposing the charge of a penalty fare on the person liable to pay it under the regulations in each particular case;

"document", without prejudice to the generality of the expression, includes any badge, token, or photograph or any other form of identification, certification or authentication;

"prescribed" means specified in, or determined in accordance with, regulations;

"regulations" means regulations under subsection (1) above;

"station" includes a reference to a part of a station;

"ticket or other authority" shall be construed in accordance with subsection (1) above;

"train" includes a reference to a part of a train;

and, subject to that, expressions used in Part I above and in this section have the same meaning in this section as they have in that Part.

131.—(1) The Restrictive Trade Practices Act 1976 (the "1976 Act") shall not apply to an agreement relating to the provision of railway services if the making of the agreement, and the inclusion in it of each provision by virtue of which the 1976 Act would (apart from this subsection) apply to the agreement, is required or approved— *[margin: Modification of Restrictive Trade Practices Act 1976. 1976 c.34.]*

(a) by the Secretary of State or the Regulator, in pursuance of any function assigned or transferred to him under or by virtue of any provision of this Act (other than this section);

(b) by or under any agreement the making of which is required or approved by the Secretary of State or the Regulator in pursuance of any such function; or

(c) by or under a licence granted under Part I above.

(2) In subsection (3) below, "relevant agreement" means an agreement—

(a) which relates to the provision of railway services; and

(b) to which (notwithstanding the provisions of subsection (1) above) the 1976 Act applies.

(3) If it appears to the Secretary of State—

(a) that those provisions of a relevant agreement, or of relevant agreements of some particular class or description, by virtue of which the 1976 Act applies to that agreement or those agreements do not have, and are not intended or likely to have, to any significant extent the effect of restricting, distorting or preventing competition, or

(b) that all or any of those provisions have, or are intended or likely to have, that effect to a significant extent, but that the effect is not greater than is necessary for—

(i) the protection of the interests of users of railway services,

(ii) the promotion of the use of any railway network in Great Britain or elsewhere for the carriage of passengers and goods or the development of any such railway network,

(iii) the promotion of efficiency and economy on the part of persons providing railway services, or

PART III

    (iv) the promotion of measures designed to facilitate the making by passengers of journeys which involve use of the services of more than one passenger service operator,

he may give a direction to the Director requiring him not to make an application to the Restrictive Practices Court under Part I of the 1976 Act in respect of that relevant agreement or, as the case may be, any relevant agreement of that class or description.

(4) The Secretary of State may vary or revoke any direction given under subsection (3) above if he is satisfied that there has been a material change of circumstances such that—

  (a) the grounds for the direction have ceased to exist; or

  (b) there are grounds for giving a different direction;

and where the Secretary of State so varies or revokes any direction, he shall give notice of the variation or revocation to the Director.

(5) In this section "agreement" has the same meaning as in the 1976 Act; and, subject to that, expressions which are used in this section and in Part I above have the same meaning in this section as they have in that Part.

Transport police

Schemes for the organisation etc. of transport police.

132.—(1) The Secretary of State may make a scheme for the organisation, control and administration of the transport police employed by the Board.

(2) A scheme may only be made after consultation with the Board and with—

  (a) persons to whom the Board is for the time being making available the services of transport police, or

  (b) such bodies or persons appearing to the Secretary of State to be representative of those persons as he may consider appropriate.

(3) A scheme may make provision enabling the Board to make an agreement—

  (a) with any such person as may be specified in the scheme, or

  (b) with any person falling within any such class or description of person as may be so specified,

for making the services of transport police available to that person for such period, to such extent, and on such terms, as may be specified in the agreement.

(4) A scheme which makes such provision as is mentioned in subsection (3) above shall also make provision for the method of settling any dispute in relation to transport police which may arise between the Board and the person with whom any such agreement as is mentioned in that subsection is made.

(5) Where the Board makes any such agreement as is mentioned in subsection (3) above, transport police may act, in accordance with the terms of the agreement, as constables in, on and in the vicinity of any premises owned by the person with whom the agreement is made, notwithstanding the provisions of section 53(1) of the British Transport Commission Act 1949 or section 53(4) of that Act as it applies to Scotland (which restrict the places in which they may so act).

1949 c. xxix.

(6) A scheme may contain such supplemental, incidental, consequential or transitional provision as the Secretary of State may consider appropriate.

(7) A scheme may make modifications consequential on its provisions in section 53 of the British Transport Commission Act 1949.

1949 c. xxix.

(8) Schedule 10 to this Act shall have effect for the purpose of making provision consequential upon the provisions of this section.

(9) The power to make a scheme shall be exercisable by statutory instrument, and a statutory instrument containing a scheme shall be subject to annulment in pursuance of a resolution of either House of Parliament.

(10) In this section—

(a) "transport police" means constables appointed under section 53 of the British Transport Commission Act 1949; and

(b) "scheme" means a scheme made under subsection (1) above.

133.—(1) There shall continue to be a conference consisting of an equal number of representatives of the Board and of transport police to which all questions relating to rates of pay, hours of duty and conditions of service of transport police shall be referred.

Terms and conditions of employment of transport police.

(2) In the event of disagreement between the two sides of the conference, an independent chairman shall be appointed with power to give decisions which shall have effect as decisions of the conference.

(3) The independent chairman shall be chosen by agreement between the two sides of the conference or, failing such agreement, shall be nominated by the Secretary of State.

(4) In this section "transport police" has the meaning given in section 132(10) above.

Pensions and other benefits

134.—(1) Schedule 11 to this Act shall have effect.

Pensions.

(2) Section 74 of the Transport Act 1962 (power of Secretary of State to make orders about pensions) shall cease to have effect, so far as relating to the Board and (within the meaning of that section) its subsidiaries, on the coming into force of subsection (1) above.

1962 c. 46.

(3) Subsection (2) above is without prejudice to the continuing validity of any orders made under that section.

135.—(1) The conditions that may be included in a passenger licence include conditions in respect of arrangements for the provision of staff concessionary travel.

Concessionary travel for railway staff etc.

(2) The Franchising Director may promote the provision of staff concessionary travel.

(3) The Franchising Director may enter into agreements or other arrangements concerning the provision of staff concessionary travel.

(4) Franchise agreements may include conditions with respect to the provision of staff concessionary travel.

PART III

(5) Agreements or arrangements under section 51 or 52 above may include provisions with respect to the provision of staff concessionary travel.

(6) The Franchising Director may perform any of his functions—

(a) under or by virtue of subsections (2) to (5) above, or

(b) under any agreements or arrangements entered into, or conditions or provisions included, by virtue of those subsections,

by entering into agreements or arrangements under which other persons (in this subsection referred to as "sub-contractors") are to perform the function in question; and subsections (2) and (3) of section 51 above shall apply in relation to agreements or arrangements under this subsection as they apply in relation to agreements or arrangements under subsection (1) of that section, but taking references to sub-contractors, within the meaning of that subsection, as references to sub-contractors, within the meaning of this subsection.

(7) Without prejudice to the generality of subsection (3) above, the agreements or arrangements that may be made under that subsection include agreements or arrangements under which the Franchising Director undertakes to secure the provision of staff concessionary travel (as well as agreements or arrangements under which some other person undertakes to provide, or to secure the provision of, staff concessionary travel).

(8) Subsection (7) above applies, with the necessary modifications, in relation to—

(a) the conditions mentioned in subsection (4) above, and

(b) the provisions mentioned in subsection (5) above,

as it applies in relation to the agreements and arrangements mentioned in subsection (3) above.

(9) This section is without prejudice to the generality of—

(a) the conditions which may be included in licences, or

(b) the provision which may be made in franchise agreements or in agreements or other arrangements under section 51 or 52 above,

whether or not with respect to free or concessionary travel; and subsections (4) and (5) above are without prejudice to the generality of subsection (3) above.

(10) Any sums required by the Franchising Director for making payments under or by virtue of this section shall be paid by the Secretary of State out of money provided by Parliament.

(11) Any sums received by the Franchising Director under or by virtue of this section shall be paid into the Consolidated Fund.

(12) Any reference in this section to the provision of "staff concessionary travel" is a reference to the provision of free travel, or travel at concessionary rates, for, or for some class or description of, persons, or dependants of persons, who are or have at any time been employed by—

(a) a person carrying on a business of providing railway services; or

(b) a person providing welfare or health care services to persons employed by a person falling within paragraph (a) above.

(13) In the application of subsection (12) above in relation to any such agreement, arrangements, conditions or provisions as are mentioned in this section, it is immaterial whether or not the provision of free travel, or travel at concessionary rates, mentioned in that subsection extends, in the case of the agreement, arrangements, conditions or provisions in question, only to persons falling within that subsection or to such persons and others; and the reference in subsection (2) above to promoting the provision of staff concessionary travel shall be construed accordingly.

(14) Expressions used in this section and in Part I above have the same meaning in this section as they have in that Part.

Financial provisions

136.—(1) The Secretary of State shall continue to be the competent authority of Great Britain in relation to the railways financial status regulations.

Grants and subsidies.

(2) The Secretary of State shall be the competent authority of Great Britain, in relation to persons who operate services for the carriage of goods by railway, for the purposes of the public service obligations regulations.

(3) The following persons, that is to say—

(a) the Secretary of State,

(b) the Franchising Director,

(c) to the extent specified in subsection (4) below, every Passenger Transport Executive, and

(d) to the extent specified in subsection (5) below—

    (i) every non-metropolitan county or district council in England or in Wales and every regional or islands council in Scotland, and

    (ii) every London borough council and the Common Council of the City of London,

shall each be the competent authority of Great Britain in relation to passenger service operators for the purposes of the public service obligations regulations.

(4) For the purposes of subsection (3) above, a Passenger Transport Executive shall only be the competent authority in relation to those railway passenger services—

(a) which the Executive provides, or secures are provided, by virtue of section 10(1) or 20(2)(b) of the Transport Act 1968; or

1968 c. 73.

(b) which, in consequence of their being specified in a statement submitted to the Franchising Director under subsection (5) of section 34 above, are provided under a franchise agreement to which the Executive is a party.

(5) For the purposes of subsection (3) above—

(a) a council falling within paragraph (d)(i) of that subsection shall only be the competent authority in relation to those railway passenger services whose provision the council secures under section 63 of the Transport Act 1985 (passenger transport in areas other than passenger transport areas); and

1985 c. 67.

PART III

(b) a council falling within paragraph (d)(ii) of that subsection shall only be the competent authority in relation to those railway passenger services in respect of which the council enters into and carries out agreements under section 59 of the London Regional Transport Act 1984 (provision of extra transport services in London).

1984 c. 32.

(6) The Secretary of State and the Franchising Director may each, in his capacity as competent authority by virtue of subsection (3) above, give directions to any passenger service operator imposing on him obligations with respect to the provision or operation of railway passenger services.

(7) It shall fall to the Secretary of State or the Franchising Director to make any payments of compensation which are required to be made to a passenger service operator by any provision of the public service obligations regulations in respect of any obligations imposed on that operator by directions under subsection (6) above, and the Secretary of State or the Franchising Director may, subject to and in accordance with the provisions of those regulations, determine the manner of calculating, and the conditions applicable to, those payments.

(8) The power of giving directions under subsection (6) above shall be so exercised that the aggregate amount of any compensation payable under the public service obligations regulations, for periods ending after 1st April 1992, in respect of all obligations imposed by directions under that subsection shall not exceed £3,000 million or such greater sum not exceeding £5,000 million as the Secretary of State may by order specify.

(9) A statutory instrument containing an order under subsection (8) above shall not be made unless a draft of the instrument has been laid before and approved by a resolution of the House of Commons.

(10) Without prejudice to any right which the Secretary of State or the Franchising Director may have under this Act to bring civil proceedings in respect of any contravention or apprehended contravention of any directions under subsection (6) above, the obligations imposed by any such directions shall not give rise to any form of duty or liability enforceable against a passenger service operator by proceedings before any court to which the passenger service operator would not otherwise be subject.

(11) In this section—

"the public service obligations regulations" means Council Regulation (EEC) No. 1191/69 on public service obligations in transport, as amended by Council Regulation (EEC) No. 1893/91;

"the railways financial status regulations" means Council Regulation (EEC) No. 1192/69 on common rules with respect to the financial status of railway undertakings.

(12) Expressions used in this section and in Part I above have the same meaning in this section as they have in that Part.

1974 c. 48.

(13) Section 3 of the Railways Act 1974 (which is superseded by this section) shall cease to have effect.

PART III

137.—(1) The Secretary of State may, for the purpose of securing the provision of adequate services for the carriage of goods by railway, enter into agreements with goods service operators under which he undertakes to make payments to the goods service operator in question in respect of all or any part of the track access charges which may be incurred by the goods service operator in connection with the provision of the services to which the agreement relates.

Payments by the Secretary of State in respect of track access charges in connection with railway goods services.

(2) The Secretary of State shall not enter into an agreement by virtue of subsection (1) above unless he is satisfied that benefits of a social or environmental nature are likely to result from the provision of those services for the carriage of goods by railway to which the agreement relates.

(3) Any sums required by the Secretary of State for making payments under agreements entered into by virtue of this section shall be paid out of money provided by Parliament.

(4) In this section—

"goods service operator" means a person who operates services for the carriage of goods by railway;

"track access charge" means any payment required to be made under an access agreement conferring any permission or right to use track;

and expressions used in this section and in Part I above have the same meaning in this section as they have in that Part.

138.—(1) Section 56 of the Transport Act 1968 (Ministerial grants and local authority payments towards capital expenditure incurred in the provision, improvement or development of facilities for public passenger transport) shall be amended in accordance with the following provisions of this section.

Grants and other payments towards facilities for public passenger transport to and from airports, harbours etc.
1968 c. 73.

(2) After subsection (2) there shall be inserted—

"(2A) Where a relevant local authority proposes to make payments under subsection (2) of this section in respect of any facilities, that authority may enter into an agreement with the Franchising Director under which the Franchising Director undertakes to exercise franchising functions of his, to refrain from exercising such functions, or to exercise such functions in a particular manner, in relation to the use of the facilities in question.

(2B) In subsection (2A) of this section, the following expressions have the following meanings respectively, that is to say—

"the Franchising Director" means the Director of Passenger Rail Franchising;

"franchising functions", in relation to the Franchising Director, has the same meaning as it has in relation to him in section 54 of the Railways Act 1993;

"relevant local authority" means—

(a) a non-metropolitan county or district council in England or in Wales;

(b) a London borough council or the Common Council of the City of London; or

PART III

(c) a regional or islands council in Scotland;

and any reference to a relevant local authority shall be taken to include a reference to any two or more such authorities acting jointly."

(3) That section shall have effect, and be taken always to have had effect, with the insertion after subsection (3) (which prevents the making of any such grants or payments for the purposes of the provision, improvement or development of an airfield, harbour, dock, pier or jetty) of the following subsection—

"(3A) Nothing in subsection (3) of this section precludes the making of grants under subsection (1) or payments under subsection (2) thereof for the purposes of the provision, improvement or development of facilities for or in connection with public passenger transport by land to or from an airfield, harbour, dock, pier or jetty."

Grants to assist the provision of facilities for freight haulage by railway.

139.—(1) The Secretary of State may, out of money provided by Parliament, make grants in accordance with this section towards the provision of any facilities which are to be provided for or in connection with the carriage of goods by railway or the loading or unloading of goods carried or intended to be carried by railway.

(2) The Secretary of State shall not make a grant under this section unless he is satisfied—

(a) that, if the facilities in question are provided, they will be used for or in connection with the carriage, or the loading or unloading, of goods of particular classes or descriptions;

(b) that if the facilities are not provided, those goods will be carried by road; and

(c) that it is in the public interest for those goods to be carried by railway.

(3) Grants under this section shall only be made towards expenditure which appears to the Secretary of State to be expenditure of a capital nature which is to be incurred in providing the facilities in question.

(4) Without prejudice to the generality of subsection (1) above, the facilities towards the provision of which grants under this section may be made include track, rolling stock, depots, access roads and equipment for use in connection with the carriage, loading or unloading of goods.

(5) No grant under this section shall be made except in pursuance of an application made to the Secretary of State by the person who intends to provide the facilities; and any such application shall be supported by such evidence as the Secretary of State may require with respect to—

(a) the use which is to be made of the facilities for or in connection with the carriage of goods by railway or the loading or unloading of goods carried or intended to be carried by railway;

(b) the amount and destination of the goods in connection with which the facilities are to be used; and

(c) the matters as to which he is required by subsection (2)(b) and (c) above to be satisfied if he is to make a grant under this section.

(6) The Secretary of State may, in making a grant under this section, impose such terms and conditions as he thinks fit.

(7) Expressions used in this section and in Part I above have the same meaning in this section as they have in that Part.

(8) Section 8 of the Railways Act 1974 (freight facilities grants) shall cease to have effect.

1974 c. 48.

140.—(1) The Secretary of State may, out of money provided by Parliament, make grants in accordance with this section towards the provision of any facilities which are to be provided for or in connection with the carriage of goods by inland waterway or the loading or unloading of goods carried or intended to be carried by inland waterway.

Grants to assist the provision of facilities for freight haulage by inland waterway.

(2) The Secretary of State shall not make a grant under this section unless he is satisfied—

(a) that, if the facilities in question are provided, they will be used for or in connection with the carriage, or the loading or unloading, of goods of particular classes or descriptions;

(b) that if the facilities are not provided, those goods will be carried by road; and

(c) that it is in the public interest for those goods to be carried by inland waterway.

(3) Grants under this section shall only be made towards expenditure which appears to the Secretary of State to be expenditure of a capital nature which is to be incurred in providing the facilities in question.

(4) Without prejudice to the generality of subsection (1) above, the facilities towards the provision of which grants under this section may be made include cargo-carrying craft, inland waterway terminals, wharves, access roads and equipment for use in connection with the carriage, loading or unloading of goods.

(5) No grant under this section shall be made except in pursuance of an application made to the Secretary of State by the person who intends to provide the facilities; and any such application shall be supported by such evidence as the Secretary of State may require with respect to—

(a) the use which is to be made of the facilities for or in connection with the carriage of goods by inland waterway or the loading or unloading of goods carried or intended to be carried by inland waterway;

(b) the amount and destination of the goods in connection with which the facilities are to be used; and

(c) the matters as to which he is required by subsection (2)(b) and (c) above to be satisfied if he is to make a grant under this section.

(6) The Secretary of State may, in making a grant under this section, impose such terms and conditions as he thinks fit.

(7) In this section—

"goods" has the same meaning as in Part I above;

"inland waterway" includes every such waterway, whether natural or artificial.

(8) Section 36 of the Transport Act 1981 (grants to assist the provision of facilities for freight haulage by inland waterway) shall cease to have effect.

1981 c. 56.

PART III

Financial assistance for employees seeking to acquire franchises or parts of the Board's undertaking etc.

141.—(1) If it appears to the Board that any persons employed by the Board, or by any subsidiary of the Board, are taking steps towards—

(a) the submission of such a tender as is mentioned in section 26 above, or

(b) the making of an offer for any part of the Board's undertaking or for any shares of any subsidiary of the Board,

the Board may provide financial assistance to those persons for the purpose of defraying, in whole or in part, any expenses incurred or to be incurred by them for the purposes of the submission of the tender or the making of the offer.

(2) Without prejudice to the generality of the expression, "steps" includes, for the purposes of subsection (1) above, the formation of, or the acquisition of interests in, a company (in this subsection referred to as an "employees' company"); and accordingly—

(a) any reference in that subsection to the submission of a tender or to the making of an offer includes a reference to the submission of a tender or, as the case may be, to the making of an offer by an employees' company; and

(b) the reference to expenses incurred or to be incurred by those persons includes a reference to expenses incurred or to be incurred by an employees' company.

(3) The Secretary of State may give the Board directions with respect to the provision of financial assistance under this section.

(4) Without prejudice to the generality of subsection (3) above, any such direction may, in particular—

(a) specify a limit on the total amount of the financial assistance which may be provided under this section or on the amount, or the total amount, which may be so provided—

(i) in cases of any particular class or description specified in the direction; or

(ii) during any period or periods so specified; or

(b) require the provision of any such financial assistance by the Board to be subject to conditions, including conditions as to repayment.

(5) Expressions used in this section and in Part I or II above have the same meaning in this section as they have in that Part.

General financial provisions.

142. There shall be paid out of money provided by Parliament—

(a) any administrative expenses incurred by the Secretary of State or the Treasury in consequence of the provisions of this Act; and

(b) any increase attributable to this Act in the sums payable out of money so provided under any other Act.

Supplemental

Regulations and orders.

143.—(1) Any power under this Act to make regulations, and any power of the Secretary of State under this Act to make orders, shall be exercisable by statutory instrument.

(2) Any statutory instrument—

(a) which contains (whether alone or with other provisions) regulations or an order under this Act made by the Secretary of State, other than an order under section 136(8) above or section 154(2) below, and

(b) which is not subject to any requirement that a draft of the instrument be laid before and approved by a resolution of each House of Parliament,

shall be subject to annulment in pursuance of a resolution of either House of Parliament.

(3) Any power conferred by this Act to make regulations, and any power conferred by this Act on the Secretary of State to make an order, includes power, exercisable in the same manner, to make such incidental, supplemental, consequential or transitional provision as may appear necessary or expedient to the authority by whom the power to make the regulations or order is exercisable.

(4) Any power under this Act to make regulations, and any power of the Secretary of State under this Act to make an order, may be exercised—

(a) in relation to all cases to which the power extends, or in relation to those cases subject to specified exceptions, or in relation to any specified cases or classes or descriptions of case;

(b) so as to make, as respects the cases in relation to which it is exercised, different provision for different cases or for different classes or descriptions of case.

144.—(1) It shall be the duty of any person to whom a direction is given under this Act to comply with and give effect to that direction; and, without prejudice to the generality of the foregoing, the Board shall, in particular, comply with and give effect to any direction given under section 84, 85, 89, 90 or 113 above—

Directions.

(a) notwithstanding any duty imposed upon the Board by section 3(1) of the Transport Act 1962 or section 41(2) of the Transport Act 1968; and

1962 c. 46.
1968 c. 73.

(b) in the case of a direction under section 89 or 90 above which relates to a subsidiary of the Board, notwithstanding the interests of the subsidiary or any other member of the subsidiary;

and a Passenger Transport Executive shall, in particular, comply with and give effect to any direction under section 33 or 34(17) above, notwithstanding any duty imposed upon the Executive by section 9A or 20 of the Transport Act 1968.

(2) Without prejudice to any right which any person may have to bring civil proceedings in respect of any contravention or apprehended contravention of any direction given under this Act, compliance with any such direction shall be enforceable by civil proceedings, by the person by whom the direction was given, for an injunction or interdict or for any other appropriate relief.

(3) Any power conferred by this Act to give a direction shall, unless the context otherwise requires, include power to vary or revoke the direction.

(4) Any direction given under this Act shall be in writing.

PART III

General restrictions on disclosure of information.

145.—(1) Subject to the following provisions of this section, no information with respect to any particular business which—

(a) has been obtained under or by virtue of any of the provisions of this Act; and

(b) relates to the affairs of any individual or to any particular business,

shall, during the lifetime of that individual or so long as that business continues to be carried on, be disclosed without the consent of that individual or the person for the time being carrying on that business.

(2) Subsection (1) above does not apply to any disclosure of information which is made—

(a) for the purpose of facilitating the carrying out by the Secretary of State, the Regulator, the Franchising Director or the Monopolies Commission of any of his or, as the case may be, their functions under this Act;

(b) for the purpose of facilitating the carrying out by—

(i) any Minister of the Crown,

(ii) the Director General of Fair Trading,

(iii) the Monopolies Commission,

(iv) the Director General of Telecommunications,

(v) the Director General of Gas Supply,

(vi) the Director General of Water Supply,

(vii) the Director General of Electricity Supply,

(viii) the Civil Aviation Authority,

(ix) the Insolvency Practitioners Tribunal, or

(x) a local weights and measures authority in Great Britain,

of any of his or, as the case may be, their functions under any of the enactments or instruments specified in subsection (3) below;

1986 c. 60.

(c) for the purpose of enabling or assisting the Secretary of State or the Treasury to exercise any powers conferred by the Financial Services Act 1986 or by the enactments relating to companies, insurance companies or insolvency or for the purpose of enabling or assisting any inspector appointed under the enactments relating to companies to carry out his functions;

1986 c. 45.

(d) for the purpose of enabling or assisting an official receiver to carry out his functions under the enactments relating to insolvency or for the purpose of enabling or assisting a recognised professional body for the purposes of section 391 of the Insolvency Act 1986 to carry out its functions as such;

1974 c. 37.

(e) for the purpose of facilitating the carrying out by the Health and Safety Commission or the Health and Safety Executive of any of its functions under any enactment or of facilitating the carrying out by any enforcing authority, within the meaning of Part I of the Health and Safety at Work etc. Act 1974, of any functions under a relevant statutory provision, within the meaning of that Act;

(f) for the purpose of facilitating the carrying out by the Comptroller and Auditor General of any of his functions under any enactment;

PART III

(g) for the purpose of facilitating the carrying out by the International Rail Regulator of any of his functions under any subordinate legislation made for the purpose of implementing the Directive of the Council of the European Communities dated 29th July 1991 on the development of the Community's railways;   91/440/EEC

(h) in connection with the investigation of any criminal offence or for the purposes of any criminal proceedings;

(j) for the purposes of any civil proceedings brought under or by virtue of this Act or any of the enactments or instruments specified in subsection (3) below; or

(k) in pursuance of a Community obligation.

(3) The enactments and instruments referred to in subsection (2) above are—

(a) the Trade Descriptions Act 1968;   1968 c. 29.
(b) the Fair Trading Act 1973;   1973 c. 41.
(c) the Consumer Credit Act 1974;   1974 c. 39.
(d) the Restrictive Trade Practices Act 1976;   1976 c. 34.
(e) the Resale Prices Act 1976;   1976 c. 53.
(f) the Estate Agents Act 1979;   1979 c. 38.
(g) the Competition Act 1980;   1980 c. 21.
(h) the Telecommunications Act 1984;   1984 c. 12.
(j) the Airports Act 1986;   1986 c. 31.
(k) the Gas Act 1986;   1986 c. 44.
(l) the Insolvency Act 1986;   1986 c. 45.
(m) the Consumer Protection Act 1987;   1987 c. 43.
(n) the Electricity Act 1989;   1989 c. 29.
(o) the Property Misdescriptions Act 1991;   1991 c. 29.
(p) the Water Industry Act 1991;   1991 c. 56.
(q) the Water Resources Act 1991;   1991 c. 57.
(r) any subordinate legislation made for the purpose of securing compliance with the Directive of the Council of the European Communities dated 10th September 1984 on the approximation of the laws, regulations and administrative provisions of the member States concerning misleading advertising.   84/450/EEC.

(4) The Secretary of State may by order provide that subsections (2) and (3) above shall have effect subject to such modifications as are specified in the order.

(5) Nothing in subsection (1) above shall be construed—

(a) as limiting the matters which may be published under section 71 above or may be included in, or made public as part of, a report of the Regulator, the Franchising Director, the Monopolies Commission, the Central Committee or a consultative committee under any provision of Part I above;

(b) as applying to any information—

PART III

(i) which has been so published or has been made public as part of such a report; or

(ii) which has otherwise been made available to the public by virtue of being disclosed in any circumstances in which, or for any purpose for which, disclosure is not precluded by this section.

(6) Any person who discloses any information in contravention of this section is guilty of an offence and shall be liable—

(a) on summary conviction, to a fine not exceeding the statutory maximum;

(b) on conviction on indictment, to imprisonment for a term not exceeding two years or to a fine or to both.

(7) In this section—

"the Central Committee" has the same meaning as in Part I above;

"consultative committee" has the same meaning as in Part I above and includes a reference to the London Regional Passengers' Committee.

Making of false statements etc.

146.—(1) If any person, in giving any information or making any application under or for the purposes of any provision of this Act, or of any regulations made under this Act, makes any statement which he knows to be false in a material particular, or recklessly makes any statement which is false in a material particular, he is guilty of an offence and shall be liable—

(a) on summary conviction, to a fine not exceeding the statutory maximum;

(b) on conviction on indictment, to a fine.

(2) No proceedings shall be instituted in England and Wales in respect of an offence under this section except by or with the consent of the Secretary of State or the Director of Public Prosecutions.

Offences by bodies corporate or Scottish partnerships.

147.—(1) Where a body corporate is guilty of an offence under this Act and that offence is proved to have been committed with the consent or connivance of, or to be attributable to any neglect on the part of, any director, manager, secretary or other similar officer of the body corporate or any person who was purporting to act in any such capacity he, as well as the body corporate, shall be guilty of that offence and shall be liable to be proceeded against and punished accordingly.

(2) Where the affairs of a body corporate are managed by its members, subsection (1) above shall apply in relation to the acts and defaults of a member in connection with his functions of management as if he were a director of the body corporate.

(3) Where a Scottish partnership is guilty of an offence under this Act in Scotland and that offence is proved to have been committed with the consent or connivance of, or to be attributable to any neglect on the part of, a partner, he as well as the partnership shall be guilty of that offence and shall be liable to be proceeded against and punished accordingly.

PART III
Proceedings in Scotland.

148.—(1) Subject to subsection (2) below, summary proceedings for an offence under this Act which is triable either on indictment or summarily may be commenced within a period of six months from the date on which evidence sufficient in the opinion of the procurator fiscal to warrant proceedings came to his knowledge.

(2) No such proceedings shall be commenced by virtue of this section more than three years after the commission of the offence.

(3) For the purposes of this section, a certificate signed by or on behalf of the procurator fiscal and stating the date on which evidence sufficient in his opinion to warrant proceedings came to his knowledge shall be conclusive evidence of that fact.

(4) A certificate stating that matter and purporting to be so signed shall be deemed to be so signed unless the contrary is proved.

(5) Subsection (3) of section 331 of the Criminal Procedure (Scotland) Act 1975 (which relates to the date of commencement of proceedings) shall apply for the purposes of this section as it applies for the purposes of that section. 1975 c. 21.

(6) This section extends to Scotland only.

Service of documents.

149.—(1) Any document required or authorised by virtue of this Act to be served (whether the expression "serve" or the expression "give" or "send" or any other expression is used) on any person may be served—

(a) by delivering it to him or by leaving it at his proper address or by sending it by post to him at that address; or

(b) if the person is a body corporate, by serving it in accordance with paragraph (a) above on the secretary of that body; or

(c) if the person is a partnership, by serving it in accordance with paragraph (a) above on a partner or a person having the control or management of the partnership business.

(2) For the purposes of this section and section 7 of the Interpretation Act 1978 (which relates to the service of documents by post) in its application to this section, the proper address of any person on whom a document is to be served shall be his last known address, except that— 1978 c. 30.

(a) in the case of service on a body corporate or its secretary, it shall be the address of the registered or principal office of the body;

(b) in the case of service on a partnership or a partner or a person having the control or management of a partnership business, it shall be the address of the principal office of the partnership;

and for the purposes of this subsection the principal office of a company constituted under the law of a country or territory outside the United Kingdom or of a partnership carrying on business outside the United Kingdom is its principal office within the United Kingdom.

(3) If a person to be served by virtue of this Act with any document by another has specified to that other an address within the United Kingdom other than his proper address (as determined in pursuance of subsection (2) above) as the one at which he or someone on his behalf will accept documents of the same description as that document, then, in relation to that document, that address shall be treated as his proper address for the

PART III

purposes of this section and for the purposes of the said section 7 in its application to this section, instead of that determined in accordance with subsection (2) above.

(4) This section shall not apply to any document in relation to the service of which provision is made by rules of court.

(5) In this section—

"local authority" includes a metropolitan county passenger transport authority;

1972 c. 70.
1973 c. 65.
"secretary", in relation to a local authority, means the proper officer within the meaning of the Local Government Act 1972 or (in relation to a local authority in Scotland) the Local Government (Scotland) Act 1973;

"serve" shall be construed in accordance with subsection (1) above.

Crown application.

150.—(1) The following provisions of this Act bind the Crown—

(a) sections 17 to 22;

(b) sections 55 to 58, except sections 55(8) and 58(4) and (5);

(c) sections 59 to 62;

(d) sections 85 to 88, 91 to 94, 96 and 97;

1974 c. 37.
(e) subject to, and in accordance with, section 48 of the Health and Safety at Work etc. Act 1974, section 117 (other than subsection (5)) so far as affecting or relating to provisions of, or regulations under, Part I of that Act which bind the Crown;

(f) section 118, except subsections (7) and (8);

(g) sections 119 to 121, except sections 120(4) and (5) and 121(4) to (6);

(h) section 122;

(j) section 144, so far as relating to other provisions of this Act which bind the Crown;

(k) Schedule 4;

1986 c. 45.
(l) Schedule 6, to the extent that it applies, amends or modifies the operation of provisions of the Insolvency Act 1986 which bind the Crown so far as affecting or relating to the matters specified in paragraphs (a) to (e) of section 434 of that Act;

(m) Schedule 7;

(n) Schedule 8;

(o) the amendments and repeals made by Schedules 12 and 14, to the extent that the enactments to which they relate bind the Crown.

(2) Nothing in subsection (1) above so far as relating—

(a) to sections 55 to 58 above, or

(b) to section 144 above, so far as relating to those sections,

shall authorise proceedings to be brought against Her Majesty in her private capacity.

1947 c. 44.
(3) Subsection (2) above shall be construed as if section 38(3) of the Crown Proceedings Act 1947 (interpretation of references in that Act to Her Majesty in her private capacity) were contained in this Act.

PART III

(4) No person with whom the Franchising Director enters into an agreement or arrangement pursuant to section 51 above shall be regarded, by virtue of that agreement or arrangement, as a servant or agent of the Crown, or as having any status, immunity or privilege of the Crown.

151.—(1) In this Act, unless the context otherwise requires—

"the Board" means the British Railways Board;

"body corporate" has the meaning given by section 740 of the Companies Act 1985;

"company" means any body corporate;

"contravention", in relation to any direction, condition, requirement, regulation or order, includes any failure to comply with it and cognate expressions shall be construed accordingly;

"debentures" includes debenture stock;

"the Franchising Director" means the Director of Passenger Rail Franchising;

"functions" includes powers, duties and obligations;

"local authority" means any county council, district council, regional council, islands council or London borough council, the Common Council of the City of London or the Council of the Isles of Scilly;

"modifications" includes additions, alterations and omissions and cognate expressions shall be construed accordingly;

"the Monopolies Commission" means the Monopolies and Mergers Commission;

"notice" means notice in writing;

"publicly owned railway company" means a company which is wholly owned by the Crown and which carries on, or is to carry on,—

(a) an undertaking derived, or to be derived, (whether wholly or partly and whether directly or indirectly) from, or from some part of, an undertaking carried on by the Board or a wholly owned subsidiary of the Board; or

(b) an undertaking in the course of which the company uses, or will use, any property, rights or liabilities acquired, or to be acquired, (whether directly or indirectly) from the Board or a wholly owned subsidiary of the Board;

"the Regulator" means the Rail Regulator;

"securities" has the meaning given by section 142 of the Financial Services Act 1986;

"shares" includes stock;

"subsidiary" has the meaning given by section 736 of the Companies Act 1985;

"transfer scheme" means a scheme made under or by virtue of section 85 or 86 above;

"wholly owned subsidiary" has the meaning given by section 736 of the Companies Act 1985.

General interpretation.

1985 c. 6.

1986 c.60.

PART III

(2) For the purposes of this Act, a company shall be regarded as "wholly owned by the Crown" at any time when it has no members other than—

(a) the Secretary of State, the Franchising Director or a Government department,

(b) a company which is itself wholly owned by the Crown, or

(c) a person acting on behalf of the Secretary of State, the Franchising Director, a Government department or such a company.

(3) For the purposes of this Act, a company shall be regarded as "wholly owned by the Franchising Director" at any time when it has no members other than—

(a) the Franchising Director,

(b) a company which is itself wholly owned by the Franchising Director, or

(c) a person acting on behalf of the Franchising Director or such a company.

(4) Any consent or approval under or by virtue of this Act shall be given in writing.

(5) For the purposes of this Act any class or description may be framed by reference to any matters or circumstances whatever.

S.I. 1981/1794.

(6) Nothing in this Act affects the operation of the Transfer of Undertakings (Protection of Employment) Regulations 1981, in their application in relation to the transfer of an undertaking, or part of an undertaking, within the meaning of those Regulations.

1974 c. 37.

(7) Nothing in this Act, and nothing done under it, shall prejudice or affect the operation of any of the relevant statutory provisions (whenever made) as defined in Part I of the Health and Safety at Work etc. Act 1974.

(8) Subsection (7) above is without prejudice to section 117 above.

1972 c. 59.

(9) The provisions of section 3 of the Administration of Justice (Scotland) Act 1972 (power of arbiter to state case to Court of Session) shall not apply in relation to any determination under this Act made by an arbiter.

Minor and consequential amendments, transitional provisions and repeals.

1978 c. 30.

152.—(1) The enactments mentioned in Schedule 12 to this Act shall have effect with the amendments there specified (being minor amendments and amendments consequential on provisions of this Act).

(2) The transitional provisions contained in Schedule 13 to this Act shall have effect; but those provisions are without prejudice to sections 16 and 17 of the Interpretation Act 1978 (effect of repeals).

(3) The enactments mentioned in Schedule 14 to this Act (which include some that are spent or no longer of practical utility) are hereby repealed to the extent specified in the third column of that Schedule.

Power to make consequential modifications in other Acts etc.

153.—(1) The Secretary of State may by order make such modifications of existing provisions as appear to him to be necessary or expedient in consequence of the provisions of this Act, or of any instrument made under or by virtue of this Act, being modifications in respect of—

PART III

(a) any reference in an existing provision to the Board or any subsidiary of the Board;

(b) any reference (in whatever terms) in an existing provision to any railway, railway service or railway undertaking;

(c) any reference (in whatever terms) in an existing provision to any person who—

(i) provides a railway service, or

(ii) carries on a railway undertaking,

or who is authorised to do so under or by virtue of any enactment;

(d) any reference in an existing provision to any enactment amended or repealed by or under this Act;

(e) any existing provision, so far as appearing to the Secretary of State to be of no further practical utility, having regard to the provisions of this Act;

(f) any other inconsistency between an existing provision and this Act.

(2) In this section—

"existing provision" means a provision contained in any Act (whether public general or local) passed, or in subordinate legislation made, before the relevant date;

"railway" has its wider meaning, within the meaning of Part I above;

"railway service" has the same meaning as in Part I above;

"the relevant date", in relation to any modification, means the date of the coming into force of the provision of this Act on which the modification is consequential;

"subordinate legislation" has the same meaning as in the Interpretation Act 1978.

1978 c. 30.

154.—(1) This Act may be cited as the Railways Act 1993.

Short title, commencement and extent.

(2) Except for section 1 and Schedule 1 (which come into force on the passing of this Act), this Act shall come into force on such day as may be specified in an order made by the Secretary of State; and different days may be so specified—

(a) for different provisions;

(b) for different purposes of the same provision; and

(c) for different areas within the United Kingdom.

(3) The following provisions of this Act extend to Northern Ireland—

(a) sections 32(2) and (3) and 36(1), (4) and (5);

(b) subsections (1), (2), (4) and (5) of section 66;

(c) sections 84, 85, 87 to 97, 107, 109 to 116, 124, 126, 128 and 129(3);

(d) section 131;

(e) section 134;

(f) sections 143, 144, 146, 147(1) and (2) and 149 to 152, so far as relating to provisions of this Act which so extend;

(g) section 153;

PART III

(h) this section;

(j) paragraphs 6, 7 and 8 of Schedule 1, paragraph 10 of Schedule 2 and paragraph 9 of Schedule 3;

(k) Schedules 8 and 9;

(l) Schedule 11;

(m) the amendments and repeals made by Schedules 12 and 14, other than those relating to—

1889 c. 57. (i) section 6 of the Regulation of Railways Act 1889,
1905 c. 11. (ii) the Railway Fires Act 1905, and
1923 c. 27. (iii) the Railway Fires Act (1905) Amendment Act 1923,

to the extent that the enactments to which they relate so extend.

(4) Except as provided in subsection (3) above, this Act does not extend to Northern Ireland.

SCHEDULES

SCHEDULE 1

Section 1.

THE REGULATOR AND THE FRANCHISING DIRECTOR

Remuneration, pensions etc.

1.—(1) There shall be paid to a holder of the office of the Regulator or the Franchising Director such remuneration, and such travelling and other allowances, as the Secretary of State may determine.

(2) In the case of any such holder of the office of the Regulator or the Franchising Director as may be determined by the Secretary of State, there shall be paid such pension, allowance or gratuity to or in respect of him, or such contributions or payments towards provision for such a pension, allowance or gratuity, as may be so determined.

(3) If, when any person ceases to hold office as the Regulator or the Franchising Director, the Secretary of State determines that there are special circumstances which make it right that he should receive compensation, there may be paid to him a sum by way of compensation of such amount as may be determined by the Secretary of State.

(4) The approval of the Treasury shall be required for the making of a determination under this paragraph.

Staff

2.—(1) The Regulator and the Franchising Director may each, with the approval of the Treasury as to numbers and terms and conditions of service, appoint such staff as the Regulator, or (as the case may be) the Franchising Director, may determine.

(2) Where a person who is, by reference to his employment as a member of the staff of the Regulator or the Franchising Director, a participant in a scheme under section 1 of the Superannuation Act 1972 (superannuation schemes as respects civil servants etc) becomes a holder of the office of the Regulator or the Franchising Director, the Treasury may determine that his term of office as such shall be treated for the purposes of the scheme as employment in the civil service of the State (whether or not any benefits are payable to or in respect of him by virtue of paragraph 1(2) above).

1972 c. 11.

Expenses of the Regulator, the Franchising Director and their staff

3. There shall be paid out of money provided by Parliament—

   (a) the remuneration of, and any travelling or other allowances payable under this Act to, the Regulator or the Franchising Director or to any staff of the Regulator or the Franchising Director;

   (b) except as otherwise provided by this Act, any sums payable under this Act to or in respect of the Regulator or the Franchising Director; and

   (c) except as otherwise provided by this Act, any expenses duly incurred by the Regulator or the Franchising Director, or by any staff of the Regulator or the Franchising Director, in consequence of the provisions of this Act.

Official seal

4. The Regulator and the Franchising Director shall each have an official seal for the authentication of documents required for the purposes of their respective functions.

SCH. 1

Performance of functions

5. Anything authorised or required by or under this Act or any other enactment to be done by the Regulator or the Franchising Director may be done by any member of the staff of the Regulator or, as the case may be, the Franchising Director who is authorised generally or specially in that behalf by the Regulator or, as the case may be, the Franchising Director.

Documentary evidence

1868 c. 37.

6. The Documentary Evidence Act 1868 shall have effect as if—

   (a) the Regulator and the Franchising Director were each included in the first column of the Schedule to that Act;

   (b) the Regulator, the Franchising Director and any person authorised to act on behalf of the Regulator or the Franchising Director were mentioned in the second column of that Schedule; and

   (c) the regulations referred to in that Act included any document issued by the Regulator, the Franchising Director or any such person.

The Parliamentary Commissioner

1967 c. 13.

7. In the Parliamentary Commissioner Act 1967, in Schedule 2 (departments and authorities subject to investigation) the following entries shall be inserted at the appropriate places—

   (a) "The Director of Passenger Rail Franchising"; and

   (b) "The Rail Regulator".

Parliamentary disqualification etc.

1975 c. 24.

8. In Part III of Schedule 1 to the House of Commons Disqualification Act 1975, the following entries shall be inserted at the appropriate places—

   (a) "The Director of Passenger Rail Franchising"; and

   (b) "The Rail Regulator".

Section 2.

SCHEDULE 2

RAIL USERS' CONSULTATIVE COMMITTEES

Preliminary

1. In this Schedule any reference to the committee is a reference to each of the consultative committees.

Remuneration of, and allowances for, the chairman

2. There shall be paid to the chairman of the committee such remuneration, and such travelling and other allowances, as the Regulator may, with the approval of the Treasury, determine.

Allowances for other members

3. There shall be paid to members of the committee other than the chairman such travelling and other allowances as the Regulator with the approval of the Treasury may determine.

Administration etc.

4. The Regulator shall make arrangements for the committee to be provided with office accommodation and with such services as he considers appropriate to enable them to carry out their functions.

Proceedings

5.—(1) Subject to the following provisions of this paragraph and paragraph 6 below, the committee may regulate their own procedure, including quorum.

(2) The committee shall meet when convened by the chairman, and in any case shall meet at least twice a year.

(3) Without prejudice to the discretion of the chairman to call a meeting whenever he thinks fit, he shall call a meeting when required to do so by any three members of the committee.

(4) Minutes shall be kept of the proceedings at every meeting of the committee; and copies of those minutes shall be sent to the Central Committee and the Regulator.

(5) The committee shall have regard to any general recommendations which the Central Committee may from time to time make with respect to any matter affecting the procedure or functions of consultative committees.

(6) The validity of any proceedings of the committee shall not be affected by any vacancy amongst the members or by any defect in the appointment of a member.

Admission of public to meetings

6.—(1) Subject to sub-paragraph (2) below, meetings of the committee shall be open to the public.

(2) The public shall be excluded during any item of business where—

(a) it is likely, were members of the public to be present during that item, that information furnished in confidence to the committee by the Regulator or the Franchising Director would be disclosed in breach of the obligation of confidence;

(b) the committee have resolved that, by reason of the confidential nature of the item or for other special reasons stated in the resolution, it is desirable in the public interest that the public be excluded;

(c) it is likely, were members of the public to be present during that item, that there would be disclosed to them—

(i) any matter which relates to the affairs of an individual, or

(ii) any matter which relates specifically to the affairs of a particular body of persons, whether corporate or unincorporate,

where public disclosure of that matter would or might, in the opinion of the committee, seriously and prejudicially affect the interests of that individual or body.

(3) The committee shall give such notice—

(a) of any meeting of the committee which is open to the public, and

(b) of the business to be taken at that meeting (other than items during which the public is to be excluded),

as they consider appropriate for the purpose of bringing the meeting to the attention of interested members of the public.

SCH. 2

Sub-committees

7.—(1) The committee may, with the approval of the Regulator—

(a) establish local and other sub-committees through which the committee may carry out such of their functions as they may determine;

(b) appoint such persons (including persons who are not members of the committee) to be members of any such sub-committee as they may determine; and

(c) regulate the procedure of any such sub-committee.

(2) Persons appointed under sub-paragraph (1) above who are not members of the committee may be reimbursed for their travelling expenses and such of their out-of-pocket expenses as do not relate to loss of remuneration.

Financial provisions

8.—(1) There shall be paid by the Regulator out of money provided by Parliament—

(a) any sums payable to or in respect of any person under paragraph 2, 3 or 7 above; and

(b) any expenses incurred by the committee in accordance with any statement approved under sub-paragraph (3) below.

(2) The committee shall prepare and send to the Regulator not less than two months, or such other period as the Regulator may specify, before the beginning of each financial year a statement of the expenses which they expect to incur in respect of that year for the purposes of, or in connection with, the carrying out of their functions.

(3) The Regulator shall consider any statement sent to him under sub-paragraph (2) above and shall either approve the statement or approve it with such modifications as he considers appropriate.

Amendment of other Acts

1970 c. 44.

9. In section 14(1) of the Chronically Sick and Disabled Persons Act 1970, after the words "the Transport Users' Consultative Committees," there shall be inserted the words "the Rail Users' Consultative Committees,"

1975 c. 24.

10. In Part III of Schedule 1 to the House of Commons Disqualification Act 1975, the following entry shall be inserted at the appropriate place—

"Chairman of a rail users' consultative committee, appointed under section 2 of the Railways Act 1993".

Section 3.

SCHEDULE 3

THE CENTRAL RAIL USERS' CONSULTATIVE COMMITTEE

Preliminary

1. In this Schedule any reference to the committee is a reference to the Central Rail Users' Consultative Committee.

Remuneration of, and allowances for, the chairman

2. There shall be paid to the chairman of the committee such remuneration, and such travelling and other allowances, as the Regulator may, with the approval of the Treasury, determine.

Allowances for other members

3. There shall be paid to members of the committee other than the chairman such travelling and other allowances as the Regulator with the approval of the Treasury may determine.

Administration etc.

4. The Regulator shall make arrangements for the committee to be provided with office accommodation and with such services as he considers appropriate to enable them to carry out their functions.

Proceedings

5.—(1) Subject to the following provisions of this paragraph and paragraph 6 below, the committee may regulate their own procedure, including quorum.

(2) The committee shall meet when convened by the chairman, and in any case shall meet at least twice a year.

(3) Without prejudice to the discretion of the chairman to call a meeting whenever he thinks fit, he shall call a meeting when required to do so by any three members of the committee.

(4) Minutes shall be kept of the proceedings at every meeting of the committee; and copies of those minutes shall be sent to the Secretary of State and the Regulator.

(5) A person who is a member of the committee by virtue of being the chairman of a consultative committee may appoint another member of that consultative committee to attend any meeting of the committee in his stead.

(6) The validity of any proceedings of the committee shall not be affected by any vacancy amongst the members or by any defect in the appointment of a member.

Admission of public to meetings

6.—(1) Subject to sub-paragraph (2) below, meetings of the committee shall be open to the public.

(2) The public shall be excluded during any item of business where—

(a) it is likely, were members of the public to be present during that item, that information furnished in confidence to the committee by the Regulator or the Franchising Director would be disclosed in breach of the obligation of confidence;

(b) the committee have resolved that, by reason of the confidential nature of the item or for other special reasons stated in the resolution, it is desirable in the public interest that the public be excluded;

(c) it is likely, were members of the public to be present during that item, that there would be disclosed to them—

(i) any matter which relates to the affairs of an individual, or

(ii) any matter which relates specifically to the affairs of a particular body of persons, whether corporate or unincorporate,

where public disclosure of that matter would or might, in the opinion of the committee, seriously and prejudicially affect the interests of that individual or body.

(3) The committee shall give such notice—

(a) of any meeting of the committee which is open to the public, and

SCH. 3

(b) of the business to be taken at that meeting (other than items during which the public is to be excluded),

as they consider appropriate for the purpose of bringing the meeting to the attention of interested members of the public.

Sub-committees

7.—(1) The committee may, with the approval of the Regulator—

(a) establish sub-committees through which the committee may carry out such of their functions as they may determine;

(b) appoint such persons (including persons who are not members of the committee) to be members of any such sub-committee as they may determine; and

(c) regulate the procedure of any such sub-committee.

(2) Persons appointed under sub-paragraph (1) above who are not members of the committee may be reimbursed for their travelling expenses and such of their out-of-pocket expenses as do not relate to loss of remuneration.

Financial provisions

8.—(1) There shall be paid by the Regulator out of money provided by Parliament—

(a) any sums payable to or in respect of any person under paragraph 2, 3 or 7 above; and

(b) any expenses incurred by the committee in accordance with any statement approved under sub-paragraph (3) below.

(2) The committee shall prepare and send to the Regulator not less than two months, or such other period as the Regulator may specify, before the beginning of each financial year a statement of the expenses which they expect to incur in respect of that year for the purposes of, or in connection with, the carrying out of their functions.

(3) The Regulator shall consider any statement sent to him under sub-paragraph (2) above and shall either approve the statement or approve it with such modifications as he considers appropriate.

Amendment of other Acts

1975 c. 24.

9. In Part III of Schedule 1 to the House of Commons Disqualification Act 1975, the following entry shall be inserted at the appropriate place—

"Chairman of the Central Rail Users' Consultative Committee, appointed under section 3 of the Railways Act 1993".

Sections 17 and 19.

SCHEDULE 4

ACCESS AGREEMENTS: APPLICATIONS FOR ACCESS CONTRACTS

Interpretation

1. In this Schedule—

"application for directions" means an application for directions under section 17 of this Act;

"the facility owner" means the facility owner mentioned in section 17(1) of this Act;

"interested person" means any person whose consent is required by the facility owner, as a result of an obligation or duty owed by the facility owner which arose after the coming into force of section 17 of this Act, before the facility owner may enter into the required access contract;

"the required access contract" means the access contract which the applicant seeks to obtain by virtue of the application for directions;

and, subject to that, expressions used in this Schedule and in section 17 of this Act have the same meaning in this Schedule as they have in that section.

Making and withdrawal of application

2.—(1) Any application for directions must be made in writing to the Regulator and must—

(a) contain particulars of the required rights;

(b) specify the terms which the applicant proposes should be contained in the required access contract; and

(c) include any representations which the applicant wishes to make with regard to the required rights or the terms to be contained in the required access contract.

(2) The applicant may, by giving notice in writing to the Regulator, withdraw or suspend the application at any time.

(3) In this paragraph "the required rights" means the permission to use the railway facility in question which it is sought to obtain by virtue of the application for directions.

Notifications, representations and information

3.—(1) The Regulator shall—

(a) send a copy of any application for directions received by him to the facility owner; and

(b) invite the facility owner to make written representations to the Regulator within such period (being not less than 21 days from the date of issue of the invitation) as may be specified in the invitation.

(2) The Regulator shall send a copy of any such representations received by him to the applicant and invite him to make further written representations within such period (being not less than 10 days from the date of issue of the invitation) as may be specified in the invitation.

(3) The Regulator may from time to time request or invite further information, clarification or representations from the applicant or the facility owner.

Interested persons

4.—(1) Where the Regulator receives an application for directions, he shall issue a direction to the facility owner requiring him to furnish the name and address of every interested person to the Regulator within such period (being not less than 14 days from the date of issue of that direction) as may be specified in that direction.

(2) Where the name and address of an interested person is furnished pursuant to sub-paragraph (1) above, the Regulator shall invite the interested person to make written representations to him within such period (being not less than 14 days from the date of issue of the invitation) as may be specified in the invitation.

(3) The Regulator shall send a copy of any such representations received by him to the applicant and to the facility owner and invite each of them to make written representations within such period (being not less than 10 days from the date of issue of the invitation) as may be specified in the invitation.

(4) The Regulator may from time to time request or invite further information, clarification or representations from any interested person.

The decision and the directions

5.—(1) The Regulator shall inform the applicant, the facility owner and any interested person of his decision on an application for directions.

(2) If the Regulator decides to give directions to the facility owner requiring him to enter into an access contract—

    (a) the directions shall specify—

        (i) the terms of the access contract; and

        (ii) the date by which the access contract is to be entered into; and

    (b) the Regulator may also give directions to the applicant or the facility owner requiring him to pay compensation of such amount as may be specified in the directions to such interested person as may be so specified.

(3) Any compensation directed to be paid by virtue of sub-paragraph (2)(b) above shall be recoverable as a debt due.

(4) The facility owner shall be released from his duty to comply with the directions if the applicant fails to enter into an access contract on the terms required by the directions by the date specified for that purpose in the directions.

Effect of directions on facility owner and interested persons

6.—(1) Any directions given on an application for directions or under this Schedule shall be binding on the person to whom they are given, notwithstanding any obligation or duty he may owe to an interested person and whether or not the interested person has had an opportunity to make representations.

(2) No interested person, and no successor to an interested person, shall take any step for the purpose of enforcing or exercising any right he may have against the facility owner in respect of, or in consequence of, the facility owner's—

    (a) entering into an access contract pursuant to directions under section 17 of this Act,

    (b) performing such a contract in accordance with its terms, or

    (c) failing to take any step to protect the interests of the interested person in connection with the application for directions, or the making of the access contract,

whether or not the interested person had, or has had, an opportunity to make representations.

(3) The duty of the facility owner to furnish the Regulator with the name and address of every interested person pursuant to a direction under paragraph 4 above is a duty owed to each interested person and (subject to the defences and incidents applying in actions for breach of statutory duty) any contravention of that duty shall be actionable at the suit or instance of the interested person and the facility owner shall be liable for any loss or damage suffered by the interested person as a result of any access contract which is entered into in consequence of the application for directions.

(4) It shall be a defence in any proceedings brought by virtue of sub-paragraph (3) above for the facility owner to show that he took all reasonable steps, and exercised all due diligence, to avoid contravening the duty in question.

(5) In this paragraph "successor", in relation to an interested person, means any person—

    (a) who is a successor in title to the interested person; or

    (b) whose rights derive directly or indirectly from the interested person.

Financial provision

7.—(1) Any sums required by the Franchising Director for the payment of compensation pursuant to directions under this Schedule shall be paid by the Secretary of State out of money provided by Parliament.

(2) Any sums received by the Franchising Director under this Schedule shall be paid into the Consolidated Fund.

SCHEDULE 5

ALTERNATIVE CLOSURE PROCEDURE

Application of Schedule

1.—(1) This Schedule applies in relation to any railway passenger services, or railway passenger services of a class or description, or any part of any such service, for the time being designated in an order under section 49(3) of this Act as railway passenger services in relation to which this Schedule is to have effect.

(2) In this Schedule "qualifying services" means any services, or part of a service, falling within sub-paragraph (1) above.

Notice of proposed closure

2. Where a person (in this Schedule referred to as "the operator") who provides qualifying services proposes to discontinue the provision of all such services from any station or on any line (in this Schedule referred to as a closure), he shall, not less than six weeks before carrying the proposal into effect, publish in two successive weeks in two local newspapers circulating in the area affected, and in such other manner as appears to him appropriate, a notice—

 (a) giving the date and particulars of the proposed closure, and particulars of any alternative services which it appears to him will be available and of any proposals of his for providing or augmenting such services; and

 (b) stating that objections to the proposed closure may be lodged in accordance with this Schedule within six weeks of a date specified in the notice, being the date on which the notice is last published in a local newspaper as required by this paragraph;

and copies of the notice shall be sent to the appropriate consultative committee.

Objections

3.—(1) Where a notice has been published under paragraph 2 above, any user of any service affected, and any body representing such users, may within the period specified in the notice lodge with the appropriate consultative committee an objection in writing.

(2) Where such an objection is lodged with a consultative committee—

 (a) the committee shall forthwith inform the Secretary of State and the operator; and

 (b) the closure shall not be proceeded with until the committee has reported to the Secretary of State and the Secretary of State has given his consent.

Conditions

4.—(1) The Secretary of State may give his consent under paragraph 3(2)(b) above subject to such conditions as he thinks fit.

SCH. 5

(2) The Secretary of State may at any time vary or revoke any conditions which are for the time being required to be complied with pursuant to sub-paragraph (1) above.

Functions of the consultative committee

5.—(1) A consultative committee with whom an objection has been lodged under paragraph 3(1) above shall—

(a) consider the objection and any representations made by the operator; and

(b) report to the Secretary of State as soon as possible on the hardship, if any, which they consider will be caused by the proposed closure;

and the report may contain proposals for alleviating that hardship.

(2) Where objections with respect to any proposed closure have been lodged with more than one consultative committee, the committees in question—

(a) may report jointly to the Secretary of State; or

(b) may agree that the consideration of objections and representations relating to the closure and the making of a report to the Secretary of State shall be delegated to any of those committees appearing to them to be principally concerned.

(3) The Secretary of State may require a consultative committee to make a further report; and if in any case the Secretary of State considers that a report or further report has been unreasonably delayed he may, after consulting the committee concerned and making such enquiries as he thinks fit, consent to the proposed closure without awaiting the report or further report.

(4) Copies of every report under this paragraph shall be sent to the Central Committee and to the operator.

(5) Where for the purposes of sub-paragraph (1) or (2) above a consultative committee decide to hear an objector orally, or to hear oral representations made on behalf of the operator, they shall hear the objector or the representations, as the case may be, in public.

Interpretation

6.—(1) For the purposes of this Schedule, the appropriate consultative committee, in relation to a proposed closure, is the consultative committee for the area in which the station or the line, or any part of the line, affected by the proposed closure is situated.

(2) For the purposes of this Schedule, "railway" has its wider meaning.

Section 59.

SCHEDULE 6

RAILWAY ADMINISTRATION ORDERS

PART I

MODIFICATIONS OF THE 1986 ACT

General application of provisions of 1986 Act

1. Where a railway administration order has been made, sections 11 to 23 and 27 of the 1986 Act (which relate to administration orders under Part II of that Act) shall apply, with the modifications specified in the following provisions of this Part of this Schedule—

(a) as if references in those sections to an administration order were references to a railway administration order and references to an administrator were references to a special railway administrator; and

(b) where the company in relation to which the order has been made is a protected railway company which is an unregistered company, as if references in those sections to a company included references to such a company.

Effect of order

2. In section 11 of the 1986 Act (effect of order), as applied by this Part of this Schedule,—

(a) the requirement in subsection (1)(a) that any petition for the winding up of the company shall be dismissed shall be without prejudice to the railway administration order in a case where the order is made by virtue of section 61 of this Act; and

(b) the reference in subsection (3)(d) to proceedings shall include a reference to any proceedings under or for the purposes of section 55 of this Act.

Appointment of special railway administrator

3. In section 13 of the 1986 Act (appointment of administrator), as applied by this Part of this Schedule, for subsection (3) there shall be substituted the following subsection—

"(3) An application for an order under subsection (2) may be made—

(a) by the Secretary of State;

(b) if the company is the holder of a passenger licence under Part I of the Railways Act 1993, by the Director of Passenger Rail Franchising with the consent of the Secretary of State;

(c) by any continuing special railway administrator of the company or, where there is no such special railway administrator, by the company, the directors or any creditor or creditors of the company."

General powers of special railway administrator

4. In section 14 of the 1986 Act (general powers of administrator), as applied by this Part of this Schedule,—

(a) in subsection (1)(b), the reference to the powers specified in Schedule 1 to that Act shall be taken to include a reference to a power to act on behalf of the company for the purposes of this Act or any provision of a local or private Act which confers any power, or imposes any duty or obligation, on the company; and

(b) in subsection (4), the reference to a power conferred by the company's memorandum or articles of association—

(i) shall be taken to include a reference to any power conferred by any provision of a local or private Act which confers any power, or imposes any duty or obligation, on the company; and

(ii) in the case of a company which is an unregistered company, shall be taken also to include a reference to any power conferred by the company's constitution.

Power to deal with charged property

5.—(1) Section 15 of the 1986 Act (power to deal with charged property), as applied by this Part of this Schedule, shall have effect as follows.

(2) In subsection (5)(b) (amount to be paid to chargeholder not to be less than open market value), for the words "in the open market by a willing vendor" there shall be substituted the words "for the best price which is reasonably available on a sale which is consistent with the purposes of the railway administration order".

Duties of special railway administrator

6.—(1) Section 17 of the 1986 Act (duties of administrator), as applied by this Part of this Schedule, shall have effect in accordance with the following provisions of this paragraph.

(2) For subsection (2) there shall be substituted the following subsection—

"(2) Subject to any directions of the court, it shall be the duty of the special railway administrator to manage the affairs, business and property of the company in accordance with proposals, as for the time being revised under section 23, which have been prepared for the purposes of that section by him or any predecessor of his."

(3) In subsection (3), paragraph (a) (right of creditors to require the holding of a creditors' meeting) shall be omitted.

Discharge of order

7.—(1) Section 18 of the 1986 Act (discharge and variation of administration order), as applied by this Part of this Schedule, shall have effect as follows.

(2) For subsections (1) and (2) there shall be substituted the following subsection—

"(1) An application for a railway administration order to be discharged may be made—

(a) by the special railway administrator, on the ground that the purposes of the order have been achieved; or

(b) by the Secretary of State or, if the company is the holder of a passenger licence under Part I of the Railways Act 1993, by the Director of Passenger Rail Franchising with the consent of the Secretary of State, on the ground that it is no longer necessary that the purposes of the order are achieved."

(3) In subsection (3), the words "or vary" shall be omitted.

(4) In subsection (4), the words "or varied" and "or variation" shall be omitted and for the words "to the registrar of companies" there shall be substituted—

(a) except where the company is an unregistered company which is not subject to a requirement imposed under or by virtue of section 691(1) or 718 of the Companies Act 1985 to deliver any documents to the registrar of companies, the words "to the Rail Regulator, the Director of Passenger Rail Franchising and the registrar of companies"; and

(b) where the company is an unregistered company which is not subject to such a requirement as is mentioned in paragraph (a) above, the words "to the Rail Regulator and the Director of Passenger Rail Franchising".

Notice of making of order

8. In section 21(2) of the 1986 Act (notice of order to be given by administrator), as applied by this Part of this Schedule, for the words "to the registrar of companies" there shall be substituted—

(a) except where the company is an unregistered company which is not subject to a requirement imposed under or by virtue of section 691(1) or 718 of the Companies Act 1985 to deliver any documents to the registrar of companies, the words "to the Rail Regulator, the Director of Passenger Rail Franchising and the registrar of companies"; and

(b) where the company is an unregistered company which is not subject to such a requirement as is mentioned in paragraph (a) above, the words "to the Rail Regulator and the Director of Passenger Rail Franchising".

Statement of proposals

9. In section 23 of the 1986 Act (statement of proposals), as applied by this Part of this Schedule, for subsections (1) and (2) there shall be substituted the following subsections—

"(1) Where a railway administration order has been made, the special railway administrator shall, within 3 months (or such longer period as the court may allow) after the making of the order, send a statement of his proposals for achieving the purposes of the order—

(a) to the Secretary of State;

(b) to the Rail Regulator;

(c) to the Director of Passenger Rail Franchising;

(d) so far as he is aware of their addresses, to all creditors of the company; and

(e) except where the company is an unregistered company which is not subject to a requirement imposed under or by virtue of section 691(1) or 718 of the Companies Act 1985 to deliver any documents to the registrar of companies, to the registrar of companies;

and may from time to time revise those proposals.

(2) If at any time—

(a) the special railway administrator proposes to make revisions of the proposals for achieving the purposes of the railway administration order, and

(b) those revisions appear to him to be substantial,

the special railway administrator shall, before making those revisions, send a statement of the proposed revisions to the persons specified in subsection (2A).

(2A) The persons mentioned in subsection (2) are—

(a) the Secretary of State;

(b) the Rail Regulator;

(c) the Director of Passenger Rail Franchising;

(d) all creditors of the company, so far as the special railway administrator is aware of their addresses; and

(e) except where the company is an unregistered company which is not subject to a requirement imposed under or by virtue of section 691(1) or 718 of the Companies Act 1985 to deliver any documents to the registrar of companies, the registrar of companies.

(2B) Where the special railway administrator is required by subsection (1) or (2) to send any person a statement before the end of any period or before making any revision of any proposals, he shall also, before the end of that period or, as the case may be, before making those revisions either—

SCH. 6

(a) send a copy of the statement (so far as he is aware of their addresses) to all members of the company; or

(b) publish in the prescribed manner a notice stating an address to which members should write for copies of the statement to be sent to them free of charge."

Applications to court

10.—(1) Section 27 of the 1986 Act (protection of interests of creditors and members), as applied by this Part of this Schedule, shall have effect as follows.

(2) After subsection (1) there shall be inserted the following subsections—

"(1A) At any time when a railway administration order is in force the Secretary of State or, if the company is the holder of a passenger licence under Part I of the Railways Act 1993, the Director of Passenger Rail Franchising with the consent of the Secretary of State may apply to the High Court or the Court of Session by petition for an order under this section on the ground specified in subsection (1B).

(1B) The ground mentioned in subsection (1A) is that the special railway administrator has exercised or is exercising, or proposing to exercise, his powers in relation to the company in a manner which—

(a) will not best ensure the achievement of the purposes of the order; or

(b) without prejudice to paragraph (a) above, involves a contravention of any of the conditions of any licence under Part I of the Railways Act 1993 held by the company.

(1C) Where an application is made under subsection (1) in respect of a company in relation to which a railway administration order is in force—

(a) notice of the application shall be given to the Secretary of State; and

(b) he shall be entitled to be heard by the court in connection with that application."

(3) Subsection (3) (order not to prejudice or prevent voluntary arrangements or administrator's proposals) shall be omitted.

(4) In subsection (4) (provision that may be made in an order), the words "Subject as above" shall be omitted and for paragraph (d) there shall be substituted—

"(d) without prejudice to the powers exercisable by the court in making a railway administration order—

(i) provide that the railway administration order is to be discharged as from such date as may be specified in the order unless, before that date, such measures are taken as the court thinks fit for the purpose of protecting the interests of creditors; and

(ii) make such consequential provision as the court thinks fit."

(5) For subsection (6) there shall be substituted—

"(6) Where a railway administration order is discharged in consequence of such provision in an order under this section as is mentioned in subsection (4)(d)(i), the special railway administrator shall, within 14 days after the date on which the discharge takes effect, send an office copy of the order under this section—

(a) to the Rail Regulator;

(b) to the Director of Passenger Rail Franchising; and

(c) except where the company is an unregistered company which is not subject to a requirement imposed under or by virtue of section 691(1) or 718 of the Companies Act 1985 to deliver any documents to the registrar of companies, to the registrar of companies;

and if, without reasonable excuse, the special railway administrator fails to comply with this subsection, he is liable to a fine and, for continued contravention, to a daily default fine."

Particular powers of special railway administrator

11. In the application of Schedule 1 to the 1986 Act (which sets out certain powers of the administrator) by virtue of section 14 of that Act, as applied by this Part of this Schedule in relation to a company which is an unregistered company, paragraph 22 shall be omitted.

PART II

FURTHER MODIFICATIONS OF THE 1986 ACT: APPLICATION IN RELATION TO FOREIGN COMPANIES

Introductory

12.—(1) Where a railway administration order has been made in relation to a company which is a foreign company, sections 11 to 23 and 27 of the 1986 Act (as applied by Part I of this Schedule) shall apply in relation to that foreign company with the further modifications set out in the following provisions of this Part of this Schedule.

(2) In this Part of this Schedule, "foreign company" means a company incorporated outside Great Britain.

Effect of order

13.—(1) Section 11 of the 1986 Act (effect of administration order), as applied by this Part of this Schedule in relation to a foreign company, shall have effect as follows.

(2) In subsection (1), paragraph (b) shall be omitted.

(3) Subsection (2) shall be omitted.

(4) In subsection (3)—

(a) paragraphs (a) and (b) shall be omitted; and

(b) in paragraph (d)—

(i) the reference to the commencement or continuation of proceedings shall be taken as a reference to the commencement or continuation of proceedings in Great Britain; and

(ii) the reference to the levying of distress against the company shall be taken as a reference to the levying of distress against the foreign company to the extent of its property in England and Wales;

and any reference to property or goods shall be taken as a reference to property or (as the case may be) goods for the time being situated within Great Britain.

(5) Subsections (4) and (5) shall be omitted.

(6) At the end of that section there shall be added—

"(6) Where a railway administration order is in force in relation to a company which is a foreign company within the meaning of section 65 of the Railways Act 1993—

(a) any person appointed to perform functions equivalent to those of an administrative receiver, and

Sch. 6

(b) if the special railway administrator so requires, any person appointed to perform functions equivalent to those of a receiver,

shall refrain from performing those functions in Great Britain in relation to the foreign company and any of the company's property for the time being situated in Great Britain, during the period for which that order is in force or, in the case of such a person as is mentioned in paragraph (b) above, during so much of that period as falls after the date on which he is required to do so."

Notification of order

14. In section 12 of the 1986 Act (notification of order), as applied by this Part of this Schedule in relation to a foreign company, the reference to a statement that the affairs, business and property of the company are being managed by the administrator shall be taken as a reference to a statement that—

(a) the affairs and business of the foreign company so far as carried on in Great Britain, and

(b) the property of the foreign company so far as that property is for the time being situated within Great Britain,

are being managed by the special railway administrator.

General powers of special railway administrator

15.—(1) Section 14 of the 1986 Act (general powers of administrator), as applied by this Part of this Schedule in relation to a foreign company, shall have effect as follows.

(2) In subsection (1)(a), the reference to the affairs, business and property of the company shall be taken as a reference to—

(a) the affairs and business of the foreign company so far as carried on in Great Britain, and

(b) the property of that company so far as that property is for the time being situated within Great Britain.

(3) Subsection (2)(a) shall be omitted.

(4) In subsection (4)—

(a) the reference to any power conferred on the company or its officers shall be taken to include any power conferred on the foreign company or its officers under the law under which the foreign company is incorporated; and

(b) any reference (however expressed) to the exercise of any power conferred on the company or its officers shall be taken as a reference to the exercise of that power so far as it relates to—

(i) the affairs and business of the foreign company so far as carried on in Great Britain, or

(ii) the property of that company so far as that property is for the time being situated within Great Britain.

Power to deal with charged property

16. In section 15 of the 1986 Act (power of administrator to deal with charged property etc), as applied by this Part of this Schedule in relation to a foreign company, any reference to property or goods shall be taken as a reference to property or (as the case may be) goods for the time being situated within Great Britain.

SCH. 6

Duties of special railway administrator

17. In section 17 of the 1986 Act (general duties of administrator), as applied by this Part of this Schedule in relation to a foreign company,—

   (a) in subsection (1), the reference to property shall be taken as a reference to property for the time being situated within Great Britain; and

   (b) in subsection (2), the reference to the affairs, business and property of the company shall be taken as a reference to—

   (i) the affairs and business of the foreign company so far as carried on in Great Britain, and

   (ii) the property of that company so far as that property is for the time being situated within Great Britain.

Statement as to company's affairs

18. In section 22(1) of the 1986 Act (power of administrator to require certain persons to provide him with a statement as to company's affairs), as applied by this Part of this Schedule in relation to a foreign company, the reference to the affairs of the company shall be taken as a reference to the affairs of the foreign company so far as they are carried on in Great Britain, or relate to property of that company for the time being situated within Great Britain.

Particular powers of special railway administrator

19.—(1) The powers conferred on a special railway administrator by virtue of Schedule 1 to the 1986 Act (which sets out certain powers of an administrator), as that Schedule applies by virtue of section 14 of that Act, as applied by this Part of this Schedule in relation to a foreign company, shall be exercisable only in relation to—

   (a) the affairs and business of that company, so far as carried on in Great Britain; and

   (b) the property of that company, so far as that property is for the time being situated within Great Britain.

(2) In that Schedule, as it so applies,—

   (a) without prejudice to sub-paragraph (1) above, references to the property of that company shall be taken as references to that property, so far as that property is for the time being situated within Great Britain; and

   (b) paragraph 19 shall be omitted.

PART III

SUPPLEMENTAL

General adaptations and saving

20.—(1) Subject to the preceding provisions of this Schedule, references in the 1986 Act (except in sections 8 to 10 and 24 to 26), or in any other enactment passed before this Act, to an administration order under Part II of that Act, to an application for such an order and to an administrator shall include references, respectively, to a railway administration order, to an application for a railway administration order and to a special railway administrator.

(2) Subject as aforesaid and to sub-paragraph (3) below, references in the 1986 Act, or in any other enactment passed before this Act, to an enactment contained in Part II of that Act shall include references to that enactment as applied by section 60, 61, 62 or 65 of this Act or Part I or II of this Schedule.

(3) Sub-paragraphs (1) and (2) above shall apply in relation to a reference in an enactment contained in Part II of the 1986 Act only so far as necessary for the purposes of the operation of the provisions of that Part as so applied.

SCH. 6

(4) The provisions of this Schedule shall be without prejudice to the power conferred by section 411 of the 1986 Act (company insolvency rules), as modified by sub-paragraphs (1) and (2) above.

Interpretation

1986 c. 45.

21.—(1) In this Schedule "the 1986 Act" means the Insolvency Act 1986.

(2) In this Schedule, and in any modification of the 1986 Act made by this Schedule, "special railway administrator", in relation to a railway administration order, means any person appointed in relation to that order for the purposes of section 59(1) of this Act; and in any such modification "railway administration order" has the same meaning as in this Act.

Section 59.

SCHEDULE 7

TRANSFER OF RELEVANT ACTIVITIES IN CONNECTION WITH RAILWAY ADMINISTRATION ORDERS

Application of Schedule

1.—(1) This Schedule shall apply in any case where—

(a) the court has made a railway administration order in relation to a protected railway company ("the existing appointee"); and

(b) it is proposed that, on and after a date appointed by the court, another company ("the new appointee") should carry on the relevant activities of the existing appointee, in place of the existing appointee.

(2) In this Schedule—

"the court", in the case of any protected railway company, means the court having jurisdiction to wind up the company;

"other appointee" means any company, other than the existing appointee or the new appointee, which is the holder of a licence under section 8 of this Act and which may be affected by the proposal mentioned in sub-paragraph (1)(b) above;

"the relevant date" means such day, being a day before the discharge of the railway administration order takes effect, as the court may appoint for the purposes of this Schedule; and

"special railway administrator", in relation to a company in relation to which a railway administration order has been made, means the person for the time being holding office for the purposes of section 59(1) of this Act.

(3) Any reference in this Schedule to "assignment" shall be construed in Scotland as a reference to assignation.

Making and modification of transfer schemes

2.—(1) The existing appointee, acting with the consent of the new appointee and, in relation to the matters affecting them, of any other appointees, may make a scheme under this Schedule for the transfer of property, rights and liabilities from the existing appointee to the new appointee.

(2) A scheme under this Schedule shall not take effect unless it is approved by the Secretary of State or, in a case where the existing appointee is a protected railway company by virtue of section 59(6)(a)(i) of this Act, by the Franchising Director.

(3) Where a scheme under this Schedule is submitted to the Secretary of State or the Franchising Director, for his approval, he may, with the consent of the new appointee, of the existing appointee and, in relation to the matters affecting them, of any other appointees, modify the scheme before approving it.

(4) If at any time after a scheme under this Schedule has come into force in relation to the property, rights and liabilities of any company the Secretary of State considers it appropriate to do so and the existing appointee, the new appointee and, in relation to the provisions of the order which affect them, any other appointees consent to the making of the order, the Secretary of State may by order provide that that scheme shall for all purposes be deemed to have come into force with such modifications as may be specified in the order.

(5) An order under sub-paragraph (4) above may make, with effect from the coming into force of the scheme to which it relates, any such provision as could have been made by the scheme and, in connection with giving effect to that provision from that time, may contain such supplemental, consequential and transitional provision as the Secretary of State considers appropriate.

(6) In determining, in accordance with his duties under Part I of this Act, whether and in what manner to exercise any power conferred on him by this paragraph the Secretary of State or the Franchising Director, shall have regard to the need to ensure that any provision for the transfer of property, rights and liabilities in accordance with a scheme under this Schedule allocates property, rights and liabilities to the different companies affected by the scheme in such proportions as appear to him to be appropriate in the context of the different relevant activities of the existing appointee which will, by virtue of this Act, be carried out at different times on and after the relevant date by the new appointee, by the existing appointee and by any other appointees.

(7) It shall be the duty of the new appointee, of the existing appointee and of any other appointees to provide the Secretary of State or, in a case where the existing appointee is a protected railway company by virtue of section 59(6)(a)(i) of this Act, the Franchising Director with all such information and other assistance as he may reasonably require for the purposes of, or in connection with, the exercise of any power conferred on him by this paragraph.

(8) Without prejudice to the other provisions of this Act relating to the special railway administrator of a company, anything which is required by this paragraph to be done by a company shall, where that company is a company in relation to which a railway administration order is in force, be effective only if it is done on the company's behalf by its special railway administrator.

Transfers by scheme

3.—(1) A scheme under this Schedule for the transfer of the existing appointee's property, rights and liabilities shall come into force on the relevant date and, on coming into force, shall have effect, in accordance with its provisions and without further assurance, so as to transfer the property, rights and liabilities to which the scheme relates to the new appointee.

(2) For the purpose of making any division of property, rights or liabilities which it is considered appropriate to make in connection with the transfer of property, rights and liabilities in accordance with a scheme under this Schedule, the provisions of that scheme may—

  (a) create for the existing appointee, the new appointee or any other appointees an interest in or right over any property to which the scheme relates;

  (b) create new rights and liabilities as between any two or more of those companies; and

SCH. 7

(c) in connection with any provision made by virtue of paragraph (a) or (b) above, make incidental provision as to the interests, rights and liabilities of other persons with respect to the subject-matter of the scheme.

(3) The property, rights and liabilities of the existing appointee that shall be capable of being transferred in accordance with a scheme under this Schedule shall include—

(a) property, rights and liabilities that would not otherwise be capable of being transferred or assigned by the existing appointee;

(b) such property, rights and liabilities to which the existing appointee may become entitled or subject after the making of the scheme and before the relevant date as may be described in the scheme;

(c) property situated anywhere in the United Kingdom or elsewhere;

(d) rights and liabilities under the law of any part of the United Kingdom or of any country or territory outside the United Kingdom.

(4) The provision that may be made by virtue of sub-paragraph (2)(b) above includes—

(a) provision for treating any person who is entitled by virtue of a scheme under this Schedule to possession of a document as having given another person an acknowledgement in writing of the right of that other person to the production of the document and to delivery of copies thereof;

1925 c. 20.

(b) provision applying section 64 of the Law of Property Act 1925 (production and safe custody of documents) in relation to any case in relation to which provision falling within paragraph (a) above has effect; and

1979 c. 33.

(c) provision that where a scheme under this Schedule transfers any interest in land or other property situated in Scotland, subsections (1) and (2) of section 16 of the Land Registration (Scotland) Act 1979 (omission of certain clauses in deeds) shall have effect in relation to the transfer as if the transfer had been effected by deed and as if from each of those subsections the words "unless specially qualified" were omitted.

(5) For the avoidance of doubt, it is hereby declared that the transfers authorised by paragraph (a) of sub-paragraph (3) above include transfers which, by virtue of that paragraph, are to take effect as if there were no such contravention, liability or interference with any interest or right as there would be, in the case of a transfer or assignment otherwise than in accordance with a scheme under this Schedule, by reason of any provision having effect (whether under any enactment or agreement or otherwise) in relation to the terms on which the existing appointee is entitled or subject to the property, right or liability in question.

Transfer of licences

4.—(1) A scheme under this Schedule may provide for a licence held by the existing appointee to have effect as if it had been granted to the new appointee.

(2) Different schemes under this Schedule may provide for a licence held by the same existing appointee to have effect as if it had been granted as a separate licence to each of the new appointees under those schemes.

Supplemental provisions of schemes

5.—(1) A scheme under this Schedule may contain supplemental, consequential and transitional provision for the purposes of, or in connection with, the provision for the transfers or any other provision made by the scheme.

(2) Without prejudice to the generality of sub-paragraph (1) above, a scheme under this Schedule may provide—

(a) that for purposes connected with any transfers made in accordance with the scheme (including the transfer of rights and liabilities under an enactment) the new appointee is to be treated as the same person in law as the existing appointee;

(b) that, so far as may be necessary for the purposes of or in connection with any such transfers, agreements made, transactions effected and other things done by or in relation to the existing appointee are to be treated as made, effected or done by or in relation to the new appointee;

(c) that, so far as may be necessary for the purposes of or in connection with any such transfers, references in any agreement (whether or not in writing) or in any deed, bond, instrument or other document to, or to any officer of, the existing appointee are to have effect with such modifications as are specified in the scheme;

(d) that proceedings commenced by or against the existing appointee are to be continued by or against the new appointee;

(e) that the effect of any transfer under the scheme in relation to contracts of employment with the existing appointee is not to be to terminate any of those contracts but is to be that periods of employment with the existing appointee are to count for all purposes as periods of employment with the new appointee;

(f) that disputes as to the effect of the scheme between the existing appointee and the new appointee, between either of them and any other appointee or between different companies which are other appointees are to be referred to such arbitration as may be specified in or determined under the scheme;

(g) that determinations on such arbitrations and certificates given jointly by two or more such appointees as are mentioned in paragraph (f) above as to the effect of the scheme as between the companies giving the certificates are to be conclusive for all purposes.

Duties of existing appointee after the scheme comes into force

6.—(1) A scheme under this Schedule may provide for the imposition of duties on the existing appointee and on the new appointee to take all such steps as may be requisite to secure that the vesting in the new appointee, by virtue of the scheme, of any foreign property, right or liability is effective under the relevant foreign law.

(2) The provisions of a scheme under this Schedule may require the existing appointee to comply with any directions of the new appointee in performing any duty imposed on the existing appointee by virtue of a provision included in the scheme under sub-paragraph (1) above.

(3) A scheme under this Schedule may provide that, until the vesting of any foreign property, right or liability of the existing appointee in the new appointee is effective under the relevant foreign law, it shall be the duty of the existing appointee to hold that property or right for the benefit of, or to discharge that liability on behalf of, the new appointee.

(4) Nothing in any provision included by virtue of this paragraph in a scheme under this Schedule shall be taken as prejudicing the effect under the law of any part of the United Kingdom of the vesting by virtue of the scheme in the new appointee of any foreign property, right or liability.

(5) A scheme under this Schedule may provide that, in specified cases, foreign property, rights or liabilities that are acquired or incurred by an existing appointee after the scheme comes into force are immediately to become property, rights or liabilities of the new appointee; and such a scheme may make the same provision in relation to any such property, rights or liabilities as can be made, by

SCH. 7

virtue of the preceding provisions of this paragraph, in relation to foreign property, rights and liabilities vested in the existing appointee when the scheme comes into force.

(6) References in this paragraph to any foreign property, right or liability are references to any property, right or liability as respects which any issue arising in any proceedings would have to be determined (in accordance with the rules of private international law) by reference to the law of a country or territory outside the United Kingdom.

(7) Any expenses incurred by an existing appointee in consequence of any provision included by virtue of this paragraph in a scheme under this Schedule shall be met by the new appointee.

(8) Duties imposed on a company by virtue of this paragraph shall be enforceable in the same way as if they were imposed by a contract between the existing appointee and the new appointee.

Functions under private and local legislation etc.

7.—(1) A scheme under this Schedule may provide that any functions of the existing appointee under a statutory provision—

　(a) shall be transferred to the new appointee or any of the other appointees;

　(b) shall be concurrently exercisable by two or more companies falling within paragraph (a) above; or

　(c) shall be concurrently exercisable by the existing appointee and one or more companies falling within paragraph (a) above;

and different schemes under this Schedule may provide for any such functions of the same existing appointee to have effect as mentioned in paragraphs (a) to (c) above in relation to each of the new appointees under those schemes or of all or any of the other appointees.

(2) Sub-paragraph (1) above applies in relation to any function under a statutory provision if and to the extent that the statutory provision—

　(a) relates to any part of the existing appointee's undertaking, or to any property, which is to be transferred by the scheme; or

　(b) authorises the carrying out of works designed to be used in connection with any such part of the existing appointee's undertaking or the acquisition of land for the purpose of carrying out any such works.

(3) Sub-paragraph (1) above does not apply to any function of the Board or of any of the Board's subsidiaries under any provision of this Act or of—

1962 c. 46.　(a) the Transport Act 1962;

1968 c. 73.　(b) the Transport Act 1968;

1974 c. 48.　(c) section 4 of the Railways Act 1974; or

1985 c. 67.　(d) sections 119 to 124 of the Transport Act 1985.

(4) A scheme under this Schedule may define any functions of the existing appointee to be transferred or made concurrently exercisable by the scheme in accordance with sub-paragraph (1) above—

　(a) by specifying the statutory provisions in question;

　(b) by referring to all the statutory provisions (except those specified in sub-paragraph (3) above) which—

　　(i) relate to any part of the existing appointee's undertaking, or to any property, which is to be transferred by the scheme, or

　　(ii) authorise the carrying out of works designed to be used in connection with any such part of the existing appointee's undertaking or the acquisition of land for the purpose of carrying out any such works; or

(c) by referring to all the statutory provisions within paragraph (b) above, but specifying certain excepted provisions.

(5) In this paragraph "statutory provision" means a provision whether of a general or of a special nature contained in, or in any document made or issued under, any Act, whether of a general or a special nature.

SCHEDULE 8

Transfers by transfer scheme

Allocation of property, rights and liabilities

1.—(1) The provisions of this paragraph and paragraph 2 below shall have effect where a transfer to which this Schedule applies is a transfer of all (or of all but so much as may be excepted) of the property, rights and liabilities comprised in a specified part of the transferor's undertaking, but shall not apply to any such rights or liabilities under a contract of employment.

(2) Any property, right or liability comprised partly in the part of the transferor's undertaking which is transferred to the transferee and partly in the part of that undertaking which is retained by the transferor shall, where the nature of the property, right or liability permits, be divided or apportioned between the transferor and the transferee in such proportions as may be appropriate; and, where any estate or interest in land falls to be so divided—

(a) any rent payable under a lease in respect of that estate or interest, and

(b) any rent charged on that estate or interest,

shall be correspondingly apportioned or divided so that the one part is payable in respect of, or charged on, only one part of the estate or interest and the other part is payable in respect of, or charged on, only the other part of the estate or interest.

(3) Sub-paragraph (2) above shall apply, with any necessary modifications, in relation to any feuduty payable in respect of an estate or interest in land in Scotland as it applies in relation to any rents charged on an estate or interest in land.

(4) Any property, right or liability comprised as mentioned in sub-paragraph (2) above the nature of which does not permit its division or apportionment as so mentioned shall be transferred to the transferee or retained by the transferor according to—

(a) in the case of an estate or interest in land, whether on the transfer date the transferor or the transferee appears to be in greater need of the security afforded by that estate or interest or, where neither appears to be in greater need of that security, whether on that date the transferor or the transferee appears likely to make use of the land to the greater extent,

(b) in the case of any other property or any right or liability, whether on the transfer date the transferor or the transferee appears likely to make use of the property, or as the case may be to be affected by the right or liability, to the greater extent,

subject (in either case) to such arrangements for the protection of the other of them as may be agreed between them.

2.—(1) It shall be the duty of the transferor and the transferee, whether before or after the transfer date, so far as practicable to arrive at such written agreements and to execute such other instruments as are necessary or expedient to identify or define the property, rights and liabilities transferred to the transferee or retained by the transferor and as will—

(a) afford to the transferor and the transferee as against one another such rights and safeguards as they may require for the proper discharge of their respective functions; and

(b) make as from such date, not being earlier than the transfer date, as may be specified in the agreement or instrument such clarification and modifications of the division of the transferor's undertaking as will best serve the proper discharge of the respective functions of the transferor and the transferee.

(2) Any such agreement shall provide so far as it is expedient—

(a) for the granting of leases and for the creation of other liabilities and rights over land whether amounting in law to interests in land or not, and whether involving the surrender of any existing interest or the creation of a new interest or not;

(b) for the granting of indemnities in connection with the severance of leases and other matters; and

(c) for responsibility for registration of any matter in any statutory register.

(3) If the transferor or the transferee represents to the Secretary of State, or if it appears to the Secretary of State without such a representation, that it is unlikely in the case of any matter on which agreement is required under sub-paragraph (1) above that such agreement will be reached, the Secretary of State may, whether before or after the transfer date, give a direction determining that matter and may include in the direction any provision which might have been included in an agreement under sub-paragraph (1) above; and any property, rights or liabilities required by the direction to be transferred to the transferee shall accordingly be regarded as having been transferred to, and vested in, the transferee by virtue of the scheme.

Variation of transfers by agreement

3.—(1) The provisions of this paragraph shall have effect where a transfer to which this Schedule applies is a transfer by virtue of a transfer scheme made otherwise than under section 86 of this Act.

(2) At any time before the end of the period of twelve months beginning with the transfer date, the transferor and the transferee of the specified part may, with the approval of the Secretary of State, agree in writing that—

(a) as from such date as may be specified in or determined under the agreement, and

(b) in such circumstances (if any) as may be so specified,

there shall be transferred from the transferee to, and vested in, the transferor any property, rights and liabilities specified in the agreement; but no such agreement shall have effect in relation to rights and liabilities under a contract of employment unless the employee concerned is a party to the agreement.

(3) Subject to sub-paragraphs (4) and (5) below, in the case of an agreement under sub-paragraph (2) above, the property, rights and liabilities in question shall be transferred and vest in accordance with the agreement.

(4) Any transfer effected in pursuance of an agreement under sub-paragraph (2) above shall have effect subject to the provisions of any enactment which provides for such transactions to be registered in any statutory register.

(5) The following provisions of this Schedule shall have effect as if—

(a) any reference to a transfer to which this Schedule applies included a reference to a transfer effected in pursuance of an agreement under sub-paragraph (2) above;

(b) any reference to a transaction effected in pursuance of paragraph 2(1) above or of a direction under paragraph 2(3) above included a reference to such an agreement; and

SCH. 8

(c) any reference to a vesting by virtue of a transfer scheme included a reference to a vesting by virtue of such an agreement.

Right to production of documents of title

4.—(1) This paragraph applies where, on any transfer to which this Schedule applies, the transferor is entitled to retain possession of any document relating in part to the title to, or to the management of, any land or other property transferred to the transferee.

(2) Where the land or other property is situated in England and Wales—

(a) the transferor shall be deemed to have given to the transferee an acknowledgement in writing of the right of the transferee to production of that document and to delivery of copies of it; and

(b) section 64 of the Law of Property Act 1925 shall have effect accordingly, and on the basis that the acknowledgement did not contain any such expression of contrary intention as is mentioned in that section.

1925 c.20.

(3) Where the land or other property is situated in Scotland, subsections (1) and (2) of section 16 of the Land Registration (Scotland) Act 1979 (omission of certain clauses in deeds) shall have effect in relation to the transfer as if the transfer had been effected by deed and as if from each of those subsections the words "unless specially qualified" were omitted.

1979 c. 33.

(4) Where the land or other property is situated in Northern Ireland—

(a) the transferor shall be deemed to have given to the transferee an acknowledgement in writing of the right of the transferee to production of that document and to delivery of copies of it; and

(b) section 9 of the Conveyancing Act 1881 (which corresponds to section 64 of the Law of Property Act 1925) shall have effect accordingly, and on the basis that the acknowledgement did not contain any such expression of contrary intention as is mentioned in that section.

1881 c. 41.

Perfection of vesting of foreign property, rights and liabilities

5.—(1) This paragraph applies in any case where a transfer scheme provides for the transfer of any foreign property, rights or liabilities.

(2) It shall be the duty of the transferor and the transferee to take, as and when the transferee considers appropriate, all such steps as may be requisite to secure that the vesting in the transferee by virtue of the transfer scheme of any foreign property, right or liability is effective under the relevant foreign law.

(3) Until the vesting in the transferee by virtue of the transfer scheme of any foreign property, right or liability is effective under the relevant foreign law, it shall be the duty of the transferor to hold that property or right for the benefit of, or to discharge that liability on behalf of, the transferee.

(4) Nothing in sub-paragraphs (2) and (3) above shall be taken as prejudicing the effect under the law of the United Kingdom or of any part of the United Kingdom of the vesting in the transferee by virtue of a transfer scheme of any foreign property, right or liability.

(5) The transferor shall have all such powers as may be requisite for the performance of his duty under this paragraph, but it shall be the duty of the transferee to act on behalf of the transferor (so far as possible) in performing the duty imposed on the transferor by this paragraph.

(6) References in this paragraph to any foreign property, right or liability are references to any property, right or liability as respects which any issue arising in any proceedings would have been determined (in accordance with the rules of private international law) by reference to the law of a country or territory outside the United Kingdom.

(7) Duties imposed on the transferor or the transferee by this paragraph shall be enforceable in the same way as if the duties were imposed by a contract between the transferor and the transferee.

(8) Any expenses incurred by the transferor under this paragraph shall be met by the transferee.

Proof of title by certificate

6.—(1) In the case of any transfer to which this Schedule applies, a joint certificate by or on behalf of the transferor and the transferee that—

(a) any property specified in the certificate, or

(b) any such interest in or right over any such property as may be so specified, or

(c) any right or liability so specified,

is property, or (as the case may be) an interest, right or liability which was intended to be, and was vested by virtue of the scheme in such one of them as may be so specified (and, if it is the transferee who is so specified, that the property, interest, right or liability has not been transferred back to the transferor by virtue of an agreement under paragraph 3(2) above) shall be conclusive evidence for all purposes of that fact.

(2) If on the expiration of one month after a request from either the transferor or the transferee for the preparation of such a joint certificate as respects any property, interest, right or liability they have failed to agree on the terms of the certificate, they shall refer the matter to the Secretary of State and issue the certificate in such terms as he may direct.

(3) This paragraph is without prejudice to paragraph 14(6) and (7) below.

Restrictions on dealing with certain land

7.—(1) If the Secretary of State is satisfied on the representation of the transferor or the transferee—

(a) that, in consequence of a transfer to which this Schedule applies, different interests in land, whether the same or different land, are held by the transferor and by the transferee, and

(b) that the circumstances are such that this paragraph should have effect,

the Secretary of State may direct that this paragraph shall apply to such of that land as may be specified in the direction.

(2) While the direction mentioned in sub-paragraph (1) above remains in force—

(a) neither the transferor nor the transferee shall dispose of any interest to which they may respectively be entitled in any of the specified land, except with the consent of the Secretary of State;

(b) if, in connection with any proposal to dispose of any interest of either the transferor or the transferee in any of the specified land, it appears to the Secretary of State to be necessary or expedient for the protection of either of them, he may—

(i) require either the transferor or the transferee to dispose of any interest to which he may be entitled in any of the specified land to such person and in such manner as may be specified in the requirement;

(ii) require either the transferor or the transferee to acquire from the other any interest in any of the specified land to which that other is entitled; or

(iii) consent to the proposed disposal subject to compliance with such conditions as the Secretary of State may see fit to impose.

(3) A person other than the transferor and the transferee dealing with, or with a person claiming under, either the transferor or the transferee shall not be concerned—

(a) to see or enquire whether this paragraph applies, or has applied, in relation to any land to which the dealing relates; or

(b) as to whether the provisions of this paragraph have been complied with in connection with that, or any other, dealing with that land;

and no transaction between a person other than the transferor or the transferee on the one hand, and the transferor, the transferee or a person claiming under either of them on the other, shall be invalid by reason of any failure to comply with those provisions.

Construction of agreements, statutory provisions and documents

8.—(1) This paragraph applies where, in the case of any transfer to which this Schedule applies, any rights or liabilities transferred are rights or liabilities under an agreement to which the transferor was a party immediately before the transfer date, whether in writing or not, and whether or not of such nature that rights and liabilities under the agreement could be assigned by the transferor.

(2) So far as relating to property, rights or liabilities transferred to the transferee, the agreement shall have effect on and after the transfer date as if—

(a) the transferee had been the party to it;

(b) for any reference (whether express or implied and, if express, however worded) to the transferor there were substituted, as respects anything falling to be done on or after the transfer date, a reference to the transferee;

(c) any reference (whether express or implied and, if express, however worded) to a person employed by, or engaged in the business of, the transferor and holding a specified office or serving in a specified capacity were, as respects anything falling to be done on or after the transfer date, a reference to such a person as the transferee may appoint or, in default of appointment, to a person employed by, or engaged in the business of, the transferee who corresponds as nearly as may be to the first-mentioned person;

(d) any reference in general terms (however worded) to persons employed by, persons engaged in the business of, or agents of, the transferor were, as respects anything to be done on or after the transfer date, a reference to persons employed by, persons engaged in the business of, or agents of, the transferee.

9.—(1) Except as otherwise provided in any provision of this Act (whether expressly or by necessary implication), paragraph 8 above shall, so far as applicable, apply in relation to—

(a) any statutory provision,

(b) any provision of an agreement to which the transferor was not a party, and

(c) any provision of a document other than an agreement,

if and so far as the provision in question relates to any of the transferred property, rights and liabilities, as it applies in relation to an agreement to which the transferor was a party.

(2) In relation to any such statutory or other provision as is mentioned in sub-paragraph (1) above, references in sub-paragraph (2)(b), (c) and (d) of paragraph 8 above to the transferor and to any persons employed by, persons engaged in the business of, or agents of, the transferor include references made by means of a general reference to a class of persons of which the transferor is one, without the transferor himself being specifically referred to.

Sch. 8

1962 c. 46.

10. On and after the transfer date for any transfer to which this Schedule applies, any statutory provision to which paragraph 2(3) of Schedule 6 to the Transport Act 1962 applies if and so far as the provision in question relates to any of the transferred property, rights and liabilities, shall have effect as if—

(a) any of the references modified by paragraph (a) of the said paragraph 2(3) were, as respects anything falling to be done on or after the transfer date, a reference to such person as the transferee may appoint; and

(b) any of the references modified by paragraph (b) of the said paragraph 2(3) were, as respects a period beginning with the transfer date, a reference to so much of the undertaking of the transferee as corresponds as mentioned in the said paragraph (b).

11.—(1) The transferee under a transfer to which this Schedule applies and any other person shall, as from the transfer date, have the same rights, powers and remedies (and in particular the same rights and powers as to the taking or resisting of legal proceedings or the making or resisting of applications to any authority) for ascertaining, perfecting or enforcing any right or liability vested in the transferee by virtue of the scheme as he would have had if that right or liability had at all times been a right or liability of the transferee.

(2) Any legal proceedings or applications to any authority pending on the transfer date by or against the transferor, in so far as they relate—

(a) to any property, right or liability vested in the transferee by virtue of the scheme, or

(b) to any agreement or enactment relating to any such property, right or liability,

shall be continued by or against the transferee to the exclusion of the transferor.

(3) This paragraph is without prejudice to the generality of the provisions of paragraphs 8 to 10 above.

12. If, in the case of any transfer to which this Schedule applies, the effect of any agreement (and, in particular, any agreement under the Railway Road Transport Acts of 1928 mentioned in paragraph 1 of Part II of Schedule 2 to the Transport Act 1962)—

(a) which was executed before the passing of this Act, and

(b) to which the transferee is by virtue of this Act a party,

1968 c. 73.

depends on whether the transferee has power to carry on any activity, it shall be assumed for the purposes of the agreement that any activity which requires the consent of the Secretary of State under the Transport Act 1962 or the Transport Act 1968 has been authorised by such a consent.

13.—(1) References in paragraphs 8 to 12 above to agreements to which the transferor was a party and to statutory provisions include, in particular, references to agreements to which the transferor became a party by virtue of the Transport Act 1962 and statutory provisions which applied to the transferor by virtue of that Act.

(2) The provisions of paragraphs 8 to 12 above shall have effect for the interpretation of agreements, statutory provisions and other instruments subject to the context, and shall not apply where the context otherwise requires.

Third parties affected by vesting provisions

14.—(1) Without prejudice to the provisions of paragraphs 8 to 13 above, any transaction effected between the transferor and the transferee in pursuance of paragraph 2(1) above or of a direction under paragraph 2(3) above shall be binding on all other persons, and notwithstanding that it would, apart from this sub-paragraph, have required the consent or concurrence of any other person.

SCH. 8

(2) It shall be the duty of the transferor and the transferee, if they effect any transaction in pursuance of paragraph 2(1) above or a direction under paragraph 2(3) above, to notify any person who has rights or liabilities which thereby become enforceable as to part by or against the transferor and as to part by or against the transferee; and if, within 28 days of being notified, such a person applies to the Secretary of State and satisfies him that the transaction operated unfairly against him, the Secretary of State may give such directions to the transferor and the transferee as appear to him appropriate for varying the transaction.

(3) If in consequence of a transfer to which this Schedule applies or of anything done in pursuance of the provisions of this Schedule—

   (a) the rights or liabilities of any person other than the transferor and the transferee which are enforceable against or by the transferor become enforceable as to part against or by the transferor and as to part against or by the transferee, and

   (b) the value of any property or interest of that person is thereby diminished,

such compensation as may be just shall be paid to that person by the transferor, the transferee or both.

(4) If it appears to the transferor that a person is or may be entitled to compensation under sub-paragraph (3) above, he shall—

   (a) notify that person that he is or may be so entitled, and

   (b) invite him to make such representations as he wishes to the transferor not later than fourteen days after the date of issue of the document containing the notification required by paragraph (a) above,

or, if the transferor is not aware of the name and address of the person concerned, shall publish, in such manner as he considers appropriate, a notice containing information about the interest affected and inviting any person who thinks that he is or may be entitled to compensation to make such representations to the transferor within such period (being not less than 28 days from the date of publication of the notice) as may be specified in the notice.

(5) Any dispute as to whether any, and (if so) how much, compensation is payable under sub-paragraph (3) above, or as to the person to or by whom it shall be paid, shall be referred to and determined by—

   (a) an arbitrator appointed by the President for the time being of the Royal Institution of Chartered Surveyors, or

   (b) where the proceedings are to be held in Scotland, an arbiter appointed by the Lord President of the Court of Session, or

   (c) where the proceedings are to be held in Northern Ireland, an arbitrator appointed by the Lord Chancellor.

(6) Where, in the case of a transfer to which this Schedule applies, the transferor or the transferee purports by any conveyance or transfer to transfer to some person other than the transferor or the transferee for consideration any land or any other property transferred—

   (a) which before the transfer date belonged to the transferor, or

   (b) which is an interest in property which before that date belonged to the transferor,

the conveyance or transfer shall be as effective as if both the transferor and the transferee had been parties to it and had thereby conveyed or transferred all their interests in the property conveyed or transferred.

SCH. 8

(7) Sub-paragraph (6) above applies in relation to the grant of any lease of, or any other estate or interest in, or right over any such land or other property as is there mentioned as it applies in relation to a transfer of any such land or other property; and references in that sub-paragraph to a conveyance or transfer shall be construed accordingly.

(8) If, in the case of any transfer to which this Schedule applies, it appears to the court at any stage in any court proceedings to which the transferor or the transferee and a person other than the transferor or the transferee are parties that the issues in the proceedings—

(a) depend on the identification or definition of any of the property, rights or liabilities transferred which the transferor and the transferee have not yet effected, or

(b) raise a question of construction on the relevant provisions of this Act which would not arise if the transferor and the transferee constituted a single person,

the court may, if it thinks fit on the application of a party to the proceedings other than the transferor and the transferee, hear and determine the proceedings on the footing that such one of the transferor and the transferee as is a party to the proceedings represents and is answerable for the other of them, and that the transferor and the transferee constitute a single person, and any judgment or order given by the court shall bind both the transferor and the transferee accordingly.

(9) In the case of any transfer to which this Schedule applies, it shall be the duty of the transferor and the transferee to keep one another informed of any case where either of them may be prejudiced by sub-paragraph (6), (7) or (8) above, and if either the transferor or the transferee claims that he has been so prejudiced and that the other of them ought to indemnify or make a repayment to him on that account and has unreasonably failed to meet that claim, he may refer the matter to the Secretary of State for determination by him.

Interpretation

15. In this Schedule "statutory provision" means a provision whether of a general or of a special nature contained in, or in any document made or issued under, any Act, whether of a general or a special nature.

Section 112.

SCHEDULE 9

STAMP DUTY AND STAMP DUTY RESERVE TAX

Interpretation

1.—(1) In this Schedule—

"the Inland Revenue" means the Commissioners of Inland Revenue;

"restructuring scheme" means a transfer scheme, if and to the extent that it provides for the transfer of property, rights or liabilities from a body or person falling within any of paragraphs (a) to (e) of section 85(1) of this Act to another such body or person.

(2) For the purposes of this Schedule a transfer, instrument or agreement shall be regarded as made in pursuance of Schedule 8 to this Act if the making of that transfer, instrument or agreement is required or authorised by or under paragraph 2 or 3 of that Schedule.

Stamp duty

2.—(1) Stamp duty shall not be chargeable on any restructuring scheme which is certified to the Inland Revenue by the Secretary of State as made by him or as made pursuant to a direction given by him under this Act.

(2) Stamp duty shall not be chargeable on any instrument or agreement which is certified to the Inland Revenue by the Secretary of State as made in pursuance of Schedule 8 to this Act, in connection with a restructuring scheme made—

(a) by the Secretary of State; or

(b) pursuant to a direction given by him under this Act.

(3) Stamp duty shall not be chargeable on any instrument or agreement which is certified to the Inland Revenue by the Secretary of State—

(a) as made pursuant to an obligation imposed by any provision included, by virtue of section 91(1)(c) of this Act, in a restructuring scheme made by—

(i) the Secretary of State;

(ii) the Board, pursuant to a direction given by the Secretary of State under this Act; or

(iii) the Franchising Director, pursuant to a direction so given; and

(b) as operating in favour of no person who does not fall within paragraphs (a) to (e) of section 85(1) of this Act.

(4) Stamp duty shall not be chargeable on any instrument or agreement which is certified to the Inland Revenue by the Secretary of State as being a transfer, or an agreement for the transfer, to the Board or any of the Board's subsidiaries of property, rights or liabilities of the Board or any such subsidiary, made for the purpose of facilitating a disposal required to be made pursuant to a direction given by him under this Act.

(5) No restructuring scheme or other instrument or agreement which is certified as mentioned in any of sub-paragraphs (1) to (4) above shall be taken to be duly stamped unless—

(a) it is stamped with the duty to which it would be liable, apart from the sub-paragraph in question; or

(b) it has, in accordance with section 12 of the Stamp Act 1891, been stamped with a particular stamp denoting that it is not chargeable with that duty or that it is duly stamped.

1891 c. 39.

(6) Section 12 of the Finance Act 1895 (collection of stamp duty in cases of property vested by Act or purchased under statutory power) shall not operate to require—

(a) the delivery to the Inland Revenue of a copy of this Act, or

(b) the payment of stamp duty under that section on any copy of this Act,

and shall not apply in relation to any instrument on which, by virtue of the preceding provisions of this paragraph, stamp duty is not chargeable.

Stamp duty reserve tax

3.—(1) An agreement to transfer chargeable securities, as defined in section 99 of the Finance Act 1986, to a person falling within paragraphs (a) to (e) of section 85(1) of this Act shall not give rise to a charge to stamp duty reserve tax if the agreement is made for the purposes of, or for purposes connected with, a restructuring scheme made—

1986 c. 41.

(a) by the Secretary of State;

SCH. 9

  (b) by the Board, pursuant to a direction given by the Secretary of State under this Act; or

  (c) by the Franchising Director, pursuant to a direction so given.

(2) An agreement shall not give rise to a charge to stamp duty reserve tax if the agreement is made in pursuance of Schedule 8 to this Act in connection with a restructuring scheme made as mentioned in paragraph (a), (b) or (c) of sub-paragraph (1) above.

Section 132.

SCHEDULE 10

TRANSPORT POLICE: CONSEQUENTIAL PROVISIONS

The British Transport Commission Act 1949

1949 c. xxix.

1.—(1) Section 53 of the British Transport Commission Act 1949 (which makes provision in relation to transport police, including provision with respect to their appointment, dismissal and resignation) shall in its application to England and Wales be amended in accordance with the provisions of this paragraph.

(2) For subsection (1) of that section, other than the proviso, there shall be substituted—

  "(1) Subject to the provisions of subsection (2) of this section, any two justices may, on the application of the British Railways Board acting in pursuance of a scheme made by the Secretary of State under section 132 of the Railways Act 1993, appoint all or so many as they think fit of the persons recommended to them for that purpose by that Board acting as aforesaid to act as constables throughout England and Wales:".

(3) In the proviso to that subsection, for the words "by any of the Boards" there shall be substituted the words "by—

  "(a) the British Railways Board; or

  (b) any person who is a party to an agreement with that Board for making available to that person the services of constables so appointed."

2.—(1) The said section 53 shall in its application to Scotland be amended in accordance with the provisions of this paragraph.

(2) In subsection (1) of that section, for the definition of the approved scheme there shall be substituted—

  ""the approved scheme" means the scheme in force for the organisation of the transport police made by the Secretary of State under section 132 of the Railways Act 1993;".

(3) In subsection (4)(a), for the words "by any of the Boards or their wholly owned subsidiaries" there shall be substituted the words "by—

  (i) any of the Boards or their wholly owned subsidiaries; or

  (ii) any person who is a party to an agreement with the British Railways Board for making available to that person the services of constables so appointed."

The Transport Act 1962

1962 c. 46.

3.—(1) In the Transport Act 1962, sections 69 (organisation of transport police), 70 (adaptation of certain references to, and relating to, transport police constables) and 71 (terms and conditions of employment of transport police) shall cease to have effect.

SCH. 10

(2) Unless and until the Secretary of State by order revokes the British Transport Police Force Scheme 1963, that Scheme shall continue in force and shall be treated as if it had been made under section 132 of this Act; but the Secretary of State may, after consultation with the Board and with—

    (a) persons to whom the Board is for the time being making available the services of transport police, or

    (b) such bodies or persons appearing to the Secretary of State to be representative of those persons as he may consider appropriate,

by order make such amendments in that Scheme as he thinks fit.

(3) In sub-paragraph (2) above, "the British Transport Police Force Scheme 1963" means the scheme for the organisation of transport police which is set out in the Second Schedule to the British Transport Police Force Scheme 1963 (Amendment) Order 1992 (being an order amending that scheme as it was set out in the Schedule to the British Transport Police Force Scheme 1963 (Approval) Order 1964).

S.I.1992/364.

S.I.1964/1456.

SCHEDULE 11

Section 134.

Pensions

Interpretation

1.—(1) In this Schedule—

    "eligible persons", in the case of any pension scheme, means—

        (a) any person who is an employee of—

            (i) the Board or any subsidiary of the Board, or

            (ii) a publicly owned railway company or a franchise company, and

        (b) any other person whose membership of that scheme would not prejudice any approval of the scheme for the purposes of Chapter I of Part XIV of the Income and Corporation Taxes Act 1988 (retirement benefit schemes),

1988 c. 1.

    but does not include any such person as is mentioned in paragraph (a) above who participates in the Transport Police scheme;

    "employment" means employment under a contract of service or apprenticeship (whether express or implied and, if express, whether oral or in writing), and cognate expressions shall be construed accordingly;

    "existing scheme" means any occupational pension scheme (other than a new scheme)—

        (a) which is a scheme for the provision of pensions for or in respect of persons with service in the railway industry (whether or not pensions may also be provided under the scheme for or in respect of persons without such service); and

        (b) which the Secretary of State by order designates as an existing scheme for the purposes of this Schedule;

    "the joint industry scheme" means such occupational pension scheme as the Secretary of State may by order designate as the joint industry scheme for the purposes of this Schedule;

    "member", in relation to a pension scheme, means—

        (a) any person who participates in that scheme;

        (b) any pensioner under that scheme; and

SCH. 11

(c) any other person who has pension rights under that scheme;

and "membership" shall be construed accordingly;

"new scheme" means an occupational pension scheme established under paragraph 2 below;

1993 c. 48.
"occupational pension scheme" has the meaning given in section 1 of the Pension Schemes Act 1993;

"participant", in relation to a pension scheme or a section of a pension scheme, means a person to whom pension rights are accruing under the scheme or section by virtue of his employment in a class or description of employment to which the scheme or section relates; and cognate expressions shall be construed accordingly;

"pension", in relation to any person, means a pension of any kind payable to or in respect of him, and includes a lump sum, allowance or gratuity so payable and a return of contributions, with or without interest or any other addition;

"pension rights", in relation to any person, includes—

(a) all forms of right to or eligibility for the present or future payment of a pension to or in respect of him; and

(b) a right of allocation in respect of the present or future payment of a pension;

"prescribed" means specified in, or determined in accordance with, an order made by the Secretary of State;

"protected person" has the meaning given by paragraph 5 below;

"the Transport Police scheme" means such one of the schemes for the provision of pensions for or in respect of persons with service as officers of the British Transport Police Force (whether or not pensions may also be provided under the scheme for or in respect of persons without such service) as the Secretary of State may by order designate as the Transport Police scheme for the purposes of this Schedule;

"trustees", in relation to any pension scheme, includes a reference to any persons who, under the rules of the scheme, are under a liability to provide pensions or other benefits but who are not trustees of the scheme.

(2) Any reference in this Schedule to a pension scheme includes a reference to the scheme as amended under or by virtue of this Schedule.

(3) Any power to make an order under or by virtue of this Schedule in relation to an existing scheme, the joint industry scheme, a new scheme, the Transport Police scheme, or a designated scheme within the meaning of paragraph 10 below shall be exercisable notwithstanding that the occupational pension scheme in question only becomes such a scheme by virtue of its establishment or designation as such in the instrument which contains the order in question; and references to such schemes shall be construed accordingly.

(4) Subject to sub-paragraph (1) above, expressions used in this Schedule and in Part I or II of this Act have the same meaning in this Schedule as they have in that Part.

Establishment of new schemes

2.—(1) The Secretary of State may by order provide for the establishment, administration and management of one or more occupational pension schemes for the provision of pensions and other benefits for or in respect of eligible persons.

(2) Without prejudice to the generality of sub-paragraph (1) above, an order under that sub-paragraph may make provision with respect to—

    (a) the persons who may participate in, or otherwise be members of, the scheme;

    (b) the making of contributions by persons participating in the scheme;

    (c) the making of contributions by employers of persons who participate in the scheme;

    (d) the amendment of the scheme;

    (e) the winding up of the scheme, whether in whole or in part;

    (f) the persons by whom any function under or relating to the scheme is to be exercisable.

(3) Any occupational pension scheme established under this paragraph shall be treated for all purposes as if it were a pension scheme established under an irrevocable trust.

Amendment of existing schemes

3.—(1) The Secretary of State may by order amend—

    (a) the trust deed of any existing scheme;

    (b) the rules of any such scheme; or

    (c) any other instrument relating to the constitution, management or operation of any such scheme;

and any reference in this Schedule to amending an existing scheme accordingly includes a reference to amending any such trust deed, rules or other instrument.

(2) Without prejudice to the generality of sub-paragraph (1) above, an order under this paragraph may, in particular, amend an existing scheme so as to alter any provision, or so as to make provision, with respect to any of the matters specified in paragraphs (a) to (f) of paragraph 2(2) above.

(3) An order under this paragraph shall not make any amendment to a scheme—

    (a) which would prejudice any approval of that scheme for the purposes of Chapter I of Part XIV of the Income and Corporation Taxes Act 1988 (retirement benefit schemes);   1988 c. 1.

    (b) which would prevent the scheme from being a contracted-out scheme for the purposes of Part III of the Pension Schemes Act 1993 or Part III of the Pension Schemes (Northern Ireland) Act 1993;   1993 c. 48.   1993 c. 49.

    (c) which would to any extent deprive a member of the scheme of pension rights which accrued to him under the scheme before the coming into force of the amendment; or

    (d) which would provide for persons who are not eligible persons to become members of the scheme.

(4) The Secretary of State shall not make an order under this paragraph except after consultation with the trustees of the occupational pension scheme to which the order relates.

Transfer of pension rights and corresponding assets and liabilities

4.—(1) Where persons with pension rights under any existing or new scheme ("the transferor scheme") are eligible to be members of another scheme ("the transferee scheme") which is either—

    (a) an existing or new scheme, or

Sch. 11

(b) the Transport Police scheme,

the Secretary of State may by order make provision for those persons to be members of the transferee scheme instead of the transferor scheme and for their pension rights under the transferor scheme to be transferred so as to become pension rights under the transferee scheme.

(2) Where any pension rights are transferred under sub-paragraph (1) above, the Secretary of State may by order make provision for—

(a) such of the assets held for the purposes of the transferor scheme, and

(b) such of the liabilities under or in relation to that scheme of any employers or trustees,

as he may consider appropriate in consequence of that transfer to be correspondingly transferred so as to become assets or, as the case may be, liabilities in relation to the transferee scheme.

(3) Where any pension rights are transferred under sub-paragraph (1) above, the Secretary of State may by order—

(a) impose on the trustees of the transferee scheme, or on the employer (if any) of the person whose pension rights are transferred, duties with respect to—

(i) the participation of that person or that employer in the scheme, or

(ii) the payment of contributions by that employer under the scheme,

in accordance with the rules of the scheme; and

(b) make provision requiring any person whose approval or consent is necessary in connection with the doing of anything required to be done by virtue of an order under this paragraph to give that approval or consent.

(4) The Secretary of State may by order make provision for the winding up of the transferor scheme, whether in whole or in part, in connection with, or in consequence of, any transfers under this paragraph.

(5) The Secretary of State shall not make an order under this paragraph except after consultation with the trustees of the occupational pension schemes which are, or are to be, the transferor scheme and the transferee scheme.

Protection of pension rights: meaning of "protected person"

5. In this Schedule "protected person" means—

(a) any person who immediately before the passing of this Act—

(i) is an employee of the Board or of a subsidiary of the Board; and

(ii) is participating in an existing scheme;

(b) any person not falling within paragraph (a) above—

(i) who either is, immediately before the passing of this Act, an employee of the Board or of a subsidiary of the Board or has at some earlier time been such an employee;

(ii) who has participated in an existing scheme before the passing of this Act; and

(iii) who fulfils prescribed conditions;

(c) any person who, immediately before the passing of this Act, has pension rights under an existing scheme but is not participating in that scheme;

(d) any person who, after the passing of this Act, acquires pension rights—

(i) in consequence of the death of a person falling within paragraph (a), (b) or (c) above, and

(ii) by virtue of the participation of that other person in an existing scheme, or in an occupational pension scheme from which pension rights of that person have been transferred, whether directly or indirectly, to an existing scheme.

The powers of protection

6.—(1) The Secretary of State may by order make provision for the purpose of protecting the interests of protected persons in respect of their pension rights.

(2) Without prejudice to the generality of sub-paragraph (1) above, an order under that sub-paragraph may make provision for the purpose of securing—

(a) that the relevant pension rights of protected persons are no less favourable as a result of—

(i) any amendment of an occupational pension scheme,

(ii) any transfer of pension rights, or

(iii) any winding up of an occupational pension scheme, in whole or in part,

than they would have been apart from the amendment, transfer or winding up, as the case may be;

(b) that a person who is a protected person by virtue of paragraph (a) or (b) of paragraph 5 above is not prevented, otherwise than by reason of either of the following events, that is to say—

(i) the continuity of his period of employment is broken, or

(ii) he voluntarily withdraws from an occupational pension scheme,

from participating in some occupational pension scheme and acquiring pension rights under that scheme which are no less favourable than those which would have been provided under his former scheme in accordance with the rules of that scheme as in force immediately before the coming into force of the order; or

(c) that the employer of a person falling within paragraph (b) above is required to provide an occupational pension scheme in which the person may participate and to which pension rights of his, and assets and liabilities relating to, or representative of, those pension rights, may be transferred;

and in paragraph (b) above "former scheme", in relation to a protected person, means the existing scheme mentioned in paragraph (a) or (b), as the case may be, of paragraph 5 above.

(3) For the purposes of this paragraph, the "relevant pension rights" of a protected person are so much of his pension rights as consist of or otherwise represent—

(a) in the case of a person who is a protected person by virtue of paragraph (a), (b) or (c) of paragraph 5 above, any pension rights which, immediately before the passing of this Act, he had under the existing scheme mentioned in the paragraph in question;

(b) in the case of a person who is a protected person by virtue of paragraph 5(a) or (b) above, any pension rights which he acquires, or has acquired, by virtue of his participation in an occupational pension scheme during the protected period in his case; and

(c) in the case of a person who is a protected person by virtue of paragraph (d) of paragraph 5 above, any pension rights which he acquires, or has acquired, after the passing of this Act and in consequence of the death of the other person mentioned in the said paragraph (d) ("the deceased"), being—

(i) pension rights under the existing scheme mentioned in that paragraph, so far as referable to pension rights which the deceased had under that scheme before the passing of this Act;

(ii) pension rights under any occupational pension scheme, so far as referable to pension rights which, before the passing of this Act, the deceased had under the existing scheme mentioned in the said paragraph (d) and which have been transferred from that existing scheme, whether directly or indirectly; or

(iii) pension rights under any occupational pension scheme, so far as referable to the participation of the deceased in that or any other occupational pension scheme during the protected period.

(4) For the purposes of sub-paragraph (3) above, "the protected period" means—

(a) in the case of a person who is a protected person by virtue of paragraph (a) of paragraph 5 above, the period beginning with the passing of this Act and ending with whichever of the following events first occurs, that is to say—

(i) the continuity of the person's period of employment is broken; or

(ii) he voluntarily withdraws from an occupational pension scheme;

(b) in the case of a person who is a protected person by virtue of paragraph (b) of paragraph 5 above, a period beginning at such time as may be prescribed and ending with whichever of the following events first occurs, that is to say—

(i) the continuity of the person's period of employment is broken; or

(ii) he voluntarily withdraws from an occupational pension scheme; and

(c) in the case of a person who is a protected person by virtue of paragraph (d) of paragraph 5 above, the period (if any) which is the protected period in the case of the other person mentioned in the said paragraph (d).

(5) In determining a person's relevant pension rights for the purposes of this paragraph, where the rules of a pension scheme make provision requiring pension rights which have accrued to a person to be enhanced in consequence of increases in remuneration after the accrual of the pension rights, that provision, and any enhancement resulting from it, shall be treated, so far as relating to any enhancement in consequence of increases in remuneration after the passing of this Act, as pension rights accruing at the time of the increase in remuneration in question.

(6) An order under this paragraph may make provision for and in connection with the making of elections in a prescribed manner by protected persons for orders under this paragraph (other than orders by virtue of this sub-paragraph) not to have effect with respect to them or their surviving dependants except to such extent (if any) as may be specified in the election or subject to such conditions (if any) as may be so specified.

(7) In sub-paragraph (6) above "surviving dependant", in relation to a protected person, means any person who may acquire, in consequence of the death of the protected person, pension rights referable to relevant pension rights of the protected person.

(8) An order under this paragraph may make provision for such orders to cease to have effect in relation to a protected person if—

(a) the continuity of his period of employment is broken,

(b) he voluntarily withdraws from an occupational pension scheme, or

SCH. 11

(c) he requests that his pension rights be transferred from an occupational pension scheme,

except in such circumstances or to such extent as may be prescribed.

(9) Circumstances may be prescribed in which—

(a) a break in the continuity of a person's period of employment, or

(b) a person's voluntary withdrawal from an occupational pension scheme,

shall be disregarded for prescribed purposes of this paragraph.

(10) Apart from paragraph 18, so much of Schedule 13 to the Employment Protection (Consolidation) Act 1978 as has effect for the purpose of ascertaining whether any period of employment is continuous shall apply for the purposes of this paragraph as it applies for the purposes of that Act, except that, in the case of an employee—

1978 c. 44.

(a) who is employed for less than sixteen hours, but for at least one hour, in any week, or

(b) whose relations with the employer are governed during the whole or part of a week by a contract of employment which normally involves employment for less than sixteen hours, but for at least one hour, weekly,

that Schedule shall so apply in relation to that employee and that week with the modifications in sub-paragraph (11) below.

(11) Those modifications are that the said Schedule 13 shall have effect—

(a) as if paragraph 3 provided for any week—

(i) during the whole or part of which the employee's relations with the employer are governed otherwise than by a contract of employment which requires him to be employed for a minimum number of hours weekly, and

(ii) in which the employee is employed for one hour or more,

to count in computing a period of employment;

(b) as if paragraph 4 provided for any week during the whole or part of which the employee's relations with the employer are governed by a contract of employment which normally involves employment for at least one hour, but for less than sixteen hours, weekly to count in computing a period of employment; and

(c) as if paragraphs 5 to 7 and, in paragraphs 9, 10 and 15, the references to paragraph 5, were omitted.

(12) Expressions used in sub-paragraph (10) or (11) above and in Schedule 13 to the Employment Protection (Consolidation) Act 1978 have the same meaning in that sub-paragraph as they have in that Schedule.

Protection: supplementary provisions

7.—(1) Without prejudice to the generality of paragraph 6 above, an order under that paragraph may impose on any person falling within sub-paragraph (2) below duties with respect to—

(a) the provision of a pension scheme,

(b) the terms of any pension scheme required to be provided by virtue of paragraph (a) above,

(c) the amendment, or the preservation from amendment, of a pension scheme,

(d) the acceptance of protected persons as members of a pension scheme,

Sch. 11

(e) the acceptance (so as to become included among the property, rights and liabilities held for the purposes of a pension scheme or to which a pension scheme is subject) of property, rights and liabilities relating to, or representative of, pension rights of protected persons,

(f) the making or refunding of contributions,

(g) the purchase of annuities,

(h) the winding up of a pension scheme, in whole or in part,

and may make provision requiring any person whose approval or consent is necessary in connection with the doing of anything required to be done by virtue of such an order, so far as relating to matters specified in paragraphs (a) to (h) above, to give that approval or consent.

(2) The persons mentioned in sub-paragraph (1) above are—

(a) any person who is or has been the employer of a protected person;

(b) any person who contributes to a pension scheme as an employer, whether or not he is or has been the employer of a protected person;

(c) the trustees of any pension scheme of which a protected person is a member or to which pension rights of a protected person may be transferred;

(d) any person who has power to amend or wind up a pension scheme under which a protected person has pension rights.

(3) An order under paragraph 5 or 6 above may include provision—

(a) for disputes arising under the order to be referred to arbitration; or

(b) for provisions of the order to be enforceable on an application made to a prescribed court by the Secretary of State or by a prescribed person or a person of a prescribed description.

Entitlement to participate in the joint industry scheme

8.—(1) The Secretary of State may by order make provision conferring upon any person to whom this paragraph applies—

(a) who is participating, or who at or after the making of the order begins to participate, in the joint industry scheme, and

(b) who fulfils the qualifying conditions,

the right to continue to participate in the joint industry scheme, in accordance with the rules of that scheme, unless and until the termination conditions become fulfilled in the case of that person.

(2) The persons to whom this paragraph applies are—

(a) any person who immediately before the passing of this Act—

(i) is an employee of the Board or of a subsidiary of the Board; and

(ii) is participating in an existing scheme; and

(b) any person not falling within paragraph (a) above—

(i) who either is, immediately before the passing of this Act, an employee of the Board or of a subsidiary of the Board or has at some earlier time been such an employee;

(ii) who has participated in an existing scheme before the passing of this Act; and

(iii) who fulfils prescribed conditions.

(3) For the purposes of this paragraph a person fulfils the "qualifying conditions" if—

(a) the continuity of his period of employment has not been broken during the intervening period;

Sch. 11

(b) he has not withdrawn voluntarily from an occupational pension scheme during that period; and

(c) he has at all times during that period been in the employment of an employer engaged in the railway industry.

(4) In sub-paragraph (3) above, the "intervening period" means the period which begins at the passing of this Act and ends—

(a) at the time when the person in question begins to participate in the joint industry scheme, or

(b) at the coming into force of the order under this paragraph which confers upon that person the right mentioned in sub-paragraph (1) above (or which would have conferred that right upon him, had he satisfied the qualifying conditions),

whichever is the later.

(5) The "termination conditions" become fulfilled for the purposes of this paragraph in the case of any person if—

(a) the continuity of his period of employment is broken;

(b) he withdraws voluntarily from the joint industry scheme; or

(c) he is not in the employment of any employer engaged in the railway industry.

(6) Circumstances may be prescribed in which—

(a) a break in the continuity of a person's period of employment,

(b) a person's voluntary withdrawal from an occupational pension scheme, or

(c) a period during which a person is not in the employment of an employer engaged in the railway industry,

shall be disregarded for the purpose of determining whether the person fulfils the qualifying conditions or whether the termination conditions have become fulfilled in his case.

(7) The employers who are to be regarded for the purposes of this paragraph as "engaged in the railway industry" are those who carry on activities of a class or description specified for the purposes of this sub-paragraph by the Secretary of State in an order under this paragraph; and the Secretary of State may so specify any class or description of activity which, in his opinion, falls within, or is related to or connected with, the railway industry.

(8) An order under this paragraph may—

(a) impose on the trustees of the joint industry scheme, or on the employer (if any) of a person for the time being entitled to the right conferred by virtue of sub-paragraph (1) above, duties with respect to—

(i) the participation of that person or that employer in the scheme, or

(ii) the payment of contributions by that employer under the scheme,

in accordance with the rules of the scheme; and

(b) make provision requiring any person whose approval or consent is necessary in connection with the doing of anything required to be done by virtue of an order under this paragraph to give that approval or consent.

(9) An order under this paragraph may make provision for the purpose of preventing a person who would otherwise be entitled to the right conferred by virtue of sub-paragraph (1) above from continuing to participate in the joint industry scheme in circumstances where his continued participation in that scheme would in the opinion of a prescribed person—

SCH. 11

1988 c. 1.

    (a) prejudice any approval of that scheme for the purposes of Chapter I of Part XIV of the Income and Corporation Taxes Act 1988 (retirement benefit schemes); or

1993 c. 48.
1993 c. 49.

    (b) prevent the scheme from being a contracted-out scheme for the purposes of Part III of the Pension Schemes Act 1993 or Part III of the Pension Schemes (Northern Ireland) Act 1993.

(10) An order under this paragraph may include provision—

    (a) for disputes arising under the order to be referred to arbitration; or

    (b) for provisions of the order to be enforceable on an application made to a prescribed court by the Secretary of State or by a prescribed person or a person of a prescribed description.

(11) An order under this paragraph may make provision for and in connection with the making of elections in a prescribed manner by persons who would otherwise be entitled by virtue of sub-paragraph (1) above to the right there mentioned for orders under this paragraph (other than orders by virtue of this sub-paragraph) not to have effect with respect to them.

(12) Sub-paragraph (10) of paragraph 6 above shall have effect for the purposes of this paragraph as it has effect for the purposes of that paragraph.

Payments in discharge of liabilities under s.52(1) of the Transport Act 1980

1980 c. 34.

9.—(1) In section 52 of the Transport Act 1980, in subsection (1) (which requires the Secretary of State to make payments each year to B.R. pension schemes in respect of unfunded pension obligations owed by the Board), for the words "Subject to the provisions of this section and section 58," there shall be substituted the words "Subject to the provisions of this section and sections 52A to 52D and 58,".

(2) After that section there shall be inserted—

"Power to make payments by way of final discharge of liabilities under s.52(1).

52A.—(1) If the Minister is desirous of making to the persons administering a B.R. pension scheme one or more payments by way of final discharge of his liability to make payments to them under section 52(1) in relation to that scheme, to the extent that that liability relates to so much of the relevant pension obligations as are owed in respect of—

    (a) all pension rights under the scheme,

    (b) pension rights of some particular class or description under the scheme, or

    (c) pension rights of persons of some particular class or description under the scheme,

he may give to the persons administering the scheme a notice identifying the pension rights in question and specifying in relation to those pension rights the matters set out in subsection (2), as determined in accordance with the following provisions of this section.

(2) The matters mentioned in subsection (1) are—

    (a) the capital value of the attributable unfunded obligations in question, as at the beginning of the next financial year;

    (b) the amount or amounts, or the method of determining the amount or amounts, of the payment or payments to be made under this section by way of final discharge of the Minister's liability to make payments under section 52(1), so far as relating to the pension rights identified in the notice under subsection (1); and

SCH. 11

(c) the date or dates on which that payment or those payments are to be made.

(3) In making any determination for the purposes of paragraph (b) of subsection (2), the amount or, as the case may be, the aggregate of the amounts mentioned in that paragraph shall be such as to include—

(a) a sum equal to the capital value determined under paragraph (a) of that subsection; and

(b) interest, payable at such rate as may be determined by the Minister, on so much (if any) of that sum as may from time to time be outstanding after the beginning of the financial year mentioned in the said paragraph (a).

(4) For the purposes of this section, the capital value mentioned in paragraph (a) of subsection (2) shall either—

(a) be determined by the Minister, or

(b) if the Minister so requires in the particular case, be determined by the actuary to the scheme in question and approved by the Minister,

and it shall be for the Minister to determine the matters mentioned in paragraphs (b) and (c) of that subsection.

(5) Notice under subsection (1) above shall only be given after consultation—

(a) with the persons administering the scheme in question; and

(b) with the actuary to that scheme, except in a case where the capital value mentioned in subsection (2)(a) is determined by that actuary pursuant to subsection (4)(b);

and any such notice must be given not less than one month before the beginning of the financial year mentioned in subsection (2)(a).

(6) The giving of a notice under subsection (1) shall—

(a) terminate the liability of the Minister to make payments under section 52(1), so far as relating to the pension rights identified in the notice, for financial years beginning after the giving of the notice; and

(b) impose upon the Minister a duty—

(i) to make to the persons administering the scheme in question the payment or payments mentioned in subsection (2)(b); and

(ii) to do so at the time or times specified in pursuance of subsection (2)(c).

(7) Where notice has been given under subsection (1), the Minister may—

(a) at any time before the expiration of the period of eleven months beginning with the financial year mentioned in subsection (2)(a) as it applies in relation to that notice, and

(b) after consultation with the persons administering the scheme in question and the actuary to the scheme,

amend that notice by giving notice of the amendment to the persons administering the scheme.

SCH. 11

(8) If notice is given under subsection (7) of an amendment affecting the amount of a payment which has been made pursuant to this section, the Minister may also give notice to the persons administering the scheme in question requiring them—

(a) to repay to him so much of the payment made as exceeds the amended amount; and

(b) to pay interest to him, at such rate as he may determine, on the amount to be repaid, as from the date on which the payment in question was made by him;

and where notice is given under paragraph (a) or (b), the amount required to be repaid or, as the case may be, the amount of interest required to be paid from time to time, shall be treated as a debt due from those persons to the Minister.

(9) In any case where—

(a) notice has been given under subsection (1), the effect of which (whether taken alone or with other notices under that subsection) is that notice has been given under that subsection in respect of all pension rights under the scheme in question, and

(b) for that financial year in which the notice mentioned in paragraph (a) is given, the aggregate amount of the payments made under section 52(1) in relation to the scheme requires adjustment for the reason set out in section 52(3)(a) or (b), but

(c) the required adjustment cannot be made as mentioned in section 52(3), because (in consequence of the notice mentioned in paragraph (a)) no payments under section 52(1) fall to be made in relation to that scheme for subsequent financial years,

payments by way of adjustment, of an amount equal in the aggregate to the amount of the required adjustment, shall instead be made by the Minister to the persons administering the scheme or, as the case may require, by those persons to the Minister, before the expiration of the period of six months beginning with the date on which the amount of the required adjustment is determined.

(10) The Minister may give a direction to the persons administering a B.R. pension scheme requiring them to furnish to him—

(a) information from which the proportion mentioned in section 55(1)(a) can be finally determined for the financial year mentioned in subsection (9)(b) in the case of the scheme; or

(b) information about any such unforeseen increase or reduction in the aggregate amount of the pensions, increases and expenses payable under or incurred in connection with the scheme for that financial year as is mentioned in section 52(3)(b).

(11) Where payments by way of adjustment fall to be made under subsection (9), interest shall be payable from the end of the financial year in which the notice mentioned in subsection (9)(a) is given, by the person liable to make those payments, at such intervals and rates as may be determined by the Minister, on so much of the aggregate amount of the payments in question as for the time being remains unpaid.

SCH. 11

(12) So much of—

(a) any payment by way of adjustment under subsection (9) which falls to be made, or

(b) any interest accrued under subsection (11),

as has not been paid shall be treated as a debt due.

(13) Nothing in this section affects the liability of the Board in respect of any relevant pension obligations.

(14) For the purposes of this section, the "capital value of the attributable unfunded obligations", in the case of any B.R. pension scheme, means such amount as is, in the opinion of the person determining that capital value pursuant to subsection (4), the capital equivalent of the payments that would, apart from this section, have been expected to be made by the Minister under section 52(1), so far as relating to the pension rights identified in the notice under subsection (1), for the successive financial years beginning with the one mentioned in subsection (2)(a).

(15) Any sums required for the making of payments under this section by the Minister shall be paid out of money provided by Parliament.".

(3) After the section 52A inserted by sub-paragraph (2) above, there shall be inserted—

"Power to substitute obligations under this section for liabilities under s.52(1).

52B.—(1) The Minister may make a substitution order in relation to any occupational pension scheme—

(a) which is a new scheme, within the meaning of Schedule 11 to the Railways Act 1993;

(b) which is designated under paragraph 10(1) of that Schedule (designation of schemes which are to be treated as B.R. pension schemes for certain purposes of this Part); and

(c) in relation to which a guarantee has been given by the Secretary of State under paragraph 11 of that Schedule;

and any reference in this section to a "guaranteed pension scheme" is a reference to such an occupational pension scheme.

(2) The Minister may also make a substitution order in relation to any section of a new scheme, within the meaning of Schedule 11 to the Railways Act 1993, if the section is one—

(a) which is designated under paragraph 10(1) of that Schedule; and

(b) in relation to which a guarantee has been given by the Secretary of State under paragraph 11 of that Schedule;

and the following provisions of this section (and sections 52C and 52D) shall apply in relation to any such section of a new scheme as if any reference to a guaranteed pension scheme included a reference to such a section.

(3) For the purposes of this section, a "substitution order" is an order under this section the effect of which is—

(a) to terminate, from the termination date, the Minister's liability to make to the persons administering the guaranteed pension scheme in question payments under section 52(1) in relation to the scheme; and

SCH. 11

(b) to impose on the Minister, in substitution for that liability, an obligation to make to those persons, subject to and in accordance with the following provisions of this section, one or more other payments (the "substitution payments") in relation to that scheme.

(4) Subject to the following provisions of this section, the amount of the substitution payments to be made in the case of a guaranteed pension scheme shall be equal in the aggregate to the sum of—

(a) the amount specified pursuant to subsection (5)(a) as the capital value of the unfunded obligations in the case of the scheme; and

(b) the aggregate amount of any interest which is dealt with as mentioned in subsection (8)(b)(ii) in the case of the scheme.

(5) A substitution order must specify—

(a) the capital value of the unfunded obligations in the case of the guaranteed pension scheme in question, as at the termination date; and

(b) the date which, for the purposes of this section, is to be the termination date in relation to that scheme, being a date not earlier than one month after the coming into force of the substitution order.

(6) Any determination for the purposes of this section of the capital value of the unfunded obligations in the case of a guaranteed pension scheme shall either—

(a) be made by the Minister; or

(b) if the Minister so requires in the particular case, be made by the actuary to the guaranteed pension scheme in question and approved by the Minister.

(7) A substitution order may specify—

(a) the amount or amounts, or the method of determining the amount or amounts, of the substitution payments,

(b) the date or dates on which the substitution payments are to be made,

(c) circumstances (which may, if the Minister so desires, be defined by reference to the opinion of any person) in which substitution payments are to be made,

and may provide for the obligation to make substitution payments to be discharged if the guaranteed pension scheme in question has, in the opinion of a person specified or described in, or nominated under, the order, been wound up.

(8) A substitution order must provide—

(a) for interest to accrue from the termination date on the outstanding balance of the capital value for the time being at such rate, and at such intervals, as may be specified in, or determined under or in accordance with, the order; and

(b) for any such interest which accrues—

(i) to be paid to the persons administering the guaranteed pension scheme in question, or

SCH. 11

(ii) to be added to the outstanding balance of the capital value,

(or to be dealt with partly in one of those ways and partly in the other);

and the provision that may be made by virtue of paragraph (a) includes provision for the rate of interest to be calculated by reference to any variable or to be such rate as the Minister may from time to time determine and specify in a notice to the persons administering the scheme in question.

(9) For the purposes of subsection (8), the "outstanding balance of the capital value", in the case of a guaranteed pension scheme, means the capital value of the unfunded obligations in the case of the scheme, as specified pursuant to subsection (5)(a),—

(a) reduced by the amount of any substitution payments made in relation to that scheme; and

(b) increased by any additions of accrued interest under or by virtue of subsection (8)(b)(ii) in relation to that scheme.

(10) Nothing in this section affects the liability of the Board in respect of any relevant pension obligations.

(11) Any sums required for the making of payments under this section by the Minister shall be paid out of money provided by Parliament.

(12) In this section—

"the capital value of the unfunded obligations", in the case of any guaranteed pension scheme, means such amount as is, in the opinion of the person determining that capital value pursuant to subsection (6), the capital equivalent of the payments that would, apart from this section, have been expected to be made by the Minister under section 52(1) in relation to that scheme after the termination date in the case of that scheme;

"occupational pension scheme" means an occupational pension scheme as defined in section 1 of the Pension Schemes Act 1993;

1993 c. 48.

"the terminal period", in the case of any guaranteed pension scheme, means—

(a) if a financial year of the scheme ends with the termination date, that financial year; or

(b) in any other case, so much of the financial year of the scheme in which the termination date falls as ends with that date;

"the termination date", in the case of any guaranteed pension scheme, shall be construed in accordance with subsection (5)(b);

"the termination year", in the case of any guaranteed pension scheme, means the financial year of the scheme which consists of or includes the terminal period;

SCH. 11

"trustees", in relation to a guaranteed pension scheme, includes a reference to any persons who, under the rules of the scheme, are under a liability to provide pensions or other benefits but who are not trustees of the scheme.

Adjustments arising in connection with orders under s.52B.

52C.—(1) As soon as practicable after the termination date in the case of any guaranteed pension scheme, there shall be determined, for the terminal period, what proportion of the pensions, increases and expenses payable under, or incurred in connection with, the scheme corresponds to the relevant pension obligations.

(2) Any determination under subsection (1) shall either—

(a) be made by the Minister; or

(b) if the Minister so requires in the particular case, be made by the actuary or auditor to the guaranteed pension scheme in question and approved by the Minister.

(3) The Minister may give a direction to the persons administering a guaranteed pension scheme requiring them to determine the aggregate amount of the pensions, increases and expenses payable under or incurred in connection with the scheme for the terminal period or the termination year and to notify him in writing of their determination.

(4) As respects the termination year of a guaranteed pension scheme, the extent of the liability of the Minister to make payments under section 52(1) in relation to that scheme shall be restricted to a liability to make payments of an amount (the "termination year amount") equal in the aggregate to the product of—

(a) the proportion determined under section 54(1) for that scheme;

(b) the proportion determined pursuant to subsection (1) in the case of that scheme; and

(c) the aggregate amount of the pensions, increases and expenses payable under or incurred in connection with that scheme in the terminal period;

and payments by way of adjustment shall be made by the Minister to the persons administering the scheme, or (as the case may be) by those persons to the Minister, before the expiration of the period of six months beginning with the date of the last of the determinations made under subsection (1) or (3) with respect to the scheme.

(5) Where, in the case of a guaranteed pension scheme, the funding of the relevant pension obligations has, by virtue of subsection (3) of section 54, been left out of account in making a determination under subsection (1) of that section, the termination year amount in the case of that scheme shall be the difference between—

(a) what that amount would have been, apart from this subsection; and

(b) the amount of any income accruing for the terminal period which may be applied towards the payment of such of the pensions, increases and expenses payable under or incurred in connection with the scheme as correspond to those obligations.

(6) The Minister may give a direction to the persons administering a guaranteed pension scheme requiring them to determine the amount mentioned in subsection (5)(b) and to notify him in writing of their determination.

(7) Where payments by way of adjustment fall to be made, interest shall be payable, as from the termination date, by the person liable to make those payments, at the rates and intervals from time to time applicable for the purposes of section 52B(8)(a) in the case of the scheme in question, on so much of the aggregate amount of the payments in question as for the time being remains unpaid.

(8) So much of—

(a) any payment by way of adjustment which falls to be made, or

(b) any interest accrued under subsection (7),

as has not been paid shall be treated as a debt due.

(9) Any sums required for the making of payments under this section by the Minister shall be paid out of money provided by Parliament.

(10) In this section, "payments by way of adjustment", in the case of a guaranteed pension scheme, means—

(a) if the Minister has made payments under section 52(1) in relation to that scheme for the termination year which, in the aggregate, exceed the termination year amount, payment to the Minister by the persons administering the scheme of an amount equal to the excess;

(b) if the Minister has made no payments under section 52(1) in relation to that scheme for the termination year, payment by the Minister to those persons of the termination year amount; or

(c) if the Minister has made payments under section 52(1) in relation to that scheme for the termination year which, in the aggregate, fall short of the termination year amount, payment by the Minister to those persons of an amount equal to the shortfall.

(11) Expressions used in this section and in section 52B have the same meaning in this section as they have in that section.

Orders and directions under sections 52A to 52C: supplemental.

52D.—(1) Any power to make an order under section 52B shall be exercisable by statutory instrument made by the Minister after consultation with the trustees of the guaranteed pension scheme to which the order relates.

(2) A statutory instrument containing an order under section 52B shall be subject to annulment in pursuance of a resolution of either House of Parliament.

(3) At the time when a statutory instrument containing an order under section 52B is laid before each House of Parliament pursuant to subsection (2), the Minister shall, if he has not already done so, also lay before each House of Parliament a copy of the guarantee mentioned in subsection (1)(c) of that section; but this subsection is without prejudice to the validity of the order in question.

Sch. 11

(4) Any power to make an order under section 52B includes power, exercisable in the same manner, to make such incidental, supplemental, consequential or transitional provision as may appear necessary or expedient to the Minister.

(5) Any order under section 52B may make different provision for different cases or for different classes or descriptions of case.

(6) It shall be the duty of any person to whom a direction is given under section 52A or 52C to comply with and give effect to that direction; and compliance with any such direction shall be enforceable by civil proceedings by the Minister for an injunction or interdict or for any other appropriate relief.

(7) Any power to give a direction under section 52A or 52C includes power to vary or revoke the direction.

(8) Any direction under section 52A or 52C shall be given in writing.

(9) In this section—

"guaranteed pension scheme" has the same meaning as in section 52B;

"trustees", in relation to a guaranteed pension scheme, has the same meaning as in section 52B."

(4) In section 70 of that Act, in subsection (2) (interpretation), for the definition of "the Minister" there shall be substituted—

""the Minister" means the Secretary of State;".

Application and modification of Part III of the 1980 Act

10.—(1) The Secretary of State may by order designate—

(a) any occupational pension scheme which would not, apart from this paragraph, be included among the pension schemes which are B.R. pension schemes for the purposes of Part III of the 1980 Act, or

(b) any section of an occupational pension scheme, being a section which would not, apart from this paragraph, be included among those schemes,

as a pension scheme which is to be treated as included among those schemes for the purpose of requiring or enabling him to make to the persons administering the scheme payments under section 52(1), 52A, 52B or 52C of that Act in respect of qualifying pension rights transferred (whether under paragraph 4 above or otherwise) so as to become pension rights under that scheme.

(2) An order under sub-paragraph (1) above may make provision, in any case where qualifying pension rights of any persons are, or are to be, transferred as mentioned in that sub-paragraph, for treating those persons as constituting a section of the occupational pension scheme to which those qualifying pension rights are, or are to be, so transferred.

(3) No order shall be made under sub-paragraph (1) above except after consultation with the trustees of the occupational pension scheme to which the qualifying pension rights are, or are to be, transferred.

(4) Subject to the following provisions of this paragraph, Part III of the 1980 Act shall have effect as if any reference in that Part to a B.R. pension scheme included a reference to a designated scheme.

(5) Where qualifying pension rights are transferred to a designated scheme as mentioned in sub-paragraph (1) above, the proportion referred to in section 52(1)(a) of the 1980 Act in its application by virtue of this paragraph in relation to the designated scheme shall, instead of being determined under section 54 of

that Act, be taken to be the proportion which has been determined under that section in relation to the B.R. pension scheme from which the qualifying pension rights are transferred; and references in Part III of that Act to that proportion shall be construed accordingly.

(6) In the application of Part III of the 1980 Act in relation to a designated scheme, references in that Part to "the relevant pension obligations" shall, in relation to the designated scheme, be construed—

(a) as if the reference in section 53(1)(a) of that Act to obligations of the Board which were owed on 1st January 1975 in connection with the scheme were a reference to so much of the obligations of the Board which were owed on that date in connection with a B.R. pension scheme as are obligations in respect of qualifying pension rights transferred to the designated scheme; and

(b) as if the reference in section 53(1)(c) of that Act to an obligation of the Board arising after that date to pay or secure the payment of increases payable under the scheme included a reference to so much of any such obligation of the Board in respect of a B.R. pension scheme as is an obligation in respect of qualifying pension rights transferred to the designated scheme.

(7) In the application of section 55 of the 1980 Act in relation to a designated scheme, paragraph (a) of subsection (1) (which requires the proportion of the scheme's outgoings which corresponds to the relevant pension obligations to be determined before the beginning of each financial year or, in the case of the first financial year, as soon as practicable after the passing of that Act) shall be taken to require the proportion mentioned in that paragraph to be determined

(a) before the beginning of the financial year in question, or

(b) as soon as practicable after the coming into force of the order under sub-paragraph (1) above by virtue of which the scheme in question is a designated scheme,

and paragraph (b) of that subsection shall be construed accordingly.

(8) The power to give a direction under section 57 of the 1980 Act (which provides for certain determinations to be made as if no transfer had taken place and as if no payment representing the pension rights in question had been made) shall be exercisable in any case where the whole or any part of a person's accrued pension rights under a B.R. pension scheme or a designated scheme are transferred (whether under paragraph 4 above or otherwise) to—

(a) a designated scheme, or

(b) a pension scheme established by the Board,

as it is in the case of any such transfer as is mentioned in that section.

(9) Without prejudice to sub-paragraph (8) above, where in any financial year the whole or any part of a person's accrued pension rights under a B.R. pension scheme are transferred to a designated scheme, it shall be assumed, for the purposes of any determination of the aggregate amount of the pensions, increases and expenses payable under or incurred in connection with the B.R. pension scheme in that financial year, that the payment of any sum representing those pension rights had not been made.

(10) Without prejudice to section 59(1) of the 1980 Act (which provides that the making of payments under section 52(1) does not discharge certain relevant pension obligations), the making of any payment under section 52(1) of the 1980 Act to the persons administering a designated scheme shall not discharge any relevant pension obligation, so far as it is an obligation to pay pensions or increases of pensions under that or any other designated scheme, or under a B.R. pension scheme, or is an obligation to secure the payment of those pensions or increases.

(11) Without prejudice to section 59(2) of the 1980 Act (power to amend pension scheme for certain purposes), if the persons administering an occupational pension scheme would not otherwise have power to do so, they may amend the scheme by instrument in writing for the purpose of enabling persons to be admitted as members of the scheme on the basis that payments will fall to be made under Part III of the 1980 Act in respect of qualifying pension rights of theirs which are transferred so as to become pension rights under the scheme.

(12) Where the persons administering an occupational pension scheme have power, apart from sub-paragraph (11) above, to amend the scheme for the purpose mentioned in that sub-paragraph, they may exercise that power for that purpose without regard to any limitations on the exercise of the power and without compliance with any procedural provisions applicable to its exercise.

(13) Any reference in Part III of the 1980 Act to a "financial year" shall, in relation to a designated scheme, be taken as a reference—

(a) to such period as—

(i) begins with the transfer of the qualifying pension rights in question, and

(ii) ends with the last day of an accounting year of the scheme,

and is a period of not less than twelve months and less than two years; and

(b) to each successive accounting year of that scheme.

(14) Where any provision of Part III of the 1980 Act requires anything to be done in, or in relation to, the first financial year of a B.R. pension scheme, that provision shall (so far as so requiring) be disregarded in the application of that Part in relation to a designated scheme.

(15) In any case where—

(a) the whole or any part of a person's accrued pension rights under a B.R. pension scheme are transferred so as to become pension rights under a designated scheme, and

(b) immediately before that transfer takes effect, relevant pension obligations a proportion of which, as determined for the purposes of section 52(1)(a) of the 1980 Act, has not been funded are owed in respect of those pension rights by the Board to the persons administering the pension scheme from which the pension rights are so transferred,

an order under sub-paragraph (1) above may provide for the benefit of that proportion of so much of those relevant pension obligations as are owed in respect of those pension rights to be transferred, so as to become relevant pension obligations owed by the Board to the persons administering the pension scheme to which the pension rights are transferred.

(16) Where the benefit of any relevant pension obligations is transferred by virtue of sub-paragraph (15) above, the persons administering the pension scheme to which the benefit of those obligations is transferred shall have, in relation to the relevant pension obligations the benefit of which is so transferred, all the rights of the persons administering the pension scheme from which the benefit of those obligations is transferred.

(17) In this paragraph—

"the 1980 Act" means the Transport Act 1980;

"designated scheme" means an occupational pension scheme or, as the case may be, a section of any such scheme, which is designated under sub-paragraph (1) above;

"pension scheme" includes a section of a pension scheme;

"qualifying pension rights" means any pension rights as respects the whole or some part of which there are subsisting relevant pension obligations a proportion of which, as determined for the purposes of section 52(1)(a) of the 1980 Act, has not been funded;

and, subject to that, expressions used in this paragraph and in Part III of the 1980 Act have the same meaning in this paragraph as they have in that Part.

Government guarantees to trustees of certain new schemes

11.—(1) Subject to the following provisions of this paragraph, the Secretary of State—

(a) shall give to the trustees of any new scheme which satisfies the conditions in sub-paragraph (3) below, and

(b) may give to the trustees of any new scheme which satisfies the conditions in sub-paragraph (4) below,

a guarantee in respect of their liabilities to make payments in respect of pension rights under the scheme.

(2) This paragraph applies in relation to a section of a new scheme as it applies in relation to a new scheme; and any reference in this paragraph to a new scheme, a closed scheme, a pension scheme or a member shall be construed accordingly.

(3) A new scheme satisfies the conditions in this sub-paragraph if—

(a) all the members of the scheme are persons whose pension rights under the scheme are pension rights which have been transferred, so as to become pension rights under that scheme, pursuant to an order under paragraph 4 above; and

(b) the rules of the scheme prevent any member of the scheme from being a participant in the scheme.

(4) A new scheme satisfies the conditions in this sub-paragraph if—

(a) the scheme is a closed scheme; and

(b) at the date on which the scheme becomes a closed scheme, all the members of the scheme are—

(i) participants in the scheme to whom pension rights under the scheme are accruing by virtue of their employment with a relevant employer; or

(ii) pensioners or deferred pensioners under the scheme whose pension rights under the scheme derive in whole or in part from their, or some other person's, participation in an occupational pension scheme as an employee of a relevant employer.

(5) Classes or descriptions of person may be prescribed whose membership of, or participation in, a new scheme is to be disregarded for the purpose of determining whether the new scheme satisfies the conditions in sub-paragraph (3) or (4) above.

(6) The power to give a guarantee under sub-paragraph (1)(b) above becomes exercisable in the case of any new scheme if the Secretary of State is of the opinion that it is desirable to give such a guarantee for the purpose of ensuring that the trustees of the scheme are, or will be, able to meet their liabilities to make payments in respect of pension rights under the scheme as those liabilities fall to be met.

(7) The Secretary of State shall consider any representations made by the trustees of a new scheme which satisfies the conditions in sub-paragraph (4) above concerning their ability to meet their liabilities to make payments in respect of pension rights under the scheme.

SCH. 11

(8) Any guarantee under this paragraph shall be given in such manner, and on such terms and conditions, as the Secretary of State may, after consultation with the trustees of, and the actuary to, the scheme in question, think fit; and, without prejudice to the generality of the foregoing provisions of this sub-paragraph, the terms and conditions on which a guarantee under this paragraph may be given include terms and conditions—

(a) with respect to any matter relating to payment under the guarantee, including—

(i) the circumstances in which payment under the guarantee falls to be made;

(ii) the amounts, or the method of determining the amounts, of any payments that fall to be so made;

(iii) the persons to whom any such payments are to be made;

(b) with respect to any matter relating to the management, affairs or winding up of the scheme, including—

(i) the policy to be followed in relation to the investment of assets held for the purposes of the scheme; and

(ii) the distribution of any surplus which may arise under the scheme; or

(c) requiring or precluding, or otherwise with respect to, amendment of the rules of the scheme;

and the sub-paragraphs of paragraphs (a) and (b) above are without prejudice to the generality of the preceding provisions of the paragraph in question.

(9) Any sums required by the Secretary of State to fulfil a guarantee given under this section shall be paid out of money provided by Parliament.

(10) In this paragraph—

"closed scheme" means a pension scheme—

(a) to which no new members are to be admitted; but

(b) under which pensions and other benefits continue to be provided;

"deferred pensioner", in the case of any pension scheme, means a person who has pension rights under the scheme but who (so far as relating to those pension rights) is neither a participant in the scheme nor a pensioner under the scheme;

"relevant employer" means—

(a) the Board;

(b) a wholly owned subsidiary of the Board; or

(c) a publicly owned railway company, other than a company which is wholly owned by the Franchising Director.

Supplementary

12. If it appears to the Secretary of State necessary or expedient to do so, in consequence of any provision made by order under this Schedule, he may by provision made in the same manner—

(a) repeal or amend, or modify the operation of, any private or local Act of Parliament; or

(b) revoke or amend, or modify the operation of, any statutory instrument (whether local or general).

Parliamentary procedure

13.—(1) A statutory instrument containing an order under this Schedule, other than an order under paragraph 11 above, shall not be made unless a draft of the instrument has been laid before and approved by resolution of each House of Parliament.

(2) At or before the time when a draft of a statutory instrument containing an order under paragraph 3 or 4 above is laid before each House of Parliament pursuant to sub-paragraph (1) above, the Secretary of State shall also lay before each House of Parliament a copy of any comments on the order in question—

(a) which have been made in writing to the Secretary of State by the trustees mentioned in paragraph 3(4) or, as the case may be, paragraph 4(5) above;

(b) which are designated by those trustees as comments which they wish the Secretary of State to consider as comments on that order; and

(c) which have been received by the Secretary of State before the expiration of such period as has been notified by him to those trustees as being the consultation period in relation to the order in question;

but this sub-paragraph is without prejudice to the validity of the order in question.

(3) If, apart from the provisions of this sub-paragraph, the draft of an instrument containing an order under this Schedule would be treated for the purposes of the Standing Orders of either House of Parliament as a hybrid instrument, it shall proceed in that House as if it were not such an instrument.

Transitory provision

14. In this Schedule, and in any amendment made by this Schedule to any other enactment,—

(a) any reference to section 1 of the Pension Schemes Act 1993 shall, until the coming into force of that section, be construed as a reference to section 66(1) of the Social Security Pensions Act 1975; [1993 c. 48.] [1975 c. 60.]

(b) any reference to Part III of the Pension Schemes Act 1993 shall, until the coming into force of that Part, be construed as a reference to Part III of the Social Security Pensions Act 1975; and

(c) any reference to Part III of the Pension Schemes (Northern Ireland) Act 1993 shall, until the coming into force of that Part, be construed as a reference to Part IV of the Social Security Pensions (Northern Ireland) Order 1975. [1993 c. 49.] [S.I. 1975/1503 (N.I. 15).]

SCHEDULE 12

MINOR AND CONSEQUENTIAL AMENDMENTS

The Regulation of Railways Act 1889

1. Section 6 of the Regulation of Railways Act 1889 (which provides that every passenger ticket issued by any railway company in the United Kingdom shall show on its face the fare chargeable for the journey for which it was issued) shall cease to have effect. [1889 c. 57.]

The Railway Fires Act 1905

2.—(1) In section 1 of the Railway Fires Act 1905 (liability of railway companies to make good damage to crops caused by their engines), after subsection (2) there shall be inserted— [1905 c. 11.]

"(2A) Any reference in subsection (2) above to a "company" includes a reference to any person—

(a) who holds a network licence, station licence or light maintenance depot licence under Part I of the Railways Act 1993; or

(b) who is exempt, by virtue of a licence exemption under section 7 of that Act, from the requirement to be authorised by licence under that Part to be the operator of a network, station or light maintenance depot.

(2B) A person such as is mentioned in subsection (2A) above shall be regarded for the purposes of subsection (2) above as working a railway which consists of the track (if any) comprised in any network, station or light maintenance depot of which he lawfully acts as the operator by virtue of the licence or licence exemption in question."

(2) In section 4 of that Act (definitions and application) after the definition of "railway" there shall be inserted—

"The expression "railway company" includes any person—

(a) who holds a licence under Part I of the Railways Act 1993; or

(b) who is exempt, by virtue of a licence exemption under section 7 of that Act, from the requirement to be authorised by licence under that Part to be the operator of a railway asset;

The expressions "light maintenance depot", "network", "operator", "railway asset", "station" and "track" have the same meaning as they have in Part I of the Railways Act 1993."

The Railway Fires Act (1905) Amendment Act 1923

3. In section 2 of the Railway Fires Act (1905) Amendment Act 1923 (conditions precedent to application of the Act of 1905) after the words "any railway company" there shall be inserted the words "(as defined in section 4 of that Act)".

The British Transport Commission Act 1950

4. Section 43 of the British Transport Commission Act 1950 (power to supply railway equipment to the Ulster Transport Authority) shall cease to have effect.

The Transport Act 1962

5.—(1) The Transport Act 1962 shall be amended in accordance with this paragraph.

(2) The following provisions shall cease to have effect, that is to say—

(a) section 4(1)(b), (2) and (7) (which relate to the provision by the Board of certain services for the carriage of goods by road),

(b) section 5 (which gives the Board power to provide certain air transport services),

(c) section 13(3) (saving for section 43 of the British Transport Commission Act 1950), and

(d) section 53 (complaints by operators of coastal shipping about the Board's railway charges).

(3) In section 12 (power of the Boards to construct and operate pipe-lines), in subsection (1), after the words "the Boards" there shall be inserted the words ", other than the Railways Board,".

(4) In section 14(4), after the words "Each of the Boards" there shall be inserted the words ", except the Railways Board,".

SCH. 12

The Transport Act 1968

6.—(1) The Transport Act 1968 shall be amended in accordance with this paragraph.   1968 c. 73.

(2) In section 42 of that Act, subsection (3) (which confers power to vary commencing capital debt of the Board to take account of transfers under section 7(5) or (6) or 8(4) of that Act and which is spent) shall be omitted.

(3) Section 45 of that Act (duty of the Board periodically to review its organisation) shall cease to have effect.

(4) Section 48 of that Act (which confers power on the Boards and the new authorities to undertake activities including manufacture for sale) shall cease to have effect in relation to the Board.

(5) In section 50 of that Act—

   (a) subsection (2) (power of the Board to provide and manage hotels) shall cease to have effect;

   (b) in subsection (4), for the words "In subsections (2) and (3) of this section the references to hotels include references" there shall be substituted the words "In subsection (3) of this section the reference to hotels includes a reference"; and

   (c) subsection (7) (which confers power on the Boards and the new authorities to provide technical advice and assistance and which is superseded, in the case of the Board, by section 127 of this Act) shall cease to have effect in relation to the Board.

(6) In section 55 of that Act (amendments concerning Transport Consultative Committees under section 56 of the Transport Act 1962), in subsection (1)   1962 c. 46.
(services and facilities in relation to which Consultative Committees' duties are to apply)—

   (a) for the words "the Consultative Committees established under that section" there shall be substituted the words "the Central Committee and the consultative committees, within the meaning of that section,", and

   (b) the following shall be omitted, namely—

      (i) in paragraph (a), the words from "or provided" onwards,

      (ii) paragraph (b),

      (iii) paragraphs (i) and (iii), and

      (iv) the words from "and for the purposes" onwards,

and subsections (2), (3) and (4) (duties of Consultative Committees in relation to certain services and facilities provided in Scotland, and provision as to office accommodation for, defrayment of expenditure incurred by, and certain payments to members of, Consultative Committees) shall cease to have effect.

(7) In section 137 of that Act (machinery for negotiation and consultation with staff), in subsection (1) (which provides that that section applies to the Board and to certain other authorities), the words "the Railways Board" in paragraph (a) shall cease to have effect.

The Fair Trading Act 1973

7. In section 133(2) of the Fair Trading Act 1973 (exceptions from the general   1973 c. 41.
restriction on the disclosure of information obtained under or by virtue of certain provisions of that Act), in paragraph (a)—

   (a) after the words "the Director General of Electricity Supply for Northern Ireland" (which were inserted by paragraph 10(a) of Schedule 12 to the Electricity (Northern Ireland) Order 1992) there   S.I. 1992/231
   shall be inserted the words "the Rail Regulator"; and   (N.I. 1).

Sch. 12

(b) after the words "Courts and Legal Services Act 1990" there shall be inserted the words "or the Railways Act 1993".

The Consumer Credit Act 1974

1974 c. 39.

8. In section 174(3) of the Consumer Credit Act 1974 (exceptions from the general restriction on the disclosure of information obtained under or by virtue of that Act), in paragraph (a)—

(a) after the words "Courts and Legal Services Act 1990" there shall be inserted the words "or the Railways Act 1993"; and

S.I. 1992/231 (N.I. 1).

(b) after the words "the Director General of Electricity Supply for Northern Ireland" (which were inserted by paragraph 14(b) of Schedule 12 to the Electricity (Northern Ireland) Order 1992) there shall be inserted the words "the Rail Regulator".

The Railways Act 1974

1974 c. 48.

1962 c. 46.

9. In the Railways Act 1974, section 9 (which provides for an alternative basis of remuneration for chairmen of Consultative Committees set up under section 56 of the Transport Act 1962) shall cease to have effect.

The Restrictive Trade Practices Act 1976

1976 c. 34.

10. In section 41(1) of the Restrictive Trade Practices Act 1976 (exceptions from the general restriction on the disclosure of information obtained under or by virtue of that Act), in paragraph (a)—

(a) after the words "the Director General of Electricity Supply for Northern Ireland" (which were inserted by paragraph 16(a) of Schedule 12 to the Electricity (Northern Ireland) Order 1992) there shall be inserted the words "the Rail Regulator"; and

(b) after the words "Courts and Legal Services Act 1990" there shall be inserted the words "or the Railways Act 1993".

The Estate Agents Act 1979

1979 c. 38.

11. In section 10(3) of the Estate Agents Act 1979 (exceptions from the general restriction on the disclosure of information obtained under or by virtue of that Act), in paragraph (a)—

(a) after the words "Courts and Legal Services Act 1990" there shall be inserted the words "or the Railways Act 1993"; and

(b) after the words "the Director General of Electricity Supply for Northern Ireland" (which were inserted by paragraph 20(b) of Schedule 12 to the Electricity (Northern Ireland) Order 1992) there shall be inserted the words "the Rail Regulator".

The Competition Act 1980

1980 c. 21

12.—(1) In section 11 of the Competition Act 1980, in subsection (3) (public bodies and other persons who may be the subject of a reference to the Monopolies Commission under that section), after paragraph (a) there shall be inserted—

"(aa) any publicly owned railway company, within the meaning of the Railways Act 1993, which supplies network services or station services, within the meaning of Part I of that Act; or".

(2) In subsection (2) of section 19 of that Act (which provides that the general restriction, in subsection (1) of that section, on the disclosure of information obtained under or by virtue of that Act does not apply in relation to the performance by certain authorities of their functions under the provisions listed in subsection (3) of that section) in paragraph (a), after the words "the Director

General of Electricity Supply for Northern Ireland" (which were inserted by paragraph 21(a) of Schedule 12 to the Electricity (Northern Ireland) Order 1992) there shall be inserted the words "the Rail Regulator".

(3) In subsection (3) of that section (list of provisions referred to in subsection (2) of that section) after the paragraph (n) inserted by paragraph 28 of Schedule 20 to the Broadcasting Act 1990 there shall be added—

"(o) the Railways Act 1993".

The Telecommunications Act 1984

13.—(1) In subsection (2) of section 101 of the Telecommunications Act 1984 (which provides that the general restriction, in subsection (1) of that section, on the disclosure of information obtained under or by virtue of that Act does not apply in relation to the performance by certain authorities of their functions under the provisions listed in subsection (3) of that section) in paragraph (b), after the words "the Director General of Electricity Supply for Northern Ireland" (which were inserted by paragraph 29(a) of Schedule 12 to the Electricity (Northern Ireland) Order 1992) there shall be inserted the words "the Rail Regulator".

(2) In subsection (3) of that section (list of provisions referred to in subsection (2) of that section) after paragraph (l) (which was inserted by paragraph 29(b) of Schedule 12 to the Electricity (Northern Ireland) Order 1992) there shall be added—

"(m) the Railways Act 1993".

The London Regional Transport Act 1984

14.—(1) Section 2 of the London Regional Transport Act 1984 (provision of passenger transport services for Greater London) shall be amended in accordance with the following provisions of this paragraph.

(2) In subsection (1) (which requires London Regional Transport, in conjunction with the Board, to provide or secure the provision of public passenger transport services in Greater London), before the words "in conjunction with the Railways Board" there shall be inserted the words "(if and to the extent that the Railways Board continues to be under a duty by virtue of section 3 of the Transport Act 1962 to provide railway services in Greater London)".

(3) At the beginning of subsection (3) (duty of London Regional Transport and the Board to co-operate for the purpose of co-ordinating services etc) there shall be inserted the words "If and so long as the Railways Board continues to be under a duty by virtue of section 3 of the Transport Act 1962 to provide railway services in Greater London,".

(4) After that subsection there shall be inserted—

"(3A) It shall be the duty of London Regional Transport (either acting directly, or acting indirectly through subsidiaries of theirs) and the Franchising Director to co-operate with one another in the exercise and performance of their respective functions for the purpose—

(a) of co-ordinating the passenger transport services for persons travelling within, to, or from Greater London—

(i) which are provided by London Regional Transport or their subsidiaries; and

(ii) which are provided under franchise agreements, or whose provision is secured by the Franchising Director pursuant to section 30, 37 or 38 of the Railways Act 1993; and

SCH. 12

(b) of securing or facilitating the proper discharge of London Regional Transport's duty under subsection (1) above;

and to afford to one another such information as to the services mentioned in paragraph (a) above as may reasonably be required for those purposes."

(5) In subsection (4) (power of London Regional Transport and the Board to enter into arrangements for the purposes of the co-operation required by the section)—

(a) for the words "subsection (3) above" there shall be substituted the words "subsection (3) or, as the case may be, subsection (3A) above—

(a)"; and

(b) after the words "the Railways Board" there shall be inserted the words "or

(b) London Regional Transport and the Franchising Director,".

(6) After that subsection there shall be inserted—

"(4A) The references in subsections (3A) and (4) above to the respective functions of London Regional Transport and the Franchising Director shall be taken, in the case of the functions of the Franchising Director, as a reference to—

(a) his functions under sections 23 to 31 of the Railways Act 1993 (franchising of passenger services); and

(b) the duties imposed upon him by sections 37 and 38 of that Act (discontinuance of railway passenger services) to secure the provision of services."

15. In section 7 of that Act (planning of passenger transport services for Greater London) in subsection (4) (which specifies the persons with whom London Regional Transport are to consult in preparing statements under that section)—

(a) after paragraph (a), there shall be inserted—

"(aa) the Franchising Director;"; and

(b) for the word "and" at the end of paragraph (c) there shall be substituted—

"(cc) such other persons as the Secretary of State may specify in a direction given to London Regional Transport; and".

1962 c. 46.

16. In section 31 of that Act (duty of Board to consult London Regional Transport as to fares and services in London) for the words "The Railways Board shall" there shall be substituted the words "If and so long as the Railways Board continues to be under a duty by virtue of section 3 of the Transport Act 1962 to provide railway services in Greater London, the Board shall".

17. After that section there shall be inserted—

"Duty of Franchising Director to consult London Regional Transport as to fares and services in London.

31A. The Franchising Director shall from time to time consult with London Regional Transport as to—

(a) the general level and structure of the fares to be charged for the carriage of passengers by railway on journeys wholly within Greater London on services—

(i) which are, or are to be, provided under franchise agreements; or

(ii) whose provision the Franchising Director is under a duty to secure, by virtue of section 30, 37 or 38 of the Railways Act 1993; and

(b) the general level of the provision to be made for such journeys."

18.—(1) Section 40 of that Act shall have effect with the following amendments.

(2) Without prejudice to the continuing validity of appointments made before the coming into force of this sub-paragraph, for subsection (2) (appointment of chairman and members by the Secretary of State) there shall be substituted—

"(2) The Committee shall consist of—

(a) a chairman, appointed by the Secretary of State after consultation with the Rail Regulator; and

(b) such other members (not exceeding thirty) as the Secretary of State may appoint after consultation with the Rail Regulator and the chairman."

(3) In subsection (4), there shall be omitted—

(a) the words "Subject to subsection (6) below,"; and

(b) paragraph (c) (which confers functions with respect to matters affecting the services and facilities provided by the Board or any subsidiary of theirs) and the word "or" immediately preceding it.

(4) In subsection (5)—

(a) in paragraph (b) (which provides that a matter falls to be considered by the committee if it has been referred to it by certain persons or bodies), for the words "by London Regional Transport or by the Railways Board" there shall be substituted the words "or by London Regional Transport"; and

(b) the words following paragraph (c) (which relate to services provided by the Board or its subsidiaries) shall be omitted.

(5) Subsection (6) (which precludes the committee from considering charges for services and questions relating to the discontinuance or reduction of railway services) shall be omitted.

(6) In subsection (7), paragraph (b) (which requires copies of the committee's minutes, requirements and recommendations in the case of certain matters affecting the Board to be sent to the Board) shall be omitted.

(7) In subsection (8) (power of the Secretary of State to give directions to certain bodies) the words "or (as the case may require) to the Railways Board" shall be omitted.

(8) In subsection (9) (requirement for certain bodies and persons to give notice of certain decisions to the committee) the words "the Railways Board" shall be omitted.

(9) In subsection (10) (committee to make annual report to the Secretary of State), after the words "Secretary of State" where first occurring there shall be inserted the words "and the Rail Regulator".

(10) In subsection (11) (certain companies not to be treated as subsidiaries of certain bodies), the words "or the Railways Board" shall be omitted.

19. Section 41 of that Act (which provides for the committee to be treated as an Area Transport Users' Consultative Committee for certain purposes and which makes other provision in connection therewith) shall cease to have effect.

20. In section 59 of that Act (which confers power on London Borough Councils and the Common Council to enter into certain agreements with the Board) for the words "the Railways Board" there shall be substituted—

SCH. 12

"(a) the Railways Board,

(b) the Franchising Director, or

(c) any person who is the holder of a passenger licence, a network licence or a station licence, within the meaning of Part I of the Railways Act 1993,".

21. In section 68 of that Act (interpretation) the following definitions shall be inserted at the appropriate places—

(a) ""franchise agreement" has the same meaning as in Part I of the Railways Act 1993;"; and

(b) ""the Franchising Director" means the Director of Passenger Rail Franchising;".

22.—(1) In Schedule 3 to that Act, in paragraph 5 (Secretary of State to provide the committee with funds with which to meet certain expenses) after sub-paragraph (2) there shall be added—

"(3) The Committee shall prepare and send to the Secretary of State not less than two months, or such other period as the Secretary of State may specify, before the beginning of each financial year a statement of the expenses which they expect to incur in respect of that year for the purposes of, or in connection with, the carrying on of their functions.

(4) The Secretary of State shall consider any statement sent to him under sub-paragraph (3) above and shall either approve the statement or approve it with such modifications as he considers appropriate."

(2) In paragraph 9 of that Schedule, at the end of sub-paragraph (3) (which requires minutes to be kept of the proceedings of every meeting of the committee) there shall be added the words "; and copies of those minutes shall be sent to the Secretary of State, the Rail Regulator and the Central Rail Users' Consultative Committee."

(3) In sub-paragraph (4) of that paragraph (power of committee to determine own procedure) after the words "Subject to the preceding provisions of this paragraph" there shall be inserted the words "and the provisions of paragraph 11A below" and after paragraph 11 of that Schedule there shall be inserted—

"Admission of public to meetings

11A.—(1) Subject to sub-paragraph (2) below, meetings of the Committee shall be open to the public.

(2) The public shall be excluded during any item of business where—

(a) it is likely, were members of the public to be present during that item, that information furnished in confidence to the Committee by the Rail Regulator or the Franchising Director would be disclosed in breach of the obligation of confidence;

(b) the Committee have resolved that, by reason of the confidential nature of the item or for other special reasons stated in the resolution, it is desirable in the public interest that the public be excluded; or

(c) it is likely, were members of the public to be present during that item, that there would be disclosed to them—

(i) any matter which relates to the affairs of an individual, or

(ii) any matter which relates specifically to the affairs of a particular body of persons, whether corporate or unincorporate,

where public disclosure of that matter would or might, in the opinion of the committee, seriously and prejudicially affect the interests of that individual or body.

(3) The Committee shall give such notice—

(a) of any meeting of the Committee which is open to the public, and

(b) of the business to be taken at that meeting (other than items during which the public is to be excluded),

as they consider appropriate for the purpose of bringing the meeting to the attention of interested members of the public.".

The Airports Act 1986

23.—(1) In subsection (2) of section 74 of the Airports Act 1986 (which provides that the general restriction, in subsection (1) of that section, on the disclosure of information obtained under or by virtue of that Act does not apply in relation to the performance by certain authorities of their functions under the provisions listed in subsection (3) of that section) in paragraph (a), after the words "the Director General of Electricity Supply for Northern Ireland" (which were inserted by paragraph 30(a) of Schedule 12 to the Electricity (Northern Ireland) Order 1992) there shall be inserted the words "the Rail Regulator".

1986 c. 31.

S.I. 1992/231 (N.I. 1).

(2) In subsection (3) of that section (list of provisions referred to in subsection (2) of that section) after paragraph (m) (which was inserted by paragraph 30(b) of Schedule 12 to the Electricity (Northern Ireland) Order 1992) there shall be added—

"(n) the Railways Act 1993".

The Gas Act 1986

24.—(1) In subsection (2) of section 42 of the Gas Act 1986 (which provides that the general restriction, in subsection (1) of that section, on the disclosure of information obtained under or by virtue of that Act does not apply in relation to the performance by certain authorities of their functions under the provisions listed in subsection (3) of that section) in paragraph (b), after the words "the Director General of Electricity Supply" there shall be inserted the words "the Rail Regulator".

1986 c. 44.

(2) In subsection (3) of that section (list of provisions referred to in subsection (2) of that section) after paragraph (m) there shall be added—

"(n) the Railways Act 1993".

The Insolvency Act 1986

25. In section 413 of the Insolvency Act 1986, at the end of subsection (2) (which imposes a requirement to consult with the Insolvency Rules Committee, except in the case of certain provisions there specified) there shall be added the words "or by any of sections 59 to 65 of, or Schedule 6 or 7 to, the Railways Act 1993."

1986 c. 45.

The Consumer Protection Act 1987

26.—(1) Section 38 of the Consumer Protection Act 1987 (which restricts the disclosure of certain information, but provides that the restriction does not apply to certain disclosures, including those made by "relevant persons", within the meaning of that section, in relation to the performance of their functions under the provisions listed in subsection (3) of that section) shall be amended in accordance with sub-paragraphs (2) and (3) below.

1987 c. 43.

236 c. **43** *Railways Act 1993*

Sch. 12

S.I. 1992/231 (N.I. 1).

(2) In subsection (3) of that section (list of provisions referred to in subsection (2) of that section) after paragraph (n) (which was inserted by paragraph 31(a) of Schedule 12 to the Electricity (Northern Ireland) Order 1992) there shall be added—

"(o) the Railways Act 1993".

(3) In paragraph (b) of the definition of "relevant person" in subsection (6) of that section, after the words "the Director General of Electricity Supply for Northern Ireland" (which were inserted by paragraph 31(b) of Schedule 12 to the Electricity (Northern Ireland) Order 1992) there shall be inserted the words "or the Rail Regulator".

The Channel Tunnel Act 1987

1987 c. 53.
1889 c. 57.

27. In Schedule 6 to the Channel Tunnel Act 1987, in paragraph 2 (sections 4 and 6 of the Regulation of Railways Act 1889 not to apply to Concessionaires and through service operators, within the meaning of that Act), for the word "Sections" there shall be substituted the word "Section".

The Electricity Act 1989

1989 c. 29.

28.—(1) In subsection (2) of section 57 of the Electricity Act 1989 (which provides that the general restriction, in subsection (1) of that section, on the disclosure of information obtained under or by virtue of that Act does not apply in relation to the performance by certain authorities of their functions under the provisions listed in subsection (3) of that section) in paragraph (b), after sub-paragraph (vii) there shall be inserted—

"(viia) the Rail Regulator;".

(2) In subsection (3) of that section (list of provisions referred to in subsection (2) of that section) after paragraph (n) there shall be added—

"(nn) the Railways Act 1993".

The New Roads and Street Works Act 1991

1991 c. 22.
1973 c. 41.

29. In section 10 of the New Roads and Street Works Act 1991 (application of the Fair Trading Act 1973 etc in relation to persons authorised by virtue of that Act to charge tolls for the use of roads), in subsection (2), paragraph (b) (which provides that, for certain purposes, section 51(3) of the Fair Trading Act 1973 is to have effect as if the Secretary of State for Transport were among the Ministers listed in that provision, and which is superseded by the amendment made by section 66(2) of this Act), and the word "and" immediately preceding it, shall cease to have effect.

The Water Industry Act 1991

1991 c. 56.

30. In the Water Industry Act 1991 (subsection (3)(d) of section 206 of which provides that the general restriction contained in subsection (1) of that section on the disclosure of certain information obtained under or by virtue of that Act does not apply in relation to disclosures facilitating the performance by persons mentioned in Part I of Schedule 15 to that Act of their functions under the provisions listed in Part II of that Schedule), in Schedule 15—

(a) in Part I, after the entry relating to the Director General of Electricity Supply, there shall be inserted the entry—

"The Rail Regulator"; and

(b) in Part II, after the entry relating to the Electricity Act 1989, there shall be inserted the entry—

"The Railways Act 1993".

The Water Resources Act 1991

31. In the Water Resources Act 1991 (subsection (2)(d) of section 204 of which provides that the general restriction contained in subsection (1) of that section on the disclosure of certain information obtained under or by virtue of that Act does not apply in relation to disclosures facilitating the performance by persons mentioned in Part I of Schedule 24 to that Act of their functions under the provisions listed in Part II of that Schedule), in Schedule 24—

  (a) in Part I, after the entry relating to the Director General of Electricity Supply, there shall be inserted the entry—

   "The Rail Regulator"; and

  (b) in Part II, after the entry relating to the Electricity Act 1989, there shall be inserted the entry—

   "The Railways Act 1993".

The British Coal and British Rail (Transfer Proposals) Act 1993

32. The British Coal and British Rail (Transfer Proposals) Act 1993 (which provides for the Board and the British Coal Corporation to have certain powers to act to facilitate the implementation of proposals of the Secretary of State to transfer property, rights, liabilities or functions of the Board or that Corporation to other persons or bodies) shall cease to have effect, so far as relating to the Board.

SCHEDULE 13

TRANSITIONAL PROVISIONS AND SAVINGS

The Central Committee

1.—(1) Unless the Secretary of State otherwise directs, any person who, immediately before the coming into force of section 3 of this Act, is—

  (a) the chairman of the former Central Committee, or

  (b) one of the other members of that Committee appointed as such by the Secretary of State,

shall, for the remainder of the period for which he was appointed as such, be the chairman or, as the case may be, one of the other members of the Central Committee.

(2) Any reference or representation—

  (a) which was made under section 56(4)(a) or (b) of the 1962 Act to the former Central Committee,

  (b) which relates to a matter which is within the competence of the Central Committee, and

  (c) which has not been disposed of by the former Central Committee before the coming into force of section 3 of this Act,

shall be treated as a reference or representation made to the Central Committee pursuant to paragraph (a) or (b) of subsection (2) of section 76 of this Act for the purposes of subsection (1) of that section.

(3) Any matter—

  (a) which was under consideration by the former Central Committee pursuant to section 56(4)(c) of the 1962 Act,

  (b) which is within the competence of the Central Committee, and

Sch. 13

(c) which has not been disposed of by the former Central Committee before the coming into force of section 3 of this Act,

shall be treated as a matter which ought to be considered by the Central Committee under subsection (1) of section 76 of this Act by virtue of subsection (2)(c) of that section.

(4) It shall be the duty of the former Central Committee to secure that all papers and other material relating to any representation, reference or matter falling within sub-paragraph (2) or (3) above are delivered up to the Central Committee as soon as reasonably practicable after the coming into force of section 3 of this Act.

(5) In any case where—

(a) any recommendation made under section 56(4) of the 1962 Act by the former Central Committee has been received by the Secretary of State before the coming into force of section 3 of this Act, but

(b) the Secretary of State has not disposed of that recommendation before the coming into force of that section,

he may, before the expiration of the period of twelve months beginning with the coming into force of that section, give a direction to any person providing a railway service whom he considers responsible for the matters dealt with in the recommendation.

(6) As respects the financial year at the beginning of which, or during which, section 3 of this Act comes into force—

(a) the Central Committee shall as soon as practicable prepare and send to the Regulator a statement of the expenses which they expect to incur in respect of that financial year for the purposes of, or in connection with, the carrying out of their functions; and

(b) the Regulator shall consider any statement sent to him under paragraph (a) above and shall either approve the statement or approve it with such modifications as he considers appropriate.

(7) In this paragraph—

1962 c. 46.

"the 1962 Act" means the Transport Act 1962;

"the Central Committee" has the same meaning as in Part I of this Act;

"the former Central Committee" means the Central Transport Consultative Committee for Great Britain, established under section 56 of the 1962 Act.

(8) For the purposes of this paragraph the matters which are within the competence of the Central Committee are any matters of a kind which, after the coming into force of section 3 of this Act, the Central Committee has power, or is under a duty, to investigate under section 76 of this Act.

Consultative committees

2.—(1) Until such time as the Regulator otherwise directs—

(a) there shall be the same number of consultative committees as there are Area Committees immediately before the coming into force of section 2 of this Act; and

(b) there shall be a consultative committee for each area for which, immediately before the coming into force of that section, there is an Area Committee.

(2) Unless the Regulator otherwise directs, any person who, immediately before the coming into force of section 2 of this Act, is the chairman or one of the other members of an Area Committee for any area shall, for the remainder of the period for which he was appointed as such, be the chairman or, as the case may be, one of the other members of the consultative committee for that area.

SCH. 13

(3) Any reference or representation—

(a) which was made under section 56(4)(a) or (b) of the 1962 Act to an Area Committee for any area,

(b) which relates to a matter which is within the competence of the consultative committee for that area, and

(c) which has not been disposed of by the Area Committee before the coming into force of section 2 of this Act,

shall be treated as a reference or representation made to the consultative committee pursuant to paragraph (a) or (b) of subsection (2) of section 77 of this Act for the purposes of subsection (1) of that section.

(4) Any matter—

(a) which was under consideration by an Area Committee for any area pursuant to section 56(4)(c) of the 1962 Act,

(b) which is within the competence of the consultative committee for that area, and

(c) which has not been disposed of by the Area Committee before the coming into force of section 2 of this Act,

shall be treated as a matter which ought to be considered by the consultative committee under subsection (1) of section 77 of this Act by virtue of subsection (2)(c) of that section.

(5) It shall be the duty of the Area Committee for any area to secure that all papers and other material relating to any representation, reference or matter falling within sub-paragraph (3) or (4) above are delivered up to the consultative committee for that area as soon as reasonably practicable after the coming into force of section 2 of this Act.

(6) In any case where—

(a) any recommendation made under section 56(4) of the 1962 Act by an Area Committee has been received by the Secretary of State before the coming into force of section 2 of this Act, but

(b) the Secretary of State has not disposed of that recommendation before the coming into force of that section,

he may, before the expiration of the period of twelve months beginning with the coming into force of that section, give a direction to any person providing a railway service whom he considers responsible for the matters dealt with in the recommendation.

(7) As respects the financial year at the beginning of which, or during which, section 2 of this Act comes into force—

(a) each consultative committee shall as soon as practicable prepare and send to the Regulator a statement of the expenses which they expect to incur in respect of that financial year for the purposes of, or in connection with, the carrying out of their functions; and

(b) the Regulator shall consider any statement sent to him under paragraph (a) above and shall either approve the statement or approve it with such modifications as he considers appropriate.

(8) In this paragraph—

"the 1962 Act" means the Transport Act 1962;

"Area Committee" means an Area Transport Users Consultative Committee, established under section 56 of the 1962 Act;

"consultative committee" means a consultative committee established under subsection (2) of section 2 of this Act.

1962 c. 46.

Sch. 13

(9) For the purposes of this paragraph the matters which are within the competence of a consultative committee are any matters of a kind which, after the coming into force of section 2 of this Act, the committee has power, or is under a duty, to investigate under section 77 of this Act.

Proposed closures

3.—(1) This paragraph applies in any case where—

(a) notice of a proposed closure has been given pursuant to subsection (7) of section 56 of the 1962 Act before the relevant date, but

(b) the Minister has not, before that date, either given or refused his consent to the proposed closure.

(2) Where this paragraph applies, subsections (7) to (10) and (13) of section 56 of the 1962 Act (and, accordingly, section 54 of the 1968 Act) shall, notwithstanding anything in section 49(1) of this Act, continue to have effect in relation to the proposed closure in question, but with the substitution—

(a) for any reference to an Area Committee of a reference to a consultative committee, and

(b) for any reference to the former Central Committee of a reference to the Central Committee,

and the closure provisions of this Act shall not have effect in relation to that proposed closure.

(3) In this paragraph—

1962 c. 46.   "the 1962 Act" means the Transport Act 1962;

1968 c. 73.   "the 1968 Act" means the Transport Act 1968;

"Area Committee" means an Area Transport Users Consultative Committee, established under section 56 of the 1962 Act, and includes a reference to the London Regional Passengers' Committee in its
1984 c. 32.   capacity as such a Committee by virtue of section 41 of the London Regional Transport Act 1984;

"the Central Committee" has the same meaning as in Part I of this Act;

"the closure provisions of this Act" means sections 37 to 49 of this Act and Schedule 5 to this Act;

"consultative committee" has the same meaning as in Part I of this Act and includes a reference to the London Regional Passengers' Committee in its capacity as consultative committee for the Greater London area, within the meaning of section 2 of this Act;

"the former Central Committee" means the Central Transport Consultative Committee for Great Britain, established under section 56 of the 1962 Act;

"the Minister" has the same meaning as in section 56 of the 1962 Act;

"proposed closure" has the same meaning as in section 56 of the 1962 Act;

"the relevant date" means the date on which the closure provisions of this Act come into force.

Saving for section 41 of the Channel Tunnel Act 1987

1987 c. 53.   4.—(1) Section 41 of the Channel Tunnel Act 1987 (which applies certain statutory functions of consumer committees to complaints about international railway passenger services as they apply in relation to services and facilities provided by the Board and its subsidiaries) shall continue to have effect as if section 78(1) of this Act and paragraphs 6(6)(b) and 18(3) to (8) and (10) of Schedule 12 to this Act had not been enacted.

SCH. 13
1984 c. 32.
1987 c. 53.

(2) In the application of subsection (5) of section 40 of the London Regional Transport Act 1984 by virtue of section 41 of the Channel Tunnel Act 1987, for the words in that subsection from "those services or facilities are within the competence of the Committee" onwards there shall be substituted the words "those services or facilities are provided within the area which is for the time being "the Greater London area" for the purposes of section 2 of the Railways Act 1993."

SCHEDULE 14
REPEALS

Section 152.

Chapter	Short title	Extent of repeal
52 & 53 Vict. c. 57.	The Regulation of Railways Act 1889.	Section 6.
18 & 19 Geo. 5 c. ci.	The London Midland and Scottish Railway (Road Transport) Act 1928.	The whole Act.
18 & 19 Geo. 5 c. cii.	The Great Western Railway (Road Transport) Act 1928.	The whole Act.
18 & 19 Geo. 5 c. ciii.	The London and North Eastern Railway (Road Transport) Act 1928.	The whole Act.
18 & 19 Geo. 5 c. civ.	The Southern Railway (Road Transport) Act 1928.	The whole Act.
19 & 20 Geo. 5 c. liv.	The Great Western Railway (Air Transport) Act 1929.	The whole Act.
19 & 20 Geo. 5 c. lv.	The London and North Eastern Railway (Air Transport) Act 1929.	The whole Act.
19 & 20 Geo. 5 c. lvi.	The London Midland and Scottish Railway (Air Transport) Act 1929.	The whole Act.
19 & 20 Geo. 5 c. lvii.	The Southern Railway (Air Transport) Act 1929.	The whole Act.
14 Geo. 6 c. liii.	The British Transport Commission Act 1950.	Section 43.
1 & 2 Eliz. 2 c. 36.	The Post Office Act 1953.	In section 29(1), the words "Without prejudice to section forty-two of this Act". Sections 33 to 42. In section 87(1), the definitions of "railway undertakers", "regular mail train services" and "sorting carriage".
10 & 11 Eliz. 2 c. 46.	The Transport Act 1962.	In section 4, subsections (1)(b), (2) and (7). Section 5. Section 13(3).

Sch. 14

Chapter	Short title	Extent of repeal
10 & 11 Eliz. 2 c. 46.—contd.	The Transport Act 1962.—contd.	Section 53. Section 54(1)(b) and (2). In section 56, subsections (1) to (3), in subsection (5), the words from the beginning to "section; and", and subsections (7) to (10), (12) to (15) and (17). Section 56A. Sections 69, 70 and 71. In section 92(1), in the definition of "subsidiary", the words "(taking references in that section to a company as being references to any body corporate)". Schedule 2, Part II.
1968 c. 73.	The Transport Act 1968.	Sections 7 and 8. Section 40. In section 42, subsections (3) to (5) and (6)(b). Section 45. Section 50(2). Section 54. In section 55, in subsection (1), in paragraph (a), the words from "or provided" onwards, paragraph (b), paragraphs (i) and (iii) and the words from "and for the purposes" onwards, and subsections (2) to (4). In section 135(1)(a), the words "7, 8,". In section 136(4)(a), the words "7(5) or (6), 8(4),". In section 137, in subsection (1)(a), the words "the Railways Board,". In section 159(1), in the definition of "the Minister", the words "7(7), 8(5),". In section 160(5), the words "otherwise than by virtue of section 7(7)(b) thereof". In Schedule 17, in Part I, in the entry relating to Part IV, the word "40,".
1969 c. 48.	The Post Office Act 1969.	In section 20, subsection (1)(b) and (d), and, in subsection (2), in paragraph (a), the words

SCH. 14

Chapter	Short title	Extent of repeal	
1969 c. 48.—*contd.*	The Post Office Act 1969.—*contd.*	"33 to 36, 38", paragraph (b) and the word "and" immediately preceding it. In Schedule 4, in paragraph 2(1), in the Table, the entries relating to sections 33, 34, 38, 41 and 42 of the Post Office Act 1953.	1953 c. 36.
1971 c. xlv.	The British Railways Act 1971.	Section 34.	
1974 c. 48.	The Railways Act 1974.	Section 3. In section 4(5)(b), the words "section 3 of the Transport Act 1981". Section 8. Section 9. In section 10(2), the definition of "the relevant transport regulations".	
1977 c. 20.	The Transport (Financial Provisions) Act 1977.	The whole Act.	
1978 c. 55.	The Transport Act 1978.	Section 16.	
1980 c. 34.	The Transport Act 1980.	In Schedule 7, paragraphs 1, 2 and 4.	
1981 c. 32.	The Transport Act 1962 (Amendment) Act 1981.	The whole Act.	
1981 c. 56.	The Transport Act 1981.	Part I. Section 36. Schedule 1.	
1982 c. 6.	The Transport (Finance) Act 1982.	Section 2.	
1984 c. 32.	The London Regional Transport Act 1984.	Part II. In section 40, in subsection (4), paragraph (c) and the word "or" immediately preceding it; in subsection (5), the words following paragraph (c); subsection (6); in subsection (7), paragraph (b); in subsection (8), the words "or (as the case may require) to the Railways Board"; in subsection (9), the words "the Railways Board"; in subsection (11), the words "or the Railways Board". Section 41. In section 42, subsections (3), (4) and (5). In Schedule 6, paragraph 2.	
1985 c. 67.	The Transport Act 1985.	Section 118(2)(a)(ii).	

SCH. 14

Chapter	Short title	Extent of repeal
1987 c. 53.	The Channel Tunnel Act 1987.	Section 33(11). In section 41, in subsection (3)(b), the words "and section 41(3) and (5) to (7)", and subsection (5). In Schedule 6, in paragraph 2, the words from "and 6" to "the fare)".
1991 c. 22.	The New Roads and Street Works Act 1991.	In section 10(2), paragraph (b) and the word "and" immediately preceding it.
1991 c. 63.	The British Railways Board (Finance) Act 1991.	Section 2.

© Crown copyright 1993

PRINTED IN THE UNITED KINGDOM BY PAUL FREEMAN
Controller and Chief Executive of Her Majesty's Stationery Office
and Queen's Printer of Acts of Parliament